D1471976

ANCIENT MAN IN BRITAIN

Copyright, 1915, by Charles Scribner's Sons

HEAD OF A CRÔ-MAGNON MAN

After the restoration modelled by J. H. McGregor.   Reproduced by permission
from *Men of the Old Stone Age* by Henry Fairfield Osborn.

ANCIENT MAN IN BRITAIN

DONALD A. MACKENZIE

SENATE

Hertfordshire Libraries,
Arts and Information

H31 525 529 1

HEF   30-10-96

         £1·99

Ancient Man in Britain

First published in 1922 by Blackie & Son Limited, London.

This edition first published in 1996 by Senate, an imprint of
Random House UK Ltd, Random House, 20 Vauxhall Bridge
Road, London SW1V 2SA

Copyright © Donald A. Mackenzie 1922

All rights reserved. This publication may not be reproduced,
stored in a retrieval system or transmitted, in any form or by
any means, electronic, mechanical, photocopying or otherwise,
without the prior written permission of the publishers.

ISBN 1 85958 207 9

Printed and bound in Guernsey by The Guernsey Press Co. Ltd

FOREWORD

In his Presidential Address to the Royal Anthropological Institute this year the late Dr. Rivers put his finger upon the most urgent need for reform in the study of Man, when he appealed for "the Unity of Anthropology". No true conception of the nature and the early history of the human family can be acquired by investigations, however carefully they may be done, of one class of evidence only. The physical characters of a series of skulls can give no reliable information unless their exact provenance and relative age are known. But the interpretation of the meaning of these characters cannot be made unless we know something of the movements of the people and the distinctive peculiarities of the inhabitants of the foreign lands from which they may have come. No less important than the study of their physical structure is the cultural history of peoples. The real spirit of a population is revealed by its social and industrial achievements, and by its

v

customs and beliefs, rather than by the shape of
the heads and members of its units.   The revival
of the belief in the widespread diffusion of culture
in early times has, as one of its many important
effects, directed attention to the physical peculiarities of the mixed populations of important foci of
civilization throughout the world.   Such inquiries
have not only enabled the student of human
structure to detect racial affinities where he might
otherwise have neglected to look for them, but on
the other hand they have been able to give the
investigator of cultural diffusion evidence of the
most definite and irrefutable kind in corroboration
of the reality of his inferences.

At the present time students are just awakening
to the fact that no adequate idea of the anthropology of any area can be acquired unless every
kind of evidence, somatic and cultural, be taken
into account, and the problems of the particular
locality are integrated with those worldwide movements of men and of civilization of which the
people and culture of that locality form a part.

The great merit of Mr. Donald Mackenzie's
book is due in the main to the fact that he has
taken this wider vision of his subject and inter-
preted the history of early man in Britain, not
simply by describing the varieties of head-form
or of implements, customs and beliefs, but rather

by indicating how these different categories of information can be put into their appropriate setting in the history of mankind as a whole. There is nothing of technical pedantry about Mr. Mackenzie's writing. He has made himself thoroughly familiar with the customs and beliefs of the whole world, as his remarkable series of books on mythology has revealed, and in the process of acquiring this mass of information he has not sacrificed his common sense and powers of judgment. He has been able to see clearly through this amazing jumble of confusing statements the way in which every phase of civilization in all parts of the world is closely correlated with the rest; and he has given luminous expression to this clear vision of the history of man and civilization as it affects Britain.

G. ELLIOT SMITH,
The University of London.

PREFACE

This volume deals with the history of man in Britain from the Ice Age till the Roman period. The evidence is gleaned from the various sciences which are usually studied apart, including geology, archæology, philology, ethnology or anthropology, &c., and the writer has set himself to tell the story of Ancient Man in a manner which will interest a wider circle of readers than is usually reached by purely technical books. It has not been assumed that the representatives of Modern Man who first settled in Europe were simple-minded savages. The evidence afforded by the craftsmanship, the burial customs, and the art of the Crô-Magnon races, those contemporaries of the reindeer and the hairy mammoth in South-western France, suggests that they had been influenced by a centre of civilization in which considerable progress had already been achieved. There is absolutely no evidence that the pioneers were lacking in intelligence or foresight. If we are to judge merely by their skeletons and the shapes and sizes of their skulls, it would appear that they were, if anything, both physically and mentally superior to the average present-day inhabitants of Europe. Nor were they entirely isolated from the ancient culture area by which they had been originally influenced. As is shown, the evidence afforded by an Indian Ocean sea-shell, found in a Crô-

Magnon burial cavern near Mentone, indicates that much has yet to be discovered regarding the activities of the early people.

In writing the history of Ancient Man in Britain, it has been found necessary to investigate the Continental evidence. When our early ancestors came from somewhere, they brought something with them, including habits of life and habits of thought. The story unfolded by British finds is but a part of a larger story; and if this larger story is to be reconstructed, our investigations must extend even beyond the continent of Europe. The data afforded by the "Red Man of Paviland", who was buried with Crô-Magnon rites in a Welsh cave, not only emphasize that Continental and North African cultural influences reached Britain when the ice-cap was retreating in Northern Europe, but that from its very beginnings the history of our civilization cannot be considered apart from that of the early civilization of the world as a whole. The writer, however, has not assumed in this connection that in all parts of the world man had of necessity to pass through the same series of evolutionary stages of progress, and that the beliefs, customs, crafts, arts, &c., of like character found in different parts of the world were everywhere of spontaneous generation. There were inventors and discoverers and explorers in ancient times as there are at present, and many new contrivances were passed on from people to people. The man who, for instance, first discovered how to "make fire" by friction of fire-sticks was undoubtedly a great scientist and a benefactor of his kind. It is shown that shipbuilding had a definite area of origin.

The "Red Man of Paviland" also reveals to us minds pre-occupied with the problems of life and death. It is evident that the corpse of the early explorer was smeared with red earth and decorated with charms for very definite reasons. That the people who thus interred

their dead with ceremony were less intelligent than the
Ancient Egyptians who adopted the custom of mummi-
fication, or the Homeric heroes who practised cremation,
we have no justification for assuming.

At the very dawn of British history, which begins
when the earliest representatives of Modern Man reached
our native land, the influences of cultures which had
origin in distant areas of human activity came drifting
northward to leave an impress which does not appear to
be yet wholly obliterated. We are the heirs of the Ages
in a profounder sense than has hitherto been supposed.

Considered from this point of view, the orthodox
scheme of Archæological Ages, which is of comparatively
recent origin, leaves much to be desired. If anthropological data have insisted upon one thing more than
another, it is that modes of thought, which govern
action, were less affected by a change of material from
which artifacts (articles made by man) were manufactured
than they were by religious ideas and by new means for
obtaining the necessary food supply. A profounder
change was effected in the habits of early man in
Britain by the introduction of the agricultural mode of
life, and the beliefs, social customs, &c., connected with
it, than could possibly have been effected by the introduction of edged implements of stone, bone, or metal.

As a substitute for the Archæological Ages, the writer
suggests in this volume a new system, based on habits
of life, which may be found useful for historical purposes. In this system the terms " Palæolithic ", " Neolithic", &c., are confined to industries. " Neolithic
man", "Bronze Age man", "Iron Age man", and other
terms of like character may be favoured by some
archæologists, but they mean little or nothing to most
anatomists, who detect different racial types in a single
"Age". A history of ancient man cannot ignore one
set of scientists to pleasure another.

Several chapters are devoted to the religious beliefs
and customs of our ancestors, and it is shown that there
is available for study in this connection a mass of
evidence which the archæological agnostics are too prone
to ignore.   The problem of the megalithic monuments
must evidently be reconsidered in the light of the fuller
anthropological data now available.   Indeed, it would
appear that a firmer basis than that afforded by "crude
evolutionary ideas" must be found for British archæology as a whole.   The evidence of surviving beliefs and
customs, of Celtic philology and literature, of early Christian writings, and of recent discoveries in Spain, Mesopotamia, and Egypt, cannot, to say the least of it, be
wholly ignored.

In dealing with the race problem, the writer has sifted
the available data which throw light on its connection
with the history of British culture, and has written as he
has written in the hope that the growth of fuller knowledge on the subject will be accompanied by the growth
of a deeper sympathy and a deeper sense of kinship than
has hitherto prevailed in these islands of ours, which were
colonized from time to time by groups of enterprising
pioneers, who have left an enduring impress on the
national character.   The time is past for beginning a
history of Britain with the Roman invasion, and for the
too-oft-repeated assertion that before the Romans
reached Britain our ancestors were isolated and half
civilized.

DONALD A. MACKENZIE.

CONTENTS

xiii

LIST OF PLATES

ANCIENT MAN IN BRITAIN

CHAPTER I

Britons of the Stone Age

Caricatures of Early Britons—Enterprising Pioneers—Diseases and Folk-cures—Ancient Surgical Operations—Expert Artisans—Organized Communities—Introduction of Agriculture—Houses and Cooking Utensils —Spinning and Weaving—Different Habits of Life—The Seafarers.

The Early Britons of the Stone Age have suffered much at the hands of modern artists, and especially the humorous artists. They are invariably depicted as rude and irresponsible savages, with semi-negroid features, who had perforce to endure our rigorous and uncertain climate clad in loosely fitting skin garments, and to go about, even in the depth of winter, barefooted and bareheaded, their long tangled locks floating in the wind.

As a rule, the artists are found to have confused ideas regarding the geological periods. Some place the white savages in the age when the wonderful megalithic monuments were erected and civilization was well advanced, while others consign them to the far-distant Cretaceous Age in association with the monstrous reptiles that browsed on tropical vegetation, being unaware, apparently, that the reptiles in question ceased to exist before the appearance of the earliest mammals. Not unfrequently the geological ages and the early stages of human culture are hopelessly mixed up, and monsters that had been extinct for several million years are shown crawling across circles that were erected by men possessed of considerable engineering skill.

It is extremely doubtful if our remote ancestors of the Stone Age were as savage or as backward as is generally supposed. They were, to begin with, the colonists who made Britain a land fit for a strenuous people to live in. We cannot deny them either courage or enterprise, nor are we justified in assuming that they were devoid of the knowledge and experience required to enable them to face the problems of existence in their new environment. They came from somewhere, and brought something with them; their modes of life did not have origin in our native land.

Although the early people lived an open-air life, it is doubtful if they were more physically fit than are the Britons of the twentieth century. They were certainly not immune from the ravages of disease. In their graves are found skeletons of babies, youths, and maidens, as well as those of elderly men and women; some spines reveal unmistakable evidence of the effects of rheumatism, and worn-down teeth are not uncommon. It is possible that the diseases associated with marshy localities and damp and cold weather were fairly prevalent, and that there were occasional pestilences with heavy death-rates. Epidemics of influenza and measles may have cleared some areas for periods of their inhabitants, the survivors taking flight, as did many Britons of the fifth century of our own era, when the country was swept by what is referred to in a Welsh book[1] as "the yellow plague", because "it made yellow and bloodless all whom it attacked". At the same time

---

[1] *Book of Llan Daf.*

recognition must be given to the fact that the early
people were not wholly ignorant of medical science.
There is evidence that some quite effective "folk cures"
are of great antiquity—that the "medicine-men" and
sorcerers of Ancient Britain had discovered how to treat
certain diseases by prescribing decoctions in which herbs
and berries utilized in modern medical science were
important ingredients. More direct evidence is available regarding surgical knowledge and skill. On the
Continent and in England have been found skulls on
which the operation known as trepanning—the removing
of a circular piece of skull so as to relieve the brain from
pressure or irritation — was successfully performed, as
is shown by the fact that severed bones had healed
during life. The accomplished primitive surgeons had
used flint instruments, which were less liable than those
of metal to carry infection into a wound. One cannot
help expressing astonishment that such an operation
should have been possible—that an ancient man who
had sustained a skull injury in a battle, or by accident,
should have been again restored to sanity and health.
Sprains and ordinary fractures were doubtless treated
with like skill and success. In some of the incantations
and charms collected by folk-lorists are lines which
suggest that the early medicine-men were more than
mere magicians. One, for instance, dealing with the
treatment of a fracture, states:

"He put marrow to marrow; he put pith to pith; he put
bone to bone; he put membrane to membrane; he put tendon
to tendon; he put blood to blood; he put tallow to tallow;
he put flesh to flesh; he put fat to fat; he put skin to skin;
he put hair to hair; he put warm to warm; he put cool to
cool."

"This," comments a medical man, "is quite a wonderful statement of the aim of modern surgical 'co-aptation',

and we can hardly believe such an exact form of words imaginable without a very clear comprehension of the natural necessity of correct and precise setting." [1]

The discovery that Stone Age man was capable of becoming a skilled surgeon is sufficient in itself to make us revise our superficial notions regarding him. A new interest is certainly imparted to our examination of his flint instruments. Apparently these served him in good stead, and it must be acknowledged that, after all, a stone tool may, for some purposes, be quite as adequate as one of metal. It certainly does not follow that the man who uses a sharper instrument than did the early Briton is necessarily endowed with a sharper intellect, or that his ability as an individual artisan is greater. The Stone Age man displayed wonderful skill in chipping flint—a most difficult operation—and he shaped and polished stone axes with so marked a degree of mathematical precision that, when laid on one side, they can be spun round on a centre of gravity. His saws were small, but are still found to be quite serviceable for the purposes they were constructed for, such as the cutting of arrow shafts and bows, and the teeth are so minute and regular that it is necessary for us to use a magnifying glass in order to appreciate the workmanship. Some flint artifacts are comparable with the products of modern opticians. The flint workers must have had wonderfully keen and accurate eyesight to have produced, for instance, little "saws" with twenty-seven teeth to the inch, found even in the north of Scotland. In Ancient Egypt these "saws" were used as sickles.

Considerable groups of the Stone Age men of Britain had achieved a remarkable degree of progress. They lived in organized communities, and had evidently codes of laws and regularized habits of life. They were not

[1] Dr. Hugh Cameron Gillies in *Home Life of the Highlanders*, Glasgow, 1911, pp. 85 *et seq.*

entirely dependent for their food supply on the fish they caught and the animals they slew and snared. Patches of ground were tilled, and root and cereal crops cultivated with success. Corn was ground in handmills;[1] the women baked cakes of barley and wheat and rye. A rough but serviceable pottery was manufactured and used for cooking food, for storing grain, nuts, and berries, and for carrying water. Houses were constructed of wattles interwoven between wooden beams and plastered over with clay, and of turf and stones; these were no doubt thatched with heather, straw, or reeds. Only a small proportion of the inhabitants of Ancient Britain could have dwelt in caves, for the simple reason that caves were not numerous. Underground dwellings, not unlike the "dug-outs" made during the recent war, were constructed as stores for food and as winter retreats.

As flax was cultivated, there can be little doubt that comfortable under-garments were worn, if not by all, at any rate by some of the Stone Age people. Wool was also utilized, and fragments of cloth have been found on certain prehistoric sites, as well as spindle-whorls of stone, bone, and clay, wooden spindles shaped so as to serve their purpose without the aid of whorls, bone needles, and crochet or knitting-pins. Those who have assumed that the Early Britons were attired in skin garments alone, overlook the possibility that a people who could sew, spin, and weave, might also have been skilled in knitting, and that the jersey and jumper may have a respectable antiquity. The art of knitting is closely related to that of basket-making, and some would have it that many of the earliest potters plastered their clay inside baskets of reeds, and that the decorations of the early pots were suggested by the markings impressed

---

[1] A pestle or stone was used to pound grain in hollowed slabs or rocks before the mechanical mill was invented.

by these.   It is of interest to note in this connection that some Roman wares were called *bascaudæ*, or "baskets", and that the Welsh *basged—basg*, from which our word "basket" is derived, signify "network" and "plaiting".   The decoration of some pots certainly suggests the imitation of wickerwork and knitting, but there are symbols also, and these had, no doubt, a religious significance.

It does not follow, of course, that all the Early Britons of the so-called Stone Age were in the same stage of civilization, or that they all pursued the same modes of life.   There were then, as there are now, backward as well as progressive communities and individuals, and there were likewise representatives of different races— tall and short, spare and stout, dark and fair men and women, who had migrated at different periods from different areas of origin and characterization.   Some peoples clung to the sea-shore, and lived mainly on deep-sea fish and shell-fish; others were forest and moorland hunters, who never ventured to sea or cultivated the soil.   There is no evidence to indicate that conflicts took place between different communities.   It may be that in the winter season the hunters occasionally raided the houses and barns of the agriculturists.   The fact, however, that weapons were not common during the Stone Age cannot be overlooked in this connection. The military profession had not come into existence.

Certain questions, however, arise in connection with even the most backward of the Stone Age peoples. How did they reach Britain, and what attracted them from the Continent?   Man did not take to the sea except under dire necessity, and it is certain that large numbers could not possibly have crossed the English Channel on logs of wood.   The boatbuilder's craft and the science of navigation must have advanced considerably before large migrations across the sea could have taken place.

When the agricultural mode of life was introduced, the early people obtained the seeds of wheat and barley, and, as these cultivated grasses do not grow wild in Britain, they must have been introduced either by traders or settlers.

It is quite evident that the term "Stone Age" is inadequate in so far as it applies to the habits of life pursued by the early inhabitants of our native land. Nor is it even sufficient in dealing with artifacts, for some people made more use of horn and bone than of stone, and these were represented among the early settlers in Britain.

CHAPTER II

Earliest Traces of Modern Man

The Culture Ages—Ancient Races—The Neanderthals—Crô-Magnon Man—The Evolution Theory—Palæolithic Ages—The Transition Period—Neanderthal Artifacts—Birth of Crô-Magnon Art—Occupations of Flint-yielding Stations—Ravages of Disease—Duration of Glacial and Interglacial Periods.

In 1865, Sir John Lubbock (afterwards Lord Avebury), writing in the *Prehistoric Times*, suggested that the Stone Age artifacts found in Western Europe should be classified into two main periods, to which he applied the terms Palæolithic (Old Stone) and Neolithic (New Stone). The foundations of the classification had previously been laid by the French antiquaries M. Boucher de Perthes and Edouard Lartet. It was intended that Palæolithic should refer to rough stone implements, and Neolithic to those of the period when certain artifacts were polished.

At the time very little was known regarding the early peoples who had pursued the flint-chipping and polishing industries, and the science of geology was in its infancy. A great controversy, which continued for many years, was being waged in scientific circles regarding the remains of a savage primitive people that had been brought to light. Of these the most notable were a woman's skull found in 1848 in a quarry at Gibraltar, the Cannstadt skull, found in 1700, which had long been lying in Stuttgart Museum undescribed and unstudied, and portions of a male skeleton taken from a

8

limestone cave in Neanderthal, near Dusseldorf, in 1857. Some refused to believe that these, and other similar remains subsequently discovered, were human at all; others declared that the skulls were those of idiots or that they had been distorted by disease. Professor Huxley contended that evidence had been forthcoming to prove the existence in remote times of a primitive race from which modern man had evolved.

It is unnecessary here to review the prolonged controversy. One of its excellent results was the stimulation of research work. A number of important finds have been made during the present century, which have thrown a flood of light on the problem. In 1908 a skeleton was discovered in a grotto near La Chapelle-aux-Saints in France, which definitely established the fact that during the earlier or lower period of the Palæolithic Age a Neanderthal race existed on the Continent, and, as other remains testify, in England as well. This race became extinct. Some hold that there are no living descendants of Neanderthal man on our globe; others contend that some peoples, or individuals, reveal Neanderthaloid traits. The natives of Australia display certain characteristics of the extinct species, but they are more closely related to Modern Man (*Homo sapiens*). There were pre-Neanderthal peoples, including Piltdown man and Heidelberg man.

During the Palæolithic Age the ancestors of modern man appeared in Western Europe. These are now known as the Crô-Magnon races.

In dealing with the Palæolithic Age, therefore, it has to be borne in mind that the artifacts classified by the archæologists represent the activities, not only of different races, but of representatives of different species of humanity. Neanderthal man, who differed greatly from Modern man, is described as follows by Professor Elliot Smith:

"His short, thick-set, and coarsely built body was carried in a half-stooping slouch upon short, powerful, and half-flexed legs of peculiarly ungraceful form. His thick neck sloped forward from the broad shoulders to support the massive flattened head, which protruded forward, so as to form an unbroken curve of neck and back, in place of the alteration of curves, which is one of the graces of the truly erect *Homo sapiens*. The heavy overhanging eyebrow ridges, and retreating forehead, the great coarse face, with its large eye-sockets, broad nose, and receding chin, combined to complete the picture of unattractiveness, which it is more probable than not was still further emphasized by a shaggy covering of hair over most of the body. The arms were relatively short, and the exceptionally large hands lacked the delicacy and the nicely balanced co-operation of thumb and fingers, which is regarded as one of the most distinctive of human characteristics."[1]

As Professor Osborn says: "the structure of the hand is a matter of the highest interest in connection with the implement-making powers of the Neanderthals". He notes that in the large and robust Neanderthal hand, "the joint of the metacarpal bone which supports the thumb is of peculiar form, convex, and presenting a veritable convex condyle, whereas in the existing human races the articular surface of the upper part of the thumb joint is saddle-shaped, that is concave from within backward, and convex from without inward". The Neanderthal fingers were "relatively short and robust".[2]

The Crô-Magnons present a sharp contrast to the Neanderthals. In all essential features they were of modern type. They would, dressed in modern attire, pass through the streets of a modern city without particular notice being taken of them. One branch of the Crô-Magnons was particularly tall and handsome, with an average height for the males of 6 feet 1½ inches, with

---

[1] *Primitive Man.*   [2] *Men of the Old Stone Age* (1916), pp. 240-1.

chests very broad in the upper part, and remarkably long shin-bones that indicate swiftness of foot. The Neanderthals had short shins and bent knees, and their gait must have been slow and awkward. The Crô-Magnon hand was quite like that of the most civilized men of to-day.

It is of importance to bring out these facts in connection with the study of the development of early civilization in our native land, because of the prevalence of the theory that in collections of stone implements, dating from remote Palæolithic times till the Neolithic Age, a complete and orderly series of evolutionary stages can be traced. "As like needs", says one writer in this connection, "produce like means of satisfaction, the contrivances with which men in similar stages of progress overcome natural obstacles are in all times very much the same."[1] Hugh Miller, the Cromarty stone-mason and geologist, was one of the first to urge this view. In 1835, he wrote in his *Scenes and Legends*, (1st edition, pp. 31, 32):

"Man in a savage stage is the same animal everywhere, and his constructive powers, whether employed in the formation of a legendary story or of a battleaxe, seem to expatiate almost everywhere in the same rugged track of invention. For even the traditions of this first stage may be identified, like its weapons of war, all the world over."[2]

He had written in this vein after seeing the collection of stone weapons and implements in the Northern Institution at Inverness. "The most practised eye", he commented, "can hardly distinguish between the weapons of the Old Scot and the New Zealander."

---

[1] *British Museum—A Guide to the Antiquities of the Stone Age*, p. 76 (1902).

[2] Miller had adopted the "stratification theory" of Professor William Robertson of Edinburgh University, who, in his *The History of America* (1777), wrote: "Men in their savage state pass their days like the animals round them, without knowledge or veneration of any superior power".

Eyes have become more practised in dealing with flints
since Miller's time.   Andrew Lang remembered his
Miller when he wrote:

" Now just as the flint arrowheads are scattered everywhere,
in all the continents and isles—and everywhere are much
alike, and bear no very definite marks of the special influence
of race—so it is with the habits and legends investigated by
the student of folk-lore ".[1]

The recent discovery that the early flints found in
Western Europe and in England were shaped by the
Neanderthals and the pre-Neanderthals compels a revision of this complacent view of an extraordinarily
difficult and complex problem.   It is obvious that the
needs and constructive powers of the Neanderthals,
whose big clumsy hands lacked "the delicate play between the thumb and fingers characteristic of modern
races", could not have been the same as those of the
Crô-Magnons, and that the finely shaped implements of
the Crô-Magnons could not have been evolved from the
rough implements of the Neanderthals.   The craftsmen
of one race may, however, have imitated, or attempted
to imitate, the technique of those of another.

There was a distinct break in the continuity of culture
during the Palæolithic Age, caused by the arrival in
Western Europe of the ancestors of Modern Man.   The
advent of the Crô-Magnons in Europe "represents on
the cultural side", as Professor Elliot Smith says in
Primitive Man, "the most momentous event in its
history".

Some urge that the term "Palæolithic" should now
be discarded altogether, but its use has become so firmly
established that archæologists are loth to dispense with
it.   The first period of human culture has, however,
had to be divided into "Lower" and "Upper Palæo-

[1] *Custom and Myth* (1910 edition), p. 13.   Lang's views regarding flints are worthless.

Mousterian type
(from Suffolk)

Acheulian type
(from Suffolk)

Photos. Oxford University Press

Chellean type
(from the Thames gravel)

Photo. Mansell

EXAMPLES OF LOWER PALÆOLITHIC INDUSTRIES
FOUND IN ENGLAND
(British Museum)

lithic"—Lower closing with the disappearance of the Neanderthals, and Upper beginning with the arrival of the Crô-Magnons. These periods embrace the sub-divisions detected during the latter half of last century by the French archæologists, and are now classified as follows:

Lower Palæolithic—

1. Pre-Chellean.
2. Chellean (named after the town of Chelles, east of Paris).
3. Acheulian (named after St. Acheul in Somme valley).
4. Mousterian (named after the caves of Le Moustier in the valley of the River Vézère).

Upper Palæolithic—

1. Aurignacian (named after Aurignac, Haute Garonne).
2. Solutrean (named after Solutré, Saône-et-Loire).
3. Magdalenian (named after La Madeleine in the valley of the River Vézère).

Then follows, in France, the Azilian stage (named after Mas d'Azil, a town at the foot of the Pyrenees) which is regarded as the link between Upper Palæolithic and Neolithic. But in Western Europe, including Britain, there were really three distinct cultures during the so-called "Transition Period". These are the Azilian, the Tardenoisian, and the Maglemosian. These cultures were associated with the movements of new peoples in Europe.

The pre-Chellean flints (also called Eoliths) were wrought by the pre-Neanderthals. Chellean probably represents the earliest work in Europe of a pre-Neanderthal type like Piltdown man. The most characteristic implement of this phase is the *coup de poing*, or pear-shaped "hand axe", which was at first roughly shaped and unsymmetrical. It was greatly improved during the Acheulian stage, and after being finely wrought in Mousterian times, when it was not much used, was supplanted by smaller and better chipped implements. The Neanderthals practised the Mousterian industry.

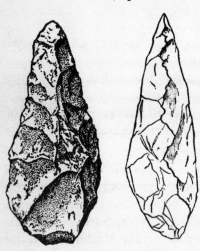

Chellean *Coup de Poing* or "Hand Axe"

Right-hand view shows sinuous cutting edge.

A profound change occurred when the Aurignacian stage of culture was inaugurated by the intruding Crô-Magnons. Skilled workers chipped flint in a new way, and, like the contemporary inhabitants of North Africa, shaped artifacts from bone; they also used reindeer horn, and the ivory tusks of mammoths. The birth of pictorial art took place in Europe after the Crô-Magnons arrived.

It would appear that the remnants of the Neanderthals in the late Mousterian stage of culture were stimulated by the arrival of the Crô-Magnons to imitate new flint forms and adopt the new methods of workmanship. There is no other evidence to indicate that the Crô-Magnons came into contact with communities of the Neanderthals. In these far-off days Europe was thinly peopled by hunters who dwelt in caves. The climate was cold, and the hairy mammoth and the reindeer browsed in the lowlands of France and Germany. Italy was linked with Africa; the grass-lands of North Africa stretched southward across the area now known as the Sahara desert, and dense forests fringed the banks of the River Nile and extended eastward to the Red Sea.

Neanderthal man had originally entered Europe when the climate was much milder than it is in our own time. He crossed over from Africa by the Italian land-bridge, and he found African fauna, including species of the elephant, rhinoceros, hippopotamus, lion, and the hyæna, jackal, and sabre-tooth tiger in Spain, France, Germany. Thousands of years elapsed and the summers became shorter, and the winters longer and more severe, until the northern fauna began to migrate southward, and the African fauna deserted the plains and decaying forests of Europe. Then followed the Fourth Glacial phase, and when it was passing away the Neanderthals, who had long been in the Mousterian phase of culture, saw bands of Crô-Magnons prospecting and hunting in southern Europe. The new-comers had migrated from some centre of culture in North Africa, and appear to have crossed over the Italian land-bridge. It is unlikely that many, if any, entered Europe from the east. At the time the Black Sea was more than twice its present size, and glaciers still blocked the passes of Asia Minor.

A great contrast was presented by the two types of mankind. The short, powerfully built, but slouching and slow-footed Neanderthals were, in a conflict, no match for the tall, active, and swift-footed Crô-Magnons, before whom they retreated, yielding up their flint-working stations, and their caves and grottoes. It may be, as some suggest, that fierce battles were fought, but there is no evidence of warfare; it may be that the Neanderthals succumbed to imported diseases, as did so many thousands of the inhabitants of the Amazon Valley, when measles and other diseases were introduced by the Spaniards. The fact remains that the Neanderthals died out as completely as did the Tasmanians

before the advance of British settlers. We do not know
whether or not they resisted, for a time, the intrusion of
strangers on their hunting-grounds. It may be that the
ravages of disease completed the tragic history of such
relations as they may have had with the ancestors of
Modern Man.

At this point, before we deal with the arrival in
Britain of the representatives of the early races, it
should be noted that differences of opinion exist among
scientists regarding the geological horizons of the Palæolithic culture stages. In the Pleistocene Age there appear to have been four great glacial epochs and two
minor ones. Geological opinion is, however, divided
in this connection.

During the First Glacial epoch the musk-ox, now
found in the Arctic regions, migrated as far south as
Sussex. The Pliocene[1] mammals were not, however,
completely exterminated; many of them survived until
the First Interglacial epoch, which lasted for about
75,000 years—that is three times longer than the First
Glacial epoch. The Second Glacial epoch is believed
to have extended over 25,000 years. It brought to the
southern shores of the Baltic Sea the reindeer and the
hairy mammoth. Then came the prolonged Second
Interglacial stage which prevailed for about 200,000
years. The climate of Europe underwent a change
until it grew warmer than it is at the present day,
and trees, not now found farther north than the Canary
Islands, flourished in the forests of southern France.
The Third Glacial stage gradually came on, grew in
intensity, and then declined during a period estimated
at about 25,000 years. It was followed by the Third
Interglacial epoch which may have extended over at
least 100,000 years. African animals returned to Europe
and mingled with those that wandered from Asia and

---

[1] The last division of the Tertiary period.

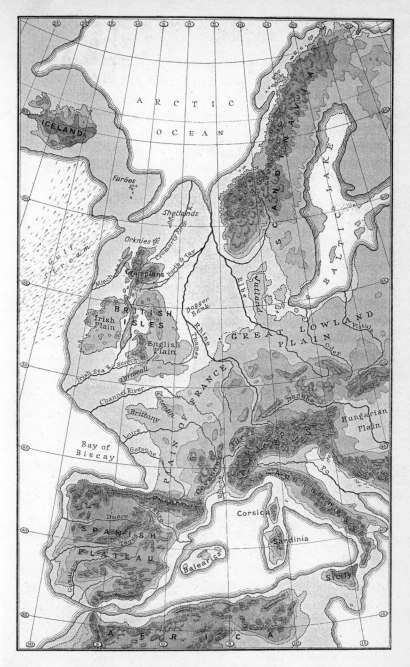

WESTERN EUROPE DURING THE THIRD
INTER-GLACIAL EPOCH

(According to the Abbé Breuil the Strait of Gibraltar was open and the
Balearic group a great island.)

the survivors in Europe of the Second Interglacial fauna. The Fourth Glacial epoch, which is believed to have lasted for about 25,000 years, was very severe. All the African or Asiatic mammals either migrated or became extinct with the exception of lions and hyænas, and the reindeer found the western plains of Europe as congenial as it does the northern plains at the present time.

During the Fourth Post-glacial epoch there were for a period of about 25,000 years [1] partial glaciations and milder intervals, until during the Neolithic Age of the archæologists the climate of Europe reached the phase that at present prevails.

When, then, did man first appear in Europe? According to some geologists, and especially Penck and James Geikie, the Chellean phase of culture originated in the Second Interglacial epoch and the Mousterian endured until the Third Interglacial stage, when the Neanderthals witnessed the arrival of the Crô-Magnon peoples. Boule, Breuil, and others, however, place the pre-Chellean, Chellean, Acheulian, and early Mousterian stages of Lower (or Early) Palæolithic culture in the Third Interglacial epoch, and fix the extermination of Neanderthal man, in his late Mousterian culture stage, at the close of the Fourth Glacial epoch. This view is now being generally accepted. It finds favour with the archæologists, and seems to accord with the evidence they have accumulated. The Upper Palæolithic culture of Crô-Magnon man, according to some, began in its Aurignacian phase about 25,000 years ago; others consider, however, that it began about five or six thousand years ago, and was contemporaneous with the long pre-Dynastic civilization of Egypt. At the time England was connected with the Continent by a land-bridge,

[1] It must be borne in mind that the lengths of these periods are subject to revision. Opinion is growing that they were not nearly so long as here stated.

and as the climate grew milder the ancestors of modern man could walk across from France to the white cliffs of Dover which were then part of a low range of mountains. As will be shown, there is evidence that the last land movement in Britain did not begin until about 3000 B.C.

CHAPTER III

The Age of the " Red Man " of Wales

An Ancient Welshman—Aurignacian Culture in Britain—Coloured Bones and Luck Charms—The Cave of Aurignac—Discovery at Crô-Magnon Village—An Ancient Tragedy—Significant Burial Customs—Crô-Magnon Characters—New Race Types in Central Europe—Galley Hill Man—The Piltdown Skull—Ancient Religious Beliefs—Life Principle in Blood—Why Body-painting was practised—"Sleepers" in Caves—Red Symbolism in different Countries—The Heart as the Seat of Life—The Green Stone Talisman—"Soul Substance".

The earliest discovery of a representative of the Crô-Magnons was made in 1823, when Dr. Buckland explored the ancient cave-dwelling of Paviland in the vicinity of Rhossilly, Gower Peninsula, South Wales. This cave, known as "Goat's Hole", is situated between 30 and 40 feet above the present sea-level, on the face of a steep sandstone cliff about 100 feet in height; it is 60 feet in length and 200 feet broad, while the roof attains an altitude of over 25 feet. When this commodious natural shelter was occupied by our remote ancestors the land was on a much lower level than it is now, and it could be easily reached from the sea-shore. Professor Sollas has shown that the Paviland cave-dwellers were in the Aurignacian stage of culture, and that they had affinities with the tall Crô-Magnon peoples on the Continent.[1]

[1] *Journal of the Royal Anthropological Institute*, Vol. XLIII, 1913.

A human skeleton of a tall man was found in the cave deposit in association with the skull and tusks of a hairy mammoth, and with implements of Aurignacian type. Apparently the Aurignacian colonists had walked over the land-bridge connecting England with France many centuries before the land sank and the Channel tides began to carve out the white cliffs of Dover.

In his description of the bones of the ancient caveman, who has been wrongly referred to as the "Red Lady of Paviland", Dr. Buckland wrote:

"They were all of them stained superficially with a dark brick-red colour, and enveloped by a coating of a kind of ruddle, composed of red micaceous oxide of iron, which stained the earth, and in some parts extended itself to the distance of about half an inch around the surface of the bones. The body must have been entirely surrounded or covered over at the time of its interment with this red substance."

Near the thighs were about two handfuls of small shells (*Nerita litoralis*) which had evidently formed a waist girdle. Over forty little rods of ivory, which may have once formed a long necklace, lay near the ribs. A few ivory rings and a tongue-shaped implement or ornament lay beside the body, as well as an instrument or charm made of the metacarpal bone of a wolf.

The next great discovery of this kind was made twenty-nine years later. In 1852 a French workman was trying to catch a wild rabbit on a lower slope of the Pyrenees, near the town of Aurignac in Haute Garonne, when he made a surprising find. From the rabbit's burrow he drew out a large human bone. A slab of stone was subsequently removed, and a grotto or cave shelter revealed. In the debris were found portions of seventeen skeletons of human beings of different ages and both sexes. Only two skulls were intact.

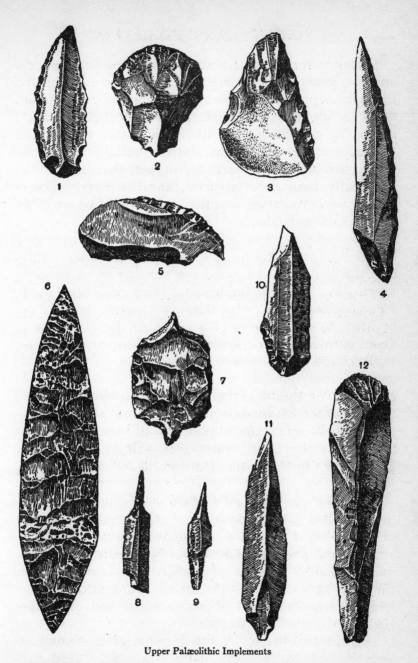

Upper Palæolithic Implements

1, Aurignacian (Chatelperron point).   2, 3, Aurignacian (keeled scrapers).   4, Aurignacian point.   5, Magdalenian ("parrot-beak" graving tool).   6, Solutrean (laurel-leaf point).   7, 8, 9, Solutrean (drill, awl, and "shouldered" point).   10, 11, 12, Magdalenian.

This discovery created a stir in the town of Aurignac, and there was much speculation regarding the tragedy that was supposed to have taken place at some distant date. A few folks were prepared to supply circumstantial details by connecting the discovery with vague local traditions. No one dreamt that the burial-place dated back a few thousand years, or, indeed, that the grotto had really been a burial-place, and the mayor of the town gave instructions that the bones should be interred in the parish cemetery.

Eight years elapsed before the grotto was visited by M. Louis Lartet, the great French archæologist. Outside the stone slab he found the remains of an ancient hearth, and a stone implement which had been used for chipping flints. In the outer debris were discovered, too, the bones of animals of the chase, and about a hundred flint artifacts, including knives, projectiles, and sling-stones, besides bone arrows, tools shaped from reindeer horns, and an implement like a bodkin of roe-deer horn. It transpired that the broken bones of animals included those of the cave-lion, the cave-bear, the hyæna, the elk, the mammoth, and the woolly-haired rhinoceros—all of which had been extinct in that part of the world for thousands of years.

As in the Paviland cave, there were indications that the dead had been interred with ornaments or charms on their bodies. Inside the grotto were found "eighteen small round and flat plates of a white shelly substance, made of some species of cockle (*Cardium*) pierced through the middle, as if for being strung into a bracelet". Perforated teeth of wild animals had evidently been used for a like purpose.

The distinct industry revealed by the grotto finds has been named Aurignacian, after Aurignac. Had the human bones not been removed, the scientists would have definitely ascertained what particular race of ancient men they represented.

It was not until the spring of 1868 that a flood of light was thrown on the Aurignacian racial problem. A gang of workmen were engaged in the construction of a railway embankment in the vicinity of the village of Crô-Magnon, near Les Eyzies, in the valley of the River Vézère, when they laid bare another grotto. Intimation was at once made to the authorities, and the Minister of Public Instruction caused an investigation to be made under the direction of M. Louis Lartet. The remains of five human skeletons were found. At the back of the grotto was the skull of an old man—now known as "the old man of Crô-Magnon"—and its antiquity was at once emphasized by the fact that some parts of it were coated by stalagmite caused by a calcareous drip from the roof of rock. Near "the old man" was found the skeleton of a woman. Her forehead bore signs of a deep wound that had been made by a cutting instrument. As the inner edge of the bone had partly healed, it was apparent she had survived her injury for a few weeks. Beside her lay the skeleton of a baby which had been prematurely born. The skeletons of two young men were found not far from those of the others. Apparently a tragic happening had occurred in ancient days in the vicinity of the Crô-Magnon grotto. The victims had been interred with ceremony, and in accordance with the religious rites prevailing at the time. Above three hundred pierced marine shells, chiefly of the periwinkle species (*Littorina littorea*), which are common on the Atlantic coasts, and a few shells of *Purpura lapillus* (a purple-yielding shell), *Turitella communis*, &c., were discovered besides the skeletons. These, it would appear, had been strung to form necklaces and other ornamental charms. M. Lartet found, too, a flat ivory pendant pierced with two holes, and was given two other pendants picked up by young people. Near the skeletons were several perforated teeth, a split block of gneiss with a smooth surface, the worked antlers of a reindeer that may have been used as a pick for excavating flint, and a few chipped flints. Other artifacts of Aurignacian type were unearthed in the debris associated with the grotto, which appears to have been used as a dwelling-place before the interments had taken place.

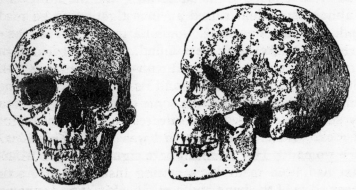

Skull of a Crô-Magnon Man: front and side views
From the Grotte des Enfants, Mentone. (After Verneau.)

The human remains of the Crô-Magnon grotto were those of a tall and handsome race of which the "Red Man" of Paviland was a representative. Other finds have shown that this race was widely distributed in Europe. The stature of the men varied from 5 feet 10½ inches to 6 feet 4½ inches on the Riviera, that of the women being slightly less. That the Crô-Magnons were people of high intelligence is suggested by the fact that the skulls of the men and women were large, and remarkably well developed in the frontal region. According to a prominent anatomist the Crô-Magnon women had bigger brains than has the average male European of to-day. All these ancient skulls are of the dolichocephalic (long-headed) type. The faces, however, were comparatively broad, and shorter than those of the modern fair North-Europeans, while the cheek bones were high—a characteristic, by the way, of so many modern Scottish faces.

This type of head—known as the "disharmonic", because a broad face is usually a characteristic of a broad skull, and a long face of a long skull—has been found to be fairly common among the modern inhabitants of the Dordogne valley. These French descendants of the Crô-Magnons are, however, short and "stocky", and most of them have dark hair and eyes. Crô-Magnon types have likewise been identified among the Berbers of North Africa, and the extinct fair-haired Guanches of the Canary Islands, in Brittany, on the islands of northern Holland, and in the British Isles.[1]

A comparatively short race, sometimes referred to as the "Combe-Capelle", after the rock-shelter at Combe-Capelle, near Montferrand, Perigord, was also active during the stage of Aurignacian culture. An adult skeleton found in this shelter was that of a man only 5 feet 3 inches in height. The skull is long and narrow, with a lofty forehead, and the chin small and well developed. It has some similarity to modern European skulls. The skeleton had been subjected for thousands of years to the dripping of water saturated with lime, and had consequently been well preserved. Near the head and neck lay a large number of perforated marine shells (*Littorina* and *Nassa*). A collection of finely-worked flints of early Aurignacian type also lay beside the body.

Reference may also be made here to the finds in Moravia. Fragmentary skull caps from Brüx and Brünn are regarded as evidence of a race which differed from the tall Crô-Magnons, and had closer affinities with

---

[1] For principal references see *The Races of Europe*, W. Z. Ripley, pp. 172 *et seq.*, and *The Anthropological History of Europe*, John Beddoe (Rhind lectures for 1891; revised edition, 1912), p. 47.

Combe-Capelle man.   Some incline to connect the Brünn
type with England, the link being provided by a skeleton called the "Galley Hill" after the place of its discovery below Gravesend and near Northfleet in Kent.
Scientists regard him as a contemporary of the Aurignacian flint-workers of Combe-Capelle and Brünn.
"Both the Brüx and Brünn skulls", writes Professor
Osborn, "are harmonic; they do not present the very
broad, high cheek-bones characteristic of the Crô-Magnon race,[1] the face being of a narrow modern type, but
not very long.   There is a possibility that the Brünn
race was ancestral to several later dolichocephalic groups
which are found in the region of the Danube and of
middle and southern Germany."[2]

The Galley Hill man had been buried in the gravels
of the "high terrace", 90 feet above the Thames.   His
bones when found were much decayed and denuded,
and the skull contorted.   The somewhat worn "wisdom
tooth" indicates that he was a "fully-grown adult,
though probably not an aged individual".   Those who
think he was not as old as the flints and the bones of
extinct animals found in the gravels, regard him as a
pioneer of the Brünn branch of the Aurignacians.

The Piltdown skull appears to date back to a period
vastly more ancient than Neanderthal times.

Our special interest in the story of early man in
Britain is with the "Red Man" of Paviland and
Galley Hill man, because these were representatives of
the species to which we ourselves belong.   The Neanderthals and pre-Neanderthals, who have left their
Eoliths and Palæoliths in our gravels, vanished like the
glaciers and the icebergs, and have left, as has been
indicated, no descendants in our midst.   Our history
begins with the arrival of the Crô-Magnon races, who

---

[1] That is, the tall representatives of the Crô-Magnon race
[2] *Men of the Old Stone Age*, pp. 335-6.

were followed in time by other peoples to whom Europe offered attractions during the period of the great thaw, when the ice-cap was shrinking towards the north, and the flooded rivers were forming the beds on which they now flow.

We have little to learn from Galley Hill man. His geological horizon is uncertain, but the balance of the available evidence tends to show he was a pioneer of the medium-sized hunters who entered Europe from the east, during the Aurignacian stage of culture. It is otherwise with the "Red Man" of Wales. We know definitely what particular family he belonged to; he was a representative of the tall variety of Crô-Magnons. We know too that those who loved him, and laid his lifeless body in the Paviland Cave, had introduced into Europe the germs of a culture that had been radiated from some centre, probably in the ancient forest land to the east of the Nile, along the North African coast at a time when it jutted far out into the Mediterranean and the Sahara was a grassy plain.

The Crô-Magnons were no mere savages who lived the life of animals and concerned themselves merely with their material needs. They appear to have been a people of active, inventive, and inquiring minds, with a social organization and a body of definite beliefs, which found expression in their art and in their burial customs. The "Red Man" was so called by the archæologists because his bones and the earth beside them were stained, as has been noted, by "red micaceous oxide of iron". Here we meet with an ancient custom of high significance. It was not the case, as some have suggested, that the skeleton was coloured after the flesh had decayed. There was no indication when the human remains were discovered that the grave had been disturbed after the corpse was laid in it. The fact that the earth as well as the bones retained the coloration affords clear proof that the corpse had been smeared over with red earth which, after the flesh had decayed, fell on the skeleton and the earth and gravel beside it.   But why, it will be asked, was the corpse so treated?   Did the Crô-Magnons paint their bodies during life, as do the Australians, the Red Indians, and others, to provide "a substitute for clothing"?   That cannot be the reason.   They could not have concerned themselves about a "substitute" for something they did not possess.   In France, the Crô-Magnons have left pictorial records of their activities and interests in their caves and other shelters.   Bas reliefs on boulders within a shelter at Laussel show that they did not wear clothing during the Aurignacian epoch which continued for many long centuries.   We know too that the Australians and Indians painted their bodies for religious and magical purposes—to protect themselves in battle or enable them to perform their mysteries—rain-getting, food-getting, and other ceremonies.   The ancient Egyptians painted their gods to "make them healthy".   Prolonged good health was immortality.

The evidence afforded by the Paviland and other Crô-Magnon burials indicates that the red colour was freshly applied before the dead was laid in the sepulchre. No doubt it was intended to serve a definite purpose, that it was an expression of a system of beliefs regarding life and the hereafter.

Apparently among the Crô-Magnons the belief was already prevalent that the "blood is the life".   The loss of life appeared to them to be due to the loss of the red vitalizing fluid which flowed in the veins.   Strong men who received wounds in conflict with their fellows, or with wild animals, were seen to faint and die in consequence of profuse bleeding; and those who were stricken with sickness grew ashen pale because, as it seemed, the supply of blood was insufficient, a condition

they may have accounted for, as did the Babylonians of
a later period, by conceiving that demons entered the
body and devoured the flesh and blood.   It is not too
much to suppose that they feared death, and that like
other Pagan religions of antiquity theirs was deeply concerned with the problem of how to restore and prolong
life.   Their medicine-men appear to have arrived at the
conclusion that the active principle in blood was the
substance that coloured it, and they identified this substance with red earth.   If cheeks grew pale in sickness,
the flush of health seemed to be restored by the application of a red face paint.   The patient did not invariably
regain strength, but when he did, the recovery was in
all likelihood attributed to the influence of the blood
substitute.   Rest and slumber were required, as experience showed, to work the cure.   When death took place,
it seemed to be a deeper and more prolonged slumber,
and the whole body was smeared over with the vitalizing
blood substitute so that, when the spell of weakness had
passed away, the sleeper might awaken, and come forth
again with renewed strength from the cave-house in
which he had been laid.

The many persistent legends about famous "sleepers"
that survive till our own day appear to have originally
been connected with a belief in the return of the dead,
the antiquity of which we are not justified in limiting,
especially when it is found that the beliefs connected
with body paint and shell ornaments and amulets were
introduced into Europe in early post-glacial times.
Ancient folk heroes might be forgotten, but from Age
to Age there arose new heroes to take their places; the
habit of placing them among the sleepers remained.
Charlemagne, Frederick of Barbarossa, William Tell,
King Arthur, the Fians, and the Irish Brian Boroimhe,
are famous sleepers.   French peasants long believed
that the sleeping Napoleon would one day return to

protect their native land from invaders, and during the Russo-Japanese war it was whispered in Russia that General Skobeleff would suddenly awake and hasten to Manchuria to lead their troops to victory. For many generations the Scots were convinced that James IV, who fell at Flodden, was a "sleeper". His place was taken in time by Thomas the Rhymer, who slept in a cave and occasionally awoke to visit markets so that he might purchase horses for the great war which was to redden Tweed and Clyde with blood. Even in our own day there were those who refused to believe that General Gordon, Sir Hector MacDonald, and Lord Kitchener, were really dead. The haunting belief in sleeping heroes dies hard.

Among the famous groups of sleeping heroes are the Seven Sleepers of Ephesus — the Christians who had been condemned to death by the Emperor Decius and concealed themselves in a cave where they slept for three and a half centuries. An eighteenth century legend tells of seven men in Roman attire, who lay in a cave in Western Germany. In Norse Mythology, the seven sons of Mimer sleep in the Underworld awaiting the blast of the horn, which will be blown at Ragnarok when the gods and demons will wage the last battle. The sleepers of Arabia once awoke to foretell the coming of Mahomet, and their sleeping dog, according to Moslem beliefs, is one of the ten animals that will enter Paradise.

A representative Scottish legend regarding the sleepers is located at the Cave of Craigiehowe in the Black Isle, Ross-shire, a few miles distant from the Rosemarkie cave. It is told that a shepherd once entered the cave and saw the sleepers and their dog. A horn, or as some say, a whistle, hung suspended from the roof. The shepherd blew it once and the sleepers shook themselves; he blew a second time, and they opened their eyes and raised themselves on their elbows. Terrified by the forbidding aspect of the mighty men, the shepherd refrained from blowing a third time, but turned and fled.   As he left the cave he heard one of the heroes call after him: "Alas! you have left us worse than you found us."   As whistles are sometimes found in Magdalenian shelters in Western and Central Europe, it may be that these were at an early period connected with the beliefs about the calling back of the Crô-Magnon dead.   The ancient whistles were made of hare- and reindeer-foot bone.   The clay whistle dates from the introduction of the Neolithic industry in Hungary.

The remarkable tendency on the part of mankind to cling to and perpetuate ancient beliefs and customs, and especially those connected with sickness and death, is forcibly illustrated by the custom of smearing the bodies of the living and dead with red ochre.   In every part of the world red is regarded as a particularly "lucky colour", which protects houses and human beings, and imparts vitality to those who use it.   The belief in the protective value of red berries is perpetuated in our own Christmas customs when houses are decorated with holly, and by those dwellers in remote parts who still tie rowan berries to their cows' tails so as to prevent witches and fairies from interfering with the milk supply. Egyptian women who wore a red jasper in their waist-girdles called the stone "a drop of the blood of Isis (the mother goddess)".

Red symbolism is everywhere connected with life-blood and the "vital spark" — the hot "blood of life".   Brinton[1] has shown that in the North American languages the word for blood is derived from the word for red or the word for fire.   The ancient Greek custom of painting red the wooden images of gods was evidently connected with the belief that a supply of life-

1 *Myths of the New World*, p. 163.

blood was thus assured, and that the colour animated
the Deity, as Homer's ghosts were animated by a blood
offering when Odysseus visited Hades. "The anoint-
ing of idols with blood for the purpose of animating
them is", says Farnell, "a part of old Mediterranean
magic."[1] The ancient Egyptians, as has been indicated, painted their gods, some of whom wore red
garments; a part of their underworld Dewat was "Red
Land", and there were "red souls" in it.[2] In India
standing stones connected with deities are either painted
red or smeared with the blood of a sacrificed animal.
The Chinese regard red as the colour of fire and light,
and in their philosophy they identify it with *Yang*, the
chief principle of life;[3] it is believed "to expel per-
nicious influences, and thus particularly to symbolize
good luck, happiness, delight, and pleasure". Red
coffins are favoured. The "red gate" on the south
side of a cemetery "is never opened except for the
passage of an Emperor".[4] The Chinese put a powdered
red stone called *hun-hong* in a drink or in food to destroy
an evil spirit which may have taken possession of one.
Red earth is eaten for a similar reason by the Polynesians and others. Many instances of this kind could
be given to illustrate the widespread persistence of the
belief in the vitalizing and protective qualities associated with red substances. In Irish Gaelic, Professor
W. J. Watson tells me, "ruadh" means both "red"
and "strong".

The Crô-Magnons regarded the heart as the seat of
life, having apparently discovered that it controls the
distribution of blood. In the cavern of Pindal, in south-
western France, is the outline of a hairy mammoth
painted in red ochre, and the seat of life is indicated by

---

[1] *Cults of the Greek States*, Vol. V, p. 243.
[2] Budge, *Gods of the Egyptians*, Vol. I, p. 203.
[3] De Groot, *The Religious System of China*, Book I, pp. 216-7.
[4] *Ibid.*, Book I, pp. 28 and 332.

a large red heart.   The painting dates back to the early
Aurignacian period.   In other cases, as in the drawing
of a large bison in the cavern of Niaux, the seat of life
and the vulnerable parts are indicated by spear- or
arrow-heads incised on the body.   The ancient Egyptians identified the heart with the mind.   To them the
heart was the seat of intelligence and will-power as well
as the seat of life.   The germ of this belief can apparently be found in the
pictorial art and burial
customs of the Auri-
gnacian Crô-Magnons.

Another   interesting
burial custom has been
traced in the Grimaldi
caves.   Some of the
skeletons were found to
have small green stones
between their teeth or
inside their mouths.[1]
No doubt these were
amulets.   Their colour
suggests that green sym-
bolism has not neces-

Outline of a Mammoth painted in red ochre in
the Cavern of Pindal, France

The seat of life is indicated by a large red
heart. (After Breuil.)

sarily a connection with agricultural religion, as some
have supposed.   The Crô-Magnons do not appear to
have paid much attention to vegetation.   In ancient
Egypt the green stone (Khepera) amulet "typified the
germ of life".   A text says, "A scarab of green stone
. . . shall be placed in the heart of a man, and it shall
perform for him the 'opening of the mouth'"—that is, it
will enable him to speak and eat again.   The scarab is
addressed in a funerary text, "My heart, my mother.
My heart whereby I came into being."   It is believed by

[1] I am indebted to the Abbé Breuil for this information which he gave me during the
course of a conversation.

Budge that the Egyptian custom of "burying green basalt scarabs inside or on the breasts of the dead" is as old as the first Dynasty (*c.* 3400 B.C.).[1] How much older it is one can only speculate. "The Mexicans", according to Brinton, "were accustomed to say that at one time all men have been stones, and that at last they would all return to stones, and acting literally on this conviction they interred with the bones of the dead a small green stone, which was called 'the principle of life'."[2] In China the custom of placing jade tongue amulets for the purpose of preserving the dead from decay and stimulating the soul to take flight to Paradise is of considerable antiquity.[3] Crystals and pebbles have been found in ancient British graves. It may well be that these pebbles were regarded as having had an intimate connection with deities, and perhaps to have been coagulated forms of what has been called "life substance". Of undoubted importance and significance was the ancient custom of adorning the dead with shells. As we have seen, this was a notable feature of the Paviland cave burial. The "Red Man" was not only smeared with red earth, but "charmed" or protected by shell amulets. In the next chapter it will be shown that this custom not only affords us a glimpse of Aurignacian religious beliefs, but indicates the area from which the Crô-Magnons came.

Professor G. Elliot Smith was the first to emphasize the importance attached in ancient times to the beliefs associated with the divine "giver of life".

---

[1] Budge, *Gods of the Egyptians,* Vol. I, p. 358. These scarabs have not been found in the early Dynastic graves. Green malachite charms, however, were used in even the pre-Dynastic period.

[2] *The Myths of the New World,* p. 294. According to Bancroft the green stones were often placed in the mouths of the dead.

[3] Laufer, *Jade,* pp. 294 *et seq.* (Chicago, 1912).

CHAPTER IV

Shell Deities and Early Trade

Early Culture and Early Races—Did Civilization originate in Europe?
—An Important Clue—Trade in Shells between Red Sea and Italy—
Traces of Early Trade in Central Europe—Religious Value of Personal
Ornaments—Importance of Shell Lore—Links between Far East and
Europe—Shell Deities—A Hebridean Shell Goddess—"Milk of Wisdom"
—Ancient Goddesses as Providers of Food—Gaelic "Spirit Shell" and
Japanese "God Body"—Influence of Deities in Jewels, &c.—A Shake-
spearean Reference—Shells in Crô-Magnon Graves—Early Sacrifices—
Hand Colours in Palæolithic Caves—Finger Lore and "Hand Spells".

When the question is asked, "Whence came the Crô-
Magnon people of the Aurignacian phase of culture?"
the answer usually given is, "Somewhere in the East".
The distribution of the Aurignacian sites indicates that
the new-comers entered south-western France by way
of Italy—that is, across the Italian land-bridge from
North Africa. Of special significance in this connection is the fact that Aurignacian culture persisted for
the longest period of time in Italy. The tallest Crô-
Magnons appear to have inhabited south-eastern
France and the western shores of Italy. "It is probable", says Osborn, referring to the men six feet four
and a half inches in height, "that in the genial
climate of the Riviera these men obtained their finest
development; the country was admirably protected
from the cold winds of the north, refuges were abundant, and game by no means scarce, to judge from the
quantity of animal bones found in the caves. Under

such conditions of life the race enjoyed a fine physical development and dispersed widely."[1]

It does not follow, however, that the tall people originated Aurignacian culture. As has been indicated, the stumpy people represented by Combe-Capelle skeletons were likewise exponents of it. "It must not be assumed", as Elliot Smith reminds us, "that the Aurignacian culture was necessarily invented by the same people who introduced it into Europe, and whose remains were associated with it . . . for any culture can be transmitted to an alien people, even when it has not been adopted by many branches of the race which was responsible for its invention, just as gas illumination, oil lamps, and even candles are still in current use by the people who invented the electric light, which has been widely adopted by many foreign peoples. This elementary consideration is so often ignored that it is necessary thus to emphasize it, because it is essential for any proper understanding of the history of early civilization."[2]

No trace of Aurignacian culture has, so far, been found outside Europe. "May it not, therefore," it may be asked, "have originated in Italy or France?" In absence of direct evidence, this possibility might be admitted. But an important discovery has been made at Grimaldi in La Grotte des Enfants (the "grotto of infants"—so called because of the discovery there of the skeletons of young Crô-Magnon children). Among the shells used as amulets by those who used the grotto as a sepulchre was one (*Cassis rufa*) that had been carried either by a migrating folk, or by traders, along the North African coast and through Italy from some southwestern Asian beach. The find has been recorded by Professor Marcellin Boule.[3]

---

[1] *Men of the Old Stone Age*, pp. 297-8.

[2] Primitive Man (*Proceedings of the British Academy*, Vol. VII).

[3] *Les Grottes de Grimaldi* (*Baousse-Rousse*), Tome I, fasc. II—*Géologie et Paléontologie* (Monaco, 1906), p. 123.

In a footnote, G. Dollfus writes:

"*Cassis rufa, L.*, an Indian ocean shell, is represented in the collection at Monaco by two fragments; one was found in the lower habitation level D, the other is probably of the same origin.   The presence of this shell is extraordinary, as it has no analogue in the Mediterranean, neither recent nor fossil; there exists no species in the North Atlantic or off Senegal with which it could be confounded.   The fragments have traces of the reddish colour preserved, and are not fossil; one of them presents a notch which has determined a hole that seems to have been made intentionally.   The species has not yet been found in the Gulf of Suez nor in the raised beaches of the Isthmus.   M. Jousseaume has found it in the Gulf of Tadjoura at Aden, but it has not yet been encountered in the Red Sea nor in the raised beaches of that region. The common habitat of *Cassis rufa* is Socotra, besides the Seychelles, Madagascar, Mauritius, New Caledonia, and perhaps Tahiti.   The fragments discovered at Mentone have therefore been brought from a great distance at a very ancient epoch by prehistoric man."

After the Crô-Magnon peoples had spread into Western and Central Europe they imported shells from the Mediterranean.   At Laugerie Basse in the Dordogne, for instance, a necklace of pierced shells from the Mediterranean was found in association with a skeleton. Atlantic shells could have been obtained from a nearer seashore.   It may be that the Rhone valley, which later became a well-known trade route, was utilized at an exceedingly remote period, and that cultural influences occasionally "flowed" along it.   "Prehistoric man" had acquired some experience as a trader even during the "hunting period", and he had formulated definite religious beliefs.

It has been the habit of some archæologists to refer to shell and other necklaces, &c., as "personal ornaments". The late Dr. Robert Munro wrote in this connection:

"We have no knowledge of any phase of humanity in which the love of personal ornament does not play an important part in the life of the individual. The savage of the present day, who paints or tattoos his body, and adorns it with shells, feathers, teeth, and trinkets made of the more gaudy materials at his disposal, may be accepted as on a parallel with the Neolithic people of Europe. . . . Teeth are often perforated and used as pendants, especially the canines of carnivorous animals, but such ornaments are not peculiar to Neolithic times, as they were equally prevalent among the later Palæolithic races of Europe." [1]

Modern savages have very definite reasons for wearing the so-called "ornaments", and for painting and tattooing their bodies. They believe that the shells, teeth, &c., afford them protection, and bring them luck. Ear-piercing, distending the lobe of the ear, disfiguring the body, the pointing, blackening, or knocking out of teeth, are all practices that have a religious significance. Even such a highly civilized people as the Chinese perpetuate, in their funerary ceremonies, customs that can be traced back to an exceedingly remote period in the history of mankind. It is not due to "love of personal ornament" that they place cowries, jade, gold, &c., in the mouth of the dead, but because they believe that by so doing the body is protected, and given a new lease of life. The Far Eastern belief that an elixir of ground oyster shells will prolong life in the next world is evidently a relic of early shell lore. Certain deities are associated with certain shells. Some deities have, like snails, shells for "houses"; others issue at birth from shells. The goddess Venus (Aphrodite) springs from the froth of the sea, and is lifted up by Tritons on a shell; she wears a love-girdle. Hathor, the Egyptian Venus, had originally a love-girdle of shells. She appears to have originated as the personification of a

[1] *Prehistoric Britain,* pp. 142-3.

shell, and afterwards to have personified the pearl within the shell. In early Egyptian graves the shell-amulets have been found in thousands. The importance of shell lore in ancient religious systems has been emphasized by Mr. J. Wilfrid Jackson in his *Shells as Evidence of the Migrations of Early Culture.*[1] He shows why the

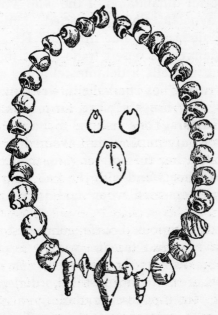

Necklace of Sea Shells, from the cave of Crô-Magnon. (After E. Lartet.)

cowry and snail shells were worn as amulets and charms, and why men were impelled "to search for them far and wide and often at great peril". "The murmur of the shell was the voice of the god, and the trumpet made of a shell became an important instrument in initiation ceremonies and in temple worship." Shells protected wearers against evil, including the evil eye. In like manner protection was afforded by the teeth and claws of carnivorous animals. In Asia and Africa the

[1] London, 1917.

belief that tigers, lions, &c., will not injure those who are thus protected is still quite widespread.

It cannot have been merely for love of personal ornaments that the Crô-Magnons of southern France imported Indian Ocean shells, and those of Central and Western Europe created a trade in Mediterranean shells. Like the ancient inhabitants of the Nile Valley who in remote pre-dynastic times imported shells, not only from the Mediterranean but from the Red Sea, along a long and dangerous desert trade-route, they evidently had imparted to shells a definite religious significance. The "luck-girdle" of snail-shells worn by the "Red Man of Paviland" has, therefore, an interesting history. When the Crô-Magnons reached Britain they brought with them not only implements invented and developed elsewhere, but a heritage of religious beliefs connected with shell ornaments and with the red earth with which the corpse was smeared when laid in its last resting-place.

The ancient religious beliefs connected with shells appear to have spread far and wide. Traces of them still survive in districts far separated from one another and from the area of origin—the borderlands of Asia and Africa.   In Japanese mythology a young god, Ohonamochie—a sort of male Cinderella—is slain by his jealous brothers.   His mother makes appeal to a sky deity who sends to her aid the two goddesses Princess Cockleshell and Princess Clam.   Princess Cockleshell burns and grinds her shell, and with water provided by Princess Clam prepares an elixir called "nurse's milk" or "mother's milk".   As soon as this "milk" is smeared over the young god, he is restored to life.   In the Hebrides it is still the custom of mothers to burn and grind the cockle-shell to prepare a lime-water for children who suffer from what in Gaelic is called "wasting".   In North America shells of *Unio* were placed in the graves of Red Indians "as food for the dead during the journey to the land of spirits". The pearls were used in India as medicines. "The burnt powder of the gems, if taken with water, cures hæmorrhages, prevents evil spirits working mischief in men's minds, cures lunacy and all mental diseases, jaundice, &c. . . . Rubbed over the body with other medicines it cures leprosy and all skin diseases."[1] The ancient Cretans, whose culture was carried into Asia and through Europe by their enterprising sea-and-land traders and prospectors, attached great importance to the cockle-shell which they connected with their mother goddess, the source of all life and the giver of medicines and food. Sir Arthur Evans found a large number of cockle-shells, some in Faeince, in the shrine of the serpent goddess in the ruins of the Palace of Knossos. The fact that the Cretans made artificial cockle-shells is of special interest, especially when we find that in Egypt the earliest use to which gold was put was in the manufacture of models of snail-shells in a necklace.[2] In different countries cowrie shells were similarly imitated in stone, ivory, and metal.[3]

Shells were thought to impart vitality and give protection, not only to human beings, but even to the plots of the earliest florists and agriculturists. "Mary, Mary, quite contrairie", who in the nursery rhyme has in her garden "cockle-shells all in row", was perpetuating an ancient custom. The cockle-shell is still favoured by conservative villagers, and may be seen in their garden plots and in graveyards. Shells placed at cottage doors, on window-sills, and round fire-places are supposed to bring luck and give security, like the horse-shoe on the door.

The mother goddess, remembered as the fairy queen,

---

[1] *Shells as Evidence of the Migrations of Early Culture*, pp. 84–91.
[2] G. A. Reisner, *Early Dynastic Cemeteries of Naga-ed-Der*, Vol. I, 1908, Plates 6 and 7.
[3] Jackson's *Shells*, pp. 128, 174, 176, 178.

is still connected with shells in Hebridean folk-lore.
A Gaelic poet refers to the goddess as "the maiden
queen of wisdom who dwelt in the beauteous bower
of the single tree where she could see the whole world
and where no fool could see her beauty". She lamented
the lack of wisdom among women, and invited them to
her knoll. When they were assembled there the goddess appeared, holding in her hand the *copan Moire*
("Cup of Mary"), as the blue-eyed limpet shell is called.
The shell contained "the ais (milk) of wisdom", which
she gave to all who sought it. "Many", we are told,
"came to the knoll too late, and there was no wisdom
left for them."[1] A Gaelic poet says the "maiden
queen" was attired in emerald green, silver, and mother-
of-pearl.

Here a particular shell is used by an old goddess for
a specific purpose. She imparts knowledge by providing a magic drink referred to as "milk". The question
arises, however, if a deity of this kind was known in
early times. Did the Crô-Magnons of the Aurignacian
stage of culture conceive of a god or goddess in human
form who nourished her human children and instructed
them as do human mothers? The figure of a woman,
holding in her hand a horn which appears to have been
used for drinking from, is of special interest in this connection. As will be shown, the Hebridean "maiden"
links with other milk-providing deities.

The earliest religious writings in the world are the

---

[1] Dr. Alexander Carmichael, *Carmina Gadelica*, Vol. II, pp. 247 *et seq*. Mr. Wilfrid
Jackson, author of *Shells as Evidence of the Migrations of Early Culture*, tells me that
the "blue-eyed limpet" is our common limpet—*Patella vulgata*—the Lepas, Patelle,
Jambe, Œil de boue, Bernicle, or Flie of the French. In Cornwall it is the "Crogan",
the "Bornigan", and the "Brennick". It is "flither" of the English, "flia" of the
Faroese, and "lapa" of the Portuguese. A Cornish giant was once, according to a
folk-tale, set to perform the hopeless task of emptying a pool with a single limpet which
had a hole in it. Limpets are found in early British graves and in the "kitchen middens".
They are met with in abundance in cromlechs, on the Channel Isles and in Brittany,
covering the bones and the skulls of the dead. Mr. Jackson thinks they were used like
cowries for vitalizing and protecting the dead.

Pyramid Texts of ancient Egypt which, as Professor
Breasted so finely says, "vaguely disclose to us a
vanished world of thought and speech". They abound
"in allusions to lost myths, to customs and usages long
since ended". Withal, they reflect the physical conditions of a particular area—the Nile Valley, in which
the sun and the river are two outstanding natural
features. There was, however, a special religious reason
for connecting the sun and the river.

In these old Pyramid Texts are survivals from a period
apparently as ancient as that of early Aurignacian civilization in Europe, and perhaps, as the clue afforded by
the Indian shell found in the Grimaldi cave, not un-
connected with it. The mother goddess, for instance,
is prayed to so that she may suckle the soul of the dead
Pharaoh as a mother suckles her child and never wean
him.[1] Milk was thus the elixir of life, and as the mother
goddess of Egypt is found to have been identified with the
cowrie—indeed to have been the spirit or personification
of the shell—the connection between shells and milk
may have obtained even in Aurignacian times in south-
western Europe. That the mother goddess of Crô-
Magnons had a human form is suggested by the
representations of mothers which have been brought
to light. An Aurignacian statuette of limestone found
in the cave of Willendorf, Lower Austria, has been
called the "Venus of Willendorf". She is very cor-
pulent—apparently because she was regarded as a giver
of life. Other statues of like character have been unearthed near Mentone, and they have a striking resemblance to the figurines of fat women found in the
pre-dynastic graves of Egypt and in Crete and Malta.
The bas-relief of the fat woman sculptured on a boulder
inside the Aurignacian shelter of Laussel may similarly
have been a goddess. In her right hand she holds a

[1] Breasted, *Religion and Thought in Ancient Egypt*, p. 130.

bison's horn—perhaps a drinking horn containing an elixir. Traces of red colouring remain on the body. A notable fact about these mysterious female forms is that the heads are formal, the features being scarcely, if at all, indicated.

Even if no such "idols" had been found, it does not follow that the early people had no ideas about supernatural beings. There are references in Gaelic to the *coich anama* (the "spirit case", or "soul shell", or "soul husk"). In Japan, which has a particularly rich and voluminous mythology, there are no idols in Shinto temples. A deity is symbolized by the *shintai* (God body), which may be a mirror, a weapon, or a round stone, a jewel or a pearl. A pearl is a *tama*; so is a precious stone, a crystal, a bit of worked jade, or a necklace of jewels, ivory, artificial beads, &c. The soul of a supernatural being is called *mi-tama*—*mi* being now a honorific prefix, but originally signifying a water serpent (dragon god). The shells, of which ancient deities were personifications, may well have been to the Crô-Magnons pretty much what a *tama* is to the Japanese, and what magic crystals were to mediæval Europeans who used them for magical purposes. It may have been believed that in the shells, green stones, and crystals remained the influence of deities as the power of beasts of prey remained in their teeth and claws. The ear-rings and other Pagan ornaments which Jacob buried with Laban's idols under the oak at Shechem were similarly supposed to be god bodies or coagulated forms of "life substance". All idols were temporary or permanent bodies of deities, and idols were not necessarily large. It would seem to be a reasonable conclusion that all the so-called ornaments found in ancient graves were supposed to have had an intimate connection with the supernatural beings who gave origin to and sustained life. These ornaments, or charms, or amulets, imparted vitality to human beings, because they were regarded as the substance of life itself. The red jasper worn in the waist girdles of the ancient Egyptians was reputed, as has been stated, to be a coagulated drop of the blood of the mother goddess Isis. Blood was the essence of life.

The red woman or goddess of the Laussel shelter was probably coloured so as to emphasize her vitalizing attributes; the red colour animated the image.

An interesting reference in Shakespeare's *Hamlet* to ancient burial customs may here be quoted, because it throws light on the problem under discussion. When Ophelia's body is carried into the graveyard[1] one of the priests says that as " her death was doubtful " she should have been buried in " ground unsanctified "— that is, among the suicides and murderers. Having taken her own life, she was unworthy of Christian burial, and should be buried in accordance with Pagan customs. In all our old churchyards the takers of life were interred on the north side, and apparently in Shakespeare's day traditional Pagan rites were observed in the burials of those regarded as Pagans. The priest in *Hamlet*, therefore, says of Ophelia:

> She should in ground unsanctified have lodged
> Till the last trumpet; *for charitable prayers,*
> *Shards, flints, and pebbles should be thrown on her.*

There are no shards (fragments of pottery) in the Crô-Magnon graves, but flints and pebbles mingle with shells, teeth, and other charms and amulets. Vast numbers of perforated shells have been found in the burial caves near Mentone. In one case the shells are so numerous that they seem to have formed a sort of burial mantle. " Similarly," says Professor Osborn, describing another of these finds, " the female skeleton

[1] *Hamlet*, V, i.

was enveloped in a bed of shells not perforated; the legs were extended, while the arms were stretched beside the body; there were a few pierced shells and a few bits of silex. One of the large male skeletons of the same grotto had the lower limbs extended, the upper limbs folded, and was decorated with a gorget and crown of perforated shells; the head rested on a block of red stone." In another case "heavy stones protected the body from disturbance; the head was decorated with a circle of perforated shells *coloured in red*, and implements of various types were carefully placed on the forehead and chest". The body of the Combe-Capelle man "was decorated with a necklace of perforated shells and surrounded with a great number of fine Aurignacian flints. It appears", adds Osborn, "that in all the numerous burials of these grottos of Aurignacian age and industry of the Crô-Magnon race we have the burial standards which prevailed in western Europe at this time."[1]

It has been suggested by one of the British archæologists that the necklaces of perforated cowrie shells and the red pigment found among the remains of early man in Britain were used by children. This theory does not accord with the evidence afforded by the Grimaldi caves, in which the infant skeletons are neither coloured nor decorated. Occasionally, however, the children were interred in burial mantles of small perforated shells, while female adults were sometimes placed in beds of unperforated shells. Shells have been found in early British graves. These include *Nerita litoralis*, and even *Patella vulgata*, the common limpet. Holes were rubbed in them so that they might be strung together. In a megalithic cist unearthed in Phœnix Park, Dublin, in 1838, two male skeletons had each beside them perforated shells (*Nerita litoralis*). During the construction of

[1] *Men of the Old Stone Age*, pp. 304-5.

the Edinburgh and Granton railway there was found beside a skeleton in a stone cist a quantity of cockle-shell rings. Two dozen perforated oyster-shells were found in a single Orkney cist. Many other examples of this kind could be referred to.[1]

In the Crô-Magnon caverns are imprints of human hands which had been laid on rock and then dusted round with coloured earth. In a number of cases it is shown that one or more finger joints of the left hand had been cut off.

The practice of finger mutilation among Bushman, Australian, and Red Indian tribes, is associated with burial customs and the ravages of disease. A Bushman woman may cut off a joint of one of her fingers when a near relative is about to die. Red Indians cut off finger-joints when burying their dead during a pestilence, so as " to cut off deaths "; they sacrificed a part of the body to save the whole. In Australia finger mutilation is occasionally practised. Highland Gaelic stories tell of heroes who lie asleep to gather power which will enable them to combat with monsters or fierce enemies. Heroines awake them by cutting off a finger joint, a part of the ear, or a portion of skin from the scalp.[2]

The colours used in drawings of hands in Palæolithic caves are black, white, red, and yellow, as the Abbé Breuil has noted. In Spain and India, the hand prints are supposed to protect dwellings from evil influences. Horse-shoes, holly with berries, various plants, shells, &c., are used for a like purpose among those who in our native land perpetuate ancient customs.

The Arabs have a custom of suspending figures of an

---

[1] A Red Sea cowry shell (*Cypræa minor*) found on the site of Hurstbourne station (L. & S. W. Railway, main line) in Hampshire, was associated with "Early Iron Age" artifacts. (Paper read by J. R. le B. Tomlin at meeting of Linnæan Society, June 14, 1911.)

[2] For references see my *Myths of Crete and Pre-Hellenic Europe*, pp. 30–31.

open hand from the necks of their children, and the Turks and Moors paint hands upon their ships and houses, " as an antidote and counter charm to an evil eye; for five is with them an unlucky number; and 'five (fingers, perhaps) in your eyes' is their proverb of cursing and defiance ". In Portugal the hand spell is called the *figa*. Southey suggests that our common phrase "a fig for him" was derived from the name of the Portuguese hand amulet.[1]

"The figo for thy friendship" is an interesting reference by Shakespeare.[2] Fig or figo is probably from *fico*, a snap of the fingers, which in French is *faire la figue*, and in Italian *far le fiche*. Finger snapping had no doubt originally a magical significance.

---

[1] Notes to *Thalaba*, Book V, Canto 36.   [2] *Henry V*, V, iii, 6.

CHAPTER V

New Races in Europe

The Solutrean Industry—A Racial and Cultural Intrusion—Decline of Aurignacian Art—A God-cult—The Solutrean Thor—Open-air Life— Magdalenian Culture — Decline of Flint Working — Horn and Bone Weapons and Implements—Revival of Crô-Magnon Art—The Lamps and Palettes of Cave Artists—The Domesticated Horse—Eskimos in Europe—Magdalenian Culture in England—The Vanishing Ice—Reindeer migrate Northward — New Industries — Tardenoisian and Azilian Industries — Pictures and Symbols of Azilians — "Long-heads" and "Broad-heads" — Maglemosian Culture of Fair Northerners — Pre-Neolithic Peoples in Britain.

In late Aurignacian times the influence of a new industry was felt in Western Europe. It first came from the south, and reached as far north as England where it can be traced in the caverns. Then, in time, it spread westward and wedge-like through Central Europe in full strength, with the force and thoroughness of an invasion, reaching the northern fringe of the Spanish coast. This was the Solutrean industry which had distinctive and independent features of its own. It was not derived from Aurignacian but had developed somewhere in Africa— perhaps in Somaliland, whence it radiated along the Libyan coast towards the west and eastward into Asia. The main or "true" Solutrean influence entered Europe from the south-east. It did not pass into Italy, which remained in the Aurignacian stage until Azilian times, nor did it cross the Pyrenees or invade Spain south of the Cantabrian Mountains. The earlier "influence" is referred to as "proto-Solutrean".

Solutrean is well represented in Hungary where no trace of Aurignacian culture has yet been found. Apparently that part of Europe had offered no attractions for the Crô-Magnons.

Who the carriers of this new culture were it is as yet impossible to say with confidence. They may have been a late "wave" of the same people who had first introduced Aurignacian culture into Europe, and they may have been representative of a different race. Some ethnologists incline to connect the Solutrean culture with a new people whose presence is indicated by the skulls found at Brünn and Brüx in Bohemia. These intruders had lower foreheads than the Crô-Magnons, narrower and longer faces, and low cheek-bones. It may be that they represented a variety of the Mediterranean race. Whoever they were, they did not make much use of ivory and bone, but they worked flint with surpassing skill and originality. Their technique was quite distinct from the Aurignacian. With the aid of wooden or bone tools, they finished their flint artifacts by pressure, gave them excellent edges and points, and shaped them with artistic skill. Their most characteristic flints are the so-called laurel-leaf (broad) and willow-leaf (narrow) lances. These were evidently used in the chase. There is no evidence that they were used in battle. Withal, their weapons had a religious significance. Fourteen laurel-leaf spear-heads of Solutrean type which were found together at Volgu, Saône-et-Loire, are believed to have been a votive offering to a deity. At any rate, these were too finely worked and too fragile, like some of the peculiar Shetland and Swedish knives of later times, to have been used as implements. One has retained traces of red colouring. It may be that the belief enshrined in the Gaelic saying, "Every weapon has its demon", had already come into existence. In Crete the double-axe was in Minoan times a symbol of a deity;[1] and in northern Egypt and on the Libyan coast the crossed arrows symbolized the goddess Neith; while in various countries, and especially in India, there are ancient stories about the spirits of weapons appearing in visions and promising to aid great hunters and warriors. The custom of giving weapons personal names, which survived for long in Europe, may have had origin in Solutrean times.

Art languished in Solutrean times. Geometrical figures were incised on ivory and bone; some engraving of mammoths, reindeer, and lions have been found in Moravia and France. When the human figure was depicted, the female was neglected and studies made of males. It may be that the Solutreans had a god-cult as distinguished from the goddess-cult of the Aurignacians, and that their "flint-god" was an early form of Zeus, or of Thor, whose earliest hammer was of flint. The Romans revered "Jupiter Lapis" (silex). When the solemn oath was taken at the ceremony of treaty-making, the representative of the Roman people struck a sacrificial pig with the *silex* and said, "Do thou, Diespiter, strike the Roman people as I strike this pig here to-day, and strike them the more, as thou art greater and stronger". Mr. Cyril Bailey (*The Religion of Ancient Rome*, p. 7) expresses the view that "in origin the stone is itself the god".

During Solutrean times the climate of Europe, although still cold, was drier than in Aurignacian times. It may be that the intruders seized the flint quarries of the Crô-Magnons, and also disputed with them the possession of hunting-grounds. The cave art declined or was suspended during what may have been a military regime and perhaps, too, under the influence of a new religion and new social customs. Open-air camps

---

[1] For other examples see Mr. Legge's article in *Proceedings of the Society of Biblical Archæology*, 1899, p. 310.

beside rock-shelters were greatly favoured. It may be, as has been suggested, that the Solutreans were as expert as the modern Eskimos in providing clothing and skin-tents. Bone needles were numerous. They fed well, and horse-flesh was a specially favoured food.

In their mountain retreats, the Aurignacians may have concentrated more attention than they had previously done on the working of bone and horn; it may be that they were reinforced by new races from north-eastern Europe, who had been developing a distinctive industry on the borders of Asia. At any rate, the industry known as Magdalenian became widespread when the ice-fields crept southward again, and southern and central Europe became as wet and cold as in early Aurignacian times. Solutrean culture gradually declined and vanished and Magdalenian became supreme.

The Magdalenian stage of culture shows affinities with Aurignacian and betrays no influence of Solutrean technique. The method of working flint was quite different. The Magdalenians, indeed, appear to have attached little importance to flint for implements of the chase. They often chipped it badly in their own way and sometimes selected flint of poor quality, but they had beautiful "scrapers" and "gravers" of flint. It does not follow, however, that they were a people on a lower stage of culture than the Solutreans. New inventions had rendered it unnecessary for them to adopt Solutrean technique. Most effective implements of horn and bone had come into use and, if wars were waged—there is no evidence of warfare—the Magdalenians were able to give a good account of themselves with javelins and exceedingly strong spears which were given a greater range by the introduction of spear-throwers—"cases" from which spears were thrown. The food supply was increased by a new method of catching fish. Barbed harpoons of reindeer-horn had been invented, and no doubt many salmon, &c., were caught at river-side stations.

The Crô-Magnons, as has been found, were again in the ascendant, and their artistic genius was given full play as in Aurignacian times, and, no doubt, as a result of the revival of religious beliefs that fostered art as a cult product. Once again the painters, engravers, and sculptors adorned the caves with representations of wild animals. Colours were used with increasing skill and taste. The artists had palettes on which to mix their colours, and used stone lamps, specimens of which have been found, to light up their "studios" in deep cave recesses. During this Magdalenian stage of culture the art of the Crô-Magnons reached its highest standard of excellence, and grew so extraordinarily rich and varied that it compares well with the later religious arts of ancient Egypt and Babylonia.

The horse appears to have been domesticated. There is at Saint Michel d'Arudy a "Celtic" horse depicted with a bridle, while at La Madeleine was found a "bâton de commandement" on which a human figure, with a stave in his right hand, walks past two horses which betray no signs of alarm.

Our knowledge is scanty regarding the races that occupied Europe during Magdalenian times. In addition to the Crô-Magnons there were other distinctive types. One of these is represented by the Chancelade skeleton found at Raymonden shelter. Some think it betrays Eskimo affinities, and represents a racial "drift" from the Russian steppes. In his *Ancient Hunters* Professor Sollas shows that there are resemblances between Eskimo and Magdalenian artifacts.

The Magdalenian culture reached England, although it never penetrated into Italy, and was shut out from the greater part of Spain. It has been traced as far north as Derbyshire, on the north-eastern border of which the

Cresswell caves have yielded Magdalenian relics, including flint-borers, engravers, &c., and bone implements, including a needle, an awl, chisels, an engraving of a horse on bone, &c. Kent's Cavern, near Torquay in Devonshire, has also yielded Magdalenian flints and implements of bone, including pins, awls, barbed harpoons, &c.

During early Magdalenian times, however, our native land did not offer great attractions to Continental people. The final glacial epoch may have been partial, but it was severe, and there was a decided lowering of the temperature. Then came a warmer and drier spell, which was followed by the sixth partial glaciation. Thereafter the "great thaw" opened up Europe to the invasion of new races from Asia and Africa.

Three distinct movements of peoples in Europe can be traced in post-Magdalenian times, and during what has been called the "Transition Period", between the Upper Palæolithic and Lower Neolithic Ages or stages. The ice-cap retreated finally from the mountains of Scotland and Sweden, and the reindeer migrated northward. Magdalenian civilization was gradually broken up, and the cave art suffered sharp decline until at length it perished utterly. Trees flourished in areas where formerly the reindeer scraped the snow to crop moss and lichen, and rich pastures attracted the northward migrating red deer, the roe-deer, the ibex, the wild boar, wild cattle, &c.

The new industries are known as the Tardenoisian, the Azilian, and the Maglemosian.

Tardenoisian flints are exceedingly small and beautifully worked, and have geometric forms; they are known as "microliths" and "pygmy flints". They were evidently used in catching fish, some being hooks and others spear-heads; and they represent a culture that spread round the Mediterranean basin: these flints are found in northern Egypt, Tunis, Algeria, and Italy; from Italy they passed through Europe into England and Scotland. A people who decorated with scenes of daily life rock shelters and caves in Spain, and hunted red deer and other animals with bows and arrows, were pressing northward across the new grass-lands towards the old Magdalenian stations. Men wore pants and

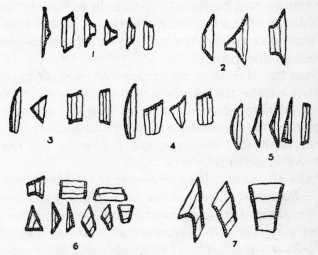

Geometric or "Pygmy" Flints. (After Breuil.)

1, From Tunis and Southern Spain. 2, From Portugal. 3, 4, Azilian types.
5, 6, 7, Tardenoisian types.

feather head-dresses; women had short gowns, blouses, and caps, as had the late Magdalenians, and both sexes wore armlets, anklets, and other ornaments of magical potency. Females were nude when engaged in the chase. The goddess Diana had evidently her human prototypes. There were ceremonial dances, as the rock pictures show; women lamented over graves, and affectionate couples—at least they seem to have been affectionate—walked hand in hand as they gradually migrated towards northern Spain, and northern France and Britain. The horse was domesticated, and is seen being

led by the halter. Wild animal "drives" were organized, and many victims fell to archer and spearman.
Arrows were feathered; bows were large and strong.
Symbolic signs indicate that a script similar to those of
the Ægean area, the northern African coast, and pre-
dynastic Egypt was freely used. Drawings became
conventional, and ultimately animals and human beings
were represented by signs. This culture lasted after the
introduction of the Neolithic industry in some areas, and
in others after the bronze industry had been adopted by
sections of the people.

When the Magdalenian harpoon of reindeer horn was
imitated by the flat harpoon of red-deer horn, this new
culture became what is known as Azilian. It met and
mingled with Tardenoisian, which appears to have
arrived later, and the combined industries are referred
to as Azilian-Tardenoisian.

While the race-drifts, represented by the carriers of
the Azilian and Tardenoisian industries, were moving
into France and Britain, another invasion from the East
was in progress. It is represented in the famous Ofnet
cave where long-heads and broad-heads were interred.
The Asiatic Armenoids (Alpine type) had begun to
arrive in Europe, the glaciers having vanished in Asia
Minor. Skulls of broad-heads found in the Belgian cave
of Furfooz, in which sixteen human skeletons were unearthed in 1867, belong to this period. The early
Armenoids met and mingled with representatives of the
blond northern race, and were the basis of the broad-
headed blonds of Holland, Denmark, and Belgium.

Maglemosian culture is believed to have been introduced by the ancestors of the fair peoples of Northern
Europe. It has been so named after the finds at Magle-
mose in the "Great Moor", near Mullerup, on the
western coast of Zeeland. A lake existed at this place
at a time when the Baltic was an inland water completely

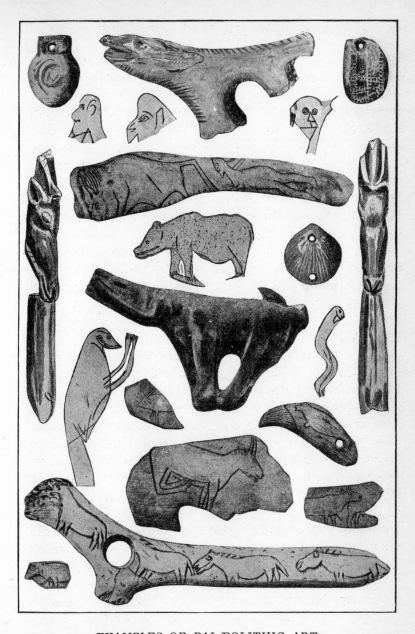

EXAMPLES OF PALÆOLITHIC ART

The objects include: handles of knives and daggers carved in ivory and bone, line drawings of wild animals, faces of masked men, of animal-headed deity or masked man with arms uplifted (compare Egyptian "Ka" attitude of adoration), of wild horses on perforated *bâton de commandement*, of man stalking a bison, of seal, cow, reindeer, cave bear, &c., and perforated amulets.

shut off from the North Sea. In a peat bog, formerly the bed of the lake, were found a large number of flint and bone artifacts. These included Tardenoisian microliths, barbed harpoons of bone, needles of bone, spears of bone, &c. Bone was more freely used than horn for implements and weapons. The animals hunted included the stag, roe-deer, moose, wild ox, and wild boar. Dogs were domesticated. It appears that the Maglemosians were lake-dwellers. Their houses, however, had not been erected on stilts, but apparently on a floating platform of logs, which was no doubt anchored or moored to the shore. There are traces of Magdalenian influence in Maglemosian culture. Although many decorative forms on bone implements and engravings on rocks are formal and symbolic, there are some fine and realistic representations of animals worthy of the Magdalenian cave artists. Traces of the Maglemosian racial drift have been obtained on both sides of the Baltic and in the Danish kitchen middens. Engravings on rocks at Lake Onega in Northern Russia closely resemble typical Maglemosian work. Apparently the northern fair peoples entered Europe from Western Siberia, and in time were influenced by Neolithic culture. But before the Europeans began to polish their stone implements and weapons, the blond hunters and fishermen settled not only in Denmark and Southern Sweden and Norway but also in Britain.

At the time when the Baltic was an inland fresh-water lake, the southern part of the North Sea was dry land, and trees grew on Dogger Bank, from which fishermen still occasionally lift in their trawls lumps of " moor-log " (peat) and the bones of animals, including those of the reindeer, the red deer, the horse, the wild ox, the bison, the Irish elk, the bear, the wolf, the beaver, the woolly rhinoceros, the mammoth, and the walrus. No doubt the Maglemosians found their way over this "land-

bridge ", crossing the rivers in rude boats, and on foot
when the rivers were frozen. Evidence has been forthcoming that they also followed the present coast line
towards Boulogne, near which a typical Maglemosian
harpoon has been discovered.

Traces of Maglemosian influence have been found
as far north as Scotland on the Hebridean islands of

A Notable Example of late Magdalenian Culture: engraving on bone of browsing
reindeer.   From Kesserloch, Switzerland.   (After Heim.)

Oronsay and Risga. The MacArthur cave at Oban
reveals Azilian artifacts. In the Victoria cave near
Settle in Yorkshire a late Magdalenian or proto-Azilian
harpoon made of reindeer-horn is of special interest,
displaying, as it does, a close connection between late
Magdalenian and early Azilian. Barbed harpoons,
found at the shelter of Druimvargie, near Oban, are
Azilian, some displaying Maglemosian features. Barbed
harpoons of bone, and especially those with barbs on
one side only, are generally Maglemosian, while those
of horn and double-barbed are typically Azilian.

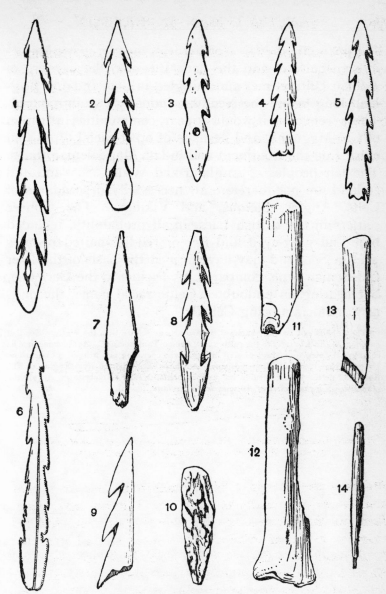

Horn and Bone Implements

Harpoons: 1 and 2, from MacArthur Cave, Oban; 3, from Laugerie Basse rock-shelter, France; 4, from shell-heap, Oronsay, Hebrides; 5, from bed of River Dee near Kirk-cudbright; 6, from Palude Brabbie, Italy—all of Azilian type. 8, Reindeer-horn harpoon of late Magdalenian, or proto-Azilian, type from Victoria Cave, near Settle, Yorks. 9, Maglemosian, or Azilian-Maglemosian, harpoon from rock-shelter, Druimvargie, Oban. 7, 10, 11, 12, 13, and 14, bone and deer-horn implements from MacArthur Cave, Oban.

Apparently the fair Northerners, the carriers of Magle-mosian culture, and the dark Iberians, the carriers of Azilian culture, met and mingled in Scotland and England long before the Neolithic industry was introduced. There were also, it would appear, communities in Britain of Crô-Magnons, and perhaps of other racial types that existed on the Continent and in late Magdalenian times. The fair peoples of England and Wales, Scotland and Ireland are not therefore all necessarily descendants of Celts, Angles, Saxons, and Vikings. The pioneer settlers in the British Isles, in all probability, included blue and grey-eyed and fair or reddish-haired peoples who in Scotland may have formed the basis of the later Caledonian type, compared by Tacitus to the Germans, but bearing an undoubted Celtic racial name, the military aristocrats being Celts.[1]

[1] The Abbé Breuil, having examined the artifacts associated with the Western Scottish harpoons, inclines to refer to the culture as "Azilian-Tardenoisian". At the same time he considers the view that Maglemosian influence was operating is worthy of consideration. He notes that traces of Maglemosian culture have been reported from England. The Abbé has detected Magdalenian influence in artifacts from Campbeltown, Argyllshire (*Proceedings of the Society of Antiquaries in Scotland*, 1921-2).

CHAPTER VI

The Faithful Dog

Transition Period between Palæolithic and Neolithic Ages—Theory of the Neolithic Edge—Crô-Magnon Civilization was broken up by Users of Bow and Arrow—Domesticated Dog of Fair Northerners—Dogs as Guides and Protectors of Man—The Dog in Early Religion—Dog Guides of Souls—The Dog of Hades—Dogs and Death—The Scape-dog in Scotland—Souls in Dog Form—Traces of Early Domesticated Dogs—Romans imported British Dogs.

The period we have now reached is regarded by some as that of transition between the Palæolithic and Neolithic Ages, and by others as the Early Neolithic period. It is necessary, therefore, that we should keep in mind that these terms have been to a great extent divested of the significance originally attached to them. The transition period was a lengthy one, extending over many centuries during which great changes occurred. It was much longer than the so-called "Neolithic Age". New races appeared in Europe and introduced new habits of life and thought, new animals appeared and animals formerly hunted by man retreated northward or became extinct; the land sank and rose; a great part of the North Sea and the English Channel was for a time dry land, and trees grew on the plateau now marked by the Dogger Bank during this "Transition Period", and before it had ended the Strait of Dover had widened and England was completely cut off from the Continent.

Compared with these great changes the invention of the polished axe edge seems almost trivial. Yet some

writers have regarded this change as being all-important.
" On the edge ever since its discovery ", writes one of
them with enthusiasm, " has depended and probably
will depend to the end of time the whole artistic and
artificial environment of human existence, in all its
infinite varied complexity. . . . By this discovery was
broken down a wall that for untold ages had dammed
up a stagnant, unprogressive past, and through the
breach were let loose all the potentialities of the future
civilization of mankind.   It was entirely due to the discovery of the edge that man was enabled, in the course
of time, to invent the art of shipbuilding."[1]

This is a very sweeping claim and hardly justified by
the evidence that of late years has come to light.   Much
progress had been achieved before the easy method of
polishing supplanted that of secondary working.   The
so-called Palæolithic implements were not devoid of
edges.   What really happened was that flint-working
was greatly simplified.   The discovery was an important one, but it was not due to it alone that great changes
in habits of life were introduced.   Long before the introduction of the Neolithic industry, the earliest traces
of which in Western Europe have been obtained at
Campigny near the village of Blangy on the River
Bresle, the Magdalenian civilization of the Crô-Magnons
had been broken up by the Azilian-Tardenoisian intruders in Central and Western Europe and by the
Maglemosians in the Baltic area.

The invading hordes in Spain, so far as can be
gathered from rock pictures, made more use of bows
and arrows than of spears, and it may be that their social
organization was superior to that of the Magdalenians.
Their animal "drives" suggest as much.   It may be
that they were better equipped for organized warfare—
if there was warfare—and for hunting by organizing

---

[1] Eirikr Magnusson in *Notes on Shipbuilding and Nautical Terms*, London, 1906.

drives than the taller and stronger Crô-Magnons. When they reached the Magdalenian stations they adopted the barbed harpoon, imitating reindeer-horn forms in red-deer horn.

The blond Maglemosians in the Baltic area introduced from Asia the domesticated dog. They were thus able to obtain their food supply with greater ease than did the Solutreans with their laurel-leaf lances, or the Magdalenians with their spears tipped with bone or horn. When man was joined by his faithful ally he met with more success than when he pursued the chase unaided. Withal, he could take greater risks when threatened by the angry bulls of a herd, and operate over more extended tracks of country with less fear of attack by beasts of prey. His dogs warned him of approaching peril and guarded his camp by night.

Hunters who dwelt in caves may have done so partly for protection against lions and bears and wolves that were attracted to hunters' camps by the scent of flesh and blood. No doubt barriers had to be erected to shield men, women, and children in the darkness; and it may be that there were fires and sentinels at cave entrances.

The introduction of the domesticated dog may have influenced the development of religious beliefs. Crô-Magnon hunters appear to have performed ceremonies in the depths of caverns where they painted and carved wild animals, with purpose to obtain power over them. Their masked dances, in which men and women represented wild animals, chiefly beasts of prey, may have had a similar significance. The fact that, during the Transition Period, a cult art passed out of existence, and the caves were no longer centres of culture and political power, may have been directly or indirectly due to the domestication of the dog and the supremacy achieved by the intruders who possessed it.

There can be no doubt that the dog played its part in the development of civilization. As much is suggested by the lore attaching to this animal. It occupies a prominent place in mythology. The dog which guided and protected the hunter in his wanderings was supposed to guide his soul to the other world.

> He thought admitted to that equal sky,
> His faithful dog would bear him company.

In Ancient Egypt the dog-headed god Anubis was the guide and protector of souls. Apuatua, an early form of Osiris, was a dog god. Yama, the Hindu god of death, as Dharma, god of justice, assumed his dog form to guide the Panadava brothers to Paradise, as is related in the Sanskrit epic the *Mahá-bhárata*[1]. The god Indra, the Hindu Jupiter, was the "big dog", and the custom still prevails among primitive Indian peoples of torturing a dog by pouring hot oil into its ears so that the "big dog" may hear and send rain. In the *Mahá-bhárata* there is a story about Indra appearing as a hunter followed by a pack of dogs. As the "Wild Huntsman" the Scandinavian god Odin rides through the air followed by dogs. The dog is in Greek mythology the sentinel of Hades; it figures in a like capacity in the Hades of Northern Mythology. Cuchullin, the Gaelic hero, kills the dog of Hades and takes its place until another dog is found and trained, and that is why he is called "Cu" (the dog) of Culann. A pool in Kildonan, Sutherland, which was reputed to contain a pot of gold, was supposed to be guarded by a big black dog with two heads. A similar legend attaches to Hound's Pool in the parish of Dean Combe, Devonshire. In different parts of the world the dog is the creator and ancestor of the human race, the symbol of kinship, &c. The star Sirius was associated with the dog. In Scotland and

---

[1] Pronounced ma-haw'-baw'-rata (the two final *a*'s are short).

Ireland "dog stones" were venerated. A common surviving belief is that dogs howl by night when a sudden death is about to occur. This association of the dog with death is echoed by Theocritus. "Hark!" cries Simaetha, "the dogs are barking through the town. Hecate is at the crossways. Haste, clash the brazen cymbals." The dog-god of Scotland is remembered as *an cù sìth* ("the supernatural dog"); it is as big as a calf, and by night passes rapidly over land and sea. A black demon-dog—the "Moddey Dhoo"—referred to by Scott in *Peveril of the Peak* was supposed to haunt Peel Castle in the Isle of Man. A former New Year's day custom in Perthshire was to send away from a house door a scape-dog with the words, "Get away you dog! Whatever death of men or loss of cattle would happen in this house till the end of the present year, may it all light on your head." A similar custom obtained among Western Himalayan peoples. Early man appears to have regarded his faithful companion as a supernatural being. There are Gaelic references to souls appearing in dog form to assist families in time of need. Not only did the dog attack beasts of prey; in Gaelic folk-tales it is the enemy of fairies and demons, and especially cave-haunting demons. Early man's gratitude to and dependence on the dog seems to be reflected in stories of this kind.

When the Baltic peoples, who are believed to be the first "wave" of blond Northerners, moved westward towards Denmark during the period of the "great thaw", they must have been greatly assisted by the domesticated dog, traces of which are found in Maglemosian stations. Bones of dogs have been found in the Danish kitchen middens and in the MacArthur cave at Oban. It may be that the famous breed of British hunting dogs which were in Roman times exported to Italy were descended from those introduced by the Maglemosian hunters.

Seven Irish dogs were in the fourth century presented to Symmachus, a Roman consul, by his brother. "All Rome", the grateful recipient wrote, "view them with wonder and thought they must have been brought hither in iron cages."

Great dogs were kept in Ancient Britain and Ireland for protection against wolves as well as for hunting wild animals. The ancient Irish made free use in battle of large fierce hounds. In the folk-stories of Scotland dogs help human beings to attack and overcome supernatural beings. Dogs were the enemies of the fairies, mermaids, &c.

Dog gods figure on the ancient sculptured stones of Scotland. The names of the Irish heroes Cuchullin and Con-chobar were derived from those of dog deities. "Con" is the genitive of "Cu" (dog).

CHAPTER VII

Ancient Mariners Reach Britain

Reindeer in Scotland—North Sea and English Channel Land-bridges—Early River Rafts and River Boats—Breaking of Land-bridges—Coast Erosion—Tilbury Man—Where were first Boats Invented?—Ancient Boats in Britain—"Dug-out" Canoes—Imitations of Earlier Papyri and Skin Boats—Cork Plug in Ancient Clyde Boat—Early Swedish Boats—An African Link—Various Types of British Boats—Daring Ancient Mariners—The Veneti Seafarers—Attractions of Early Britain for Colonists.

The Maglemosian (Baltic) and Azilian (Iberian) peoples, who reached and settled in Britain long before the introduction of the Neolithic industry, appear, as has been shown, to have crossed the great land-bridge, which is now marked by the Dogger Bank, and the narrowed land-bridge that connected England and France. No doubt they came at first in small bands, wandering along the river banks and founding fishing communities, following the herds of red deer and wild cows that had moved northward, and seeking flints, &c. The Crô-Magnons, whose civilization the new intruders had broken up on the Continent, were already in Britain, where the reindeer lingered for many centuries after they had vanished from France. The reindeer moss still grows in the north of Scotland. Bones and horns of the reindeer have been found in this area in association with human remains as late as of the Roman period. In the twelfth century the Norsemen hunted reindeer in

Caithness.[1] Cæsar refers to the reindeer in the Hercynian forest of Germany (*Gallic War*, VI, 26).

The early colonists of fair Northerners who introduced the Maglemosian culture into Britain from the Baltic area could not have crossed the North Sea land-bridge without the aid of rafts or boats. Great broad rivers were flowing towards the north. The Elbe and the Weser joined one another near the island of Heligoland, and received tributaries from marshy valleys until a long estuary wider than is the Wash at present was formed. Another long river flowed northward from the valley of the Zuyder Zee, the mouth of which has been traced on the north-east of the Dogger Bank. The Rhine reached the North Sea on the south-west of the Dogger Bank, off Flamborough Head; its tributaries included the Meuse and the Thames. The Humber and the rivers flowing at present into the Wash were united before entering the North Sea between the mouth of the Rhine and the coast of East Riding.

The Dogger Bank was then a plateau. Trawlers, as has been stated, sometimes lift from its surface in their trawl nets lumps of peat, which they call "moor-log", and also the bones of wild animals, including the wild ox, the wild horse, red deer, reindeer, the elk, the bear, the wolf, the hyæna, the beaver, the walrus the woolly rhinoceros, and the hairy mammoth. In the peat have been found the remains of the white birch, the hazel, sallow, and willow, seeds of bog-bean, fragments of fern, &c. All the plants have a northern range. In some pieces of peat have been found plants and insects that still flourish in Britain.[2]

The easiest crossing to Britain was over the English Channel land-bridge. It was ultimately cut through by

---

[1] *The Orkneyinga Saga*, p. 182, Edinburgh, 1873, and *Proceedings of the Society of Antiquaries of Scotland*, Vol. VIII.
[2] Clement Reid, *Submerged Forests*, pp. 45–7, London, 1913.

the English Channel river, so that the dark Azilian-
Tardenoisian peoples from Central and Western Europe
and the fair Maglemosians must have required and used
rafts or boats before polished implements of Neolithic
type came into use. In time the North Sea broke
through the marshes of the river land to the east of the
Thames Estuary and joined the waters of the English
Channel. The Strait of Dover was then formed. At
first it may have been narrow enough for animals to
swim across or, at any rate, for the rude river boats or
rafts of the early colonists to be paddled over in safety
between tides. Gradually, however, the strait grew
wider and wider; the chalk cliffs, long undermined by
boring molluscs and scouring shingle, were torn down
by great billows during winter storms.

It may be that for a long period after the North Sea
and English Channel were united, the Dogger Bank
remained an island, and that there were other islands
between Heligoland and the English coast. Pliny, who
had served with the Roman army in Germany, writing
in the first century of our era, refers to twenty-three
islands between the Texel and the Eider in Schleswig-
Holstein. Seven of these have since vanished. The
west coast of Schleswig has, during the past eighteen
hundred years, suffered greatly from erosion, and alluvial
plains that formerly yielded rich harvests are now represented by sandbanks. The Goodwin Sands, which
stretch for about ten miles off the Kentish coast, were
once part of the fertile estate of Earl Godwin which was
destroyed and engulfed by a great storm towards the
end of the eleventh century. The Gulf of Zuyder Zee
was formerly a green plain with many towns and villages.
Periodic inundations since the Roman period have destroyed flourishing Dutch farms and villages and eaten
far into the land. There are records of storm-floods that
drowned on one occasion 20,000, and on another no

fewer than 100,000 inhabitants.[1]   It is believed that large
tracts of land, the remnants of the ancient North Sea
land-bridge, have been engulfed since about 3000 B.C.,
as a result not merely of erosion but the gradual submergence of the land.   This date is suggested by Mr.
Clement Reid.

"The estimate", he says, "may have to be modified
as we obtain better evidence; but it is as well to realize
clearly that we are not dealing with a long period of
great geological antiquity; we are dealing with times
when the Egyptian, Babylonian, and Minoan (Cretan)
civilizations flourished.   Northern Europe was then
probably barbarous, and metals had not come into use;[2]
but the amber trade of the Baltic was probably in full
swing.   Rumours of any great disaster, such as the
submergence of thousands of square miles and the dis-
placement of large populations, might spread far and
wide along the trade routes."   It may be that the legend
of the Lost Atlantis was founded on reports of such a
disaster, that must have occurred when areas like the
Dogger Bank were engulfed.   It may be too that the
gradual wasting away of lands that have long since
vanished propelled migrations of peoples towards the
smiling coasts of England.   According to Ammianus
the Druids stated that some of the inhabitants of Gaul
were descendants of refugees from sea-invaded areas.

The gradual sinking of the land and the process of
coast erosion has greatly altered the geography of England.   The beach on which Julius Cæsar landed has
long since vanished, the dwellings of the ancient Azilian
and Maglemosian colonists, who reached England in
post-Glacial times, have been sunk below the English
Channel.   When Tilbury Docks were being excavated

---

[1] The dates of the greatest disasters on record are 1421, 1532, and 1570. There were
also terrible inundations in the seventeenth and eighteenth centuries, and in 1825 and 1855.
[2] It was not necessarily barbarous because metal weapons had not been invented.

Roman remains were found embedded in clay several feet below high-water mark. Below several layers of peat and mud, and immediately under a bank of sand in which were fragments of decomposed wood, was found the human skeleton known as "Tilbury man". The land in this area was originally 80 feet above its present level.[1] But while England was sinking Scotland was rising. The MacArthur cave at Oban, in which Azilian hunters and fishermen made their home on the sea-beach, is now about 30 feet above the old sea-level.

Before Dover Strait had been widened by the gradual sinking of the land and the process of coast erosion, and before the great islands had vanished from the southern part of the North Sea, the early hunters and fishermen could have experienced no great difficulty in reaching England. It is possible that the Azilian, Tardenoisian, and Maglemosian peoples had made considerable progress in the art of navigation. Traces of the Tardenoisian industry have been obtained in Northern Egypt, along the ancient Libyan coast of North Africa where a great deal of land has been submerged, and especially at Tunis, and in Algiers, in Italy, and in England and Scotland, as has been noted. There were boats on the Mediterranean at a very early period. The island of Crete was reached long before the introduction of copperworking by seafarers who visited the island of Melos, and there obtained obsidian (natural glass) from which sharp implements were fashioned. Egyptian mariners, who dwelt on the Delta coast, imported cedar, not only from Lebanon but from Morocco, as has been found from the evidence afforded by mummies packed with the sawdust of cedar from the Atlas Mountains.[2] When this trade with Morocco began it is impossible to say

---

[1] *Submerged Forests*, p. 120.
[2] *The Cairo Scientific Journal*, Vol. III, No. 32 (May, 1909), p. 105.

with certainty.   Long before 3000 B.C., however, the
Egyptians were building boats that were fitted with
masts and sails.   The ancient mariners were active as
explorers and traders before implements of copper came
into use.

Here we touch on a very interesting problem.   Where
were boats first invented and the art of navigation developed?   Rafts and floats formed by tying together two
trees or, as in Egypt, two bundles of reeds, were in use
at a very early period in various countries.   In Babylonia the "kufa", a great floating basket made watertight with pitch or covered with skins, was an early
invention.   It was used as it still is for river ferry boats.
But ships were not developed from "kufas".   The dug-
out canoe is one of the early prototypes of the modern
ocean-going vessel.   It reached this country before the
Neolithic industry was introduced, and during that
period when England was slowly sinking and Scotland
was gradually rising.   Dug-out canoes continued to
come during the so-called "Neolithic" stage of culture
ere yet the sinking and rising of land had ceased.
"That Neolithic man lived in Scotland during the
formation of this beach (the 45- to 50-foot beach) is
proved", wrote the late Professor James Geikie, "by
the frequent occurrence in it of his relics.   At Perth, for
example, a dug-out canoe of pine was met with towards
the bottom of the carse clays; and similar finds have
frequently been recorded from the contemporaneous
deposits in the valleys of the Forth and the Clyde."[1]

How did early man come to invent the dug-out?   Not
only did he hollow out a tree trunk by the laborious process of burning and by chipping with a flint adze, he
dressed the trunk so that his boat could be balanced on
the water.   The early shipbuilders had to learn, and

[1] *Antiquity of Man in Europe*, p. 274, Edinburgh, 1914.   The term "Neolithic" is here
rather vague.   It applies to the Azilians and Maglemosians as well as to later peoples.

did learn, for themselves, "the values of length and beam, of draught and sweet lines, of straight keel; with high stem to breast a wave and high stern to repel a following sea". The fashioning of a sea-worthy, or even a river-worthy boat, must have been in ancient times as difficult a task as was the fashioning of the first aeroplane in our own day. Many problems had to be solved, many experiments had to be made, and, no doubt, many tragedies took place before the first safe model-boat was paddled across a river. The early experimenters may have had shapes of vessels suggested to them by fish and birds, and especially by the aquatic birds that paddled past them on the river breast with dignity and ease. But is it probable that the first experiments were made with trees? Did early man undertake the laborious task of hewing down tree after tree to shape new models, until in the end he found on launching the correctly shaped vessel that its balance was perfect? Or was the dug-out canoe an imitation of a boat already in existence, just as a modern ship built of steel or concrete is an imitation of the earlier wooden ships? The available evidence regarding this important phase of the shipping problem tends to show that, before the dug-out was invented, boats were constructed of light material. Ancient Egypt was the earliest ship-building country in the world, and all ancient ships were modelled on those that traded on the calm waters of the Nile. Yet Egypt is an almost treeless land. There the earliest boats—broad, light skiffs—were made by binding together long bundles of the reeds of papyrus. Ropes were twisted from papyrus as well as from palm fibre.[1] It would appear that, before dug-outs were made, the problems of boat construction were solved by those who had invented papyri skiffs and skin boats. In the case of the latter the skins were stretched round a frame-

---

[1] Breasted, *A History of Egypt*, pp. 96-7.

work, sewed together and made watertight with pitch. We still refer to the "seams" and the "skin" of a boat.

The art of boat-building spread far and wide from the area of origin. Until recently the Chinese were building junks of the same type as they did four or five hundred years earlier. These junks have been compared by more than one writer to the deep-sea boats of the Egyptian Empire period. The Papuans make "dug-outs" and carve eyes on the prows as did the ancient Egyptians and as do the Maltese, Chinese, &c., in our own day. Even when only partly hollowed, the Papuan boats have perfect balance in the water as soon as they are launched.[1] The Polynesians performed religious ceremonies when cutting down trees and constructing boats.[2] In their incantations, &c., the lore of boat-building was enshrined and handed down. The Polynesian boat was dedicated to the *mo-o* (dragon-god). We still retain a relic of an ancient religious ceremony when a bottle of wine is broken on the bows of a vessel just as it is being launched.

After the Egyptians were able to secure supplies of cedar wood from the Atlas Mountains or Lebanon, by drifting rafts of lashed trees along the coast line, they made dug-out vessels of various shapes, as can be seen in the tomb pictures of the Old Kingdom period. These dug-outs were apparently modelled on the earlier papyri and skin boats. A ship with a square sail spread to the wind is depicted on an Ancient Egyptian two-handed jar in the British Museum, which is of pre-dynastic age and may date to anything like 4000 or 5000 B.C. At that remote period the art of navigation was already well advanced, no doubt on account of the experience gained on the calm waters of the Nile.

---

[1] Wollaston, *Pygmies and Papuans* (*The Stone Age To-day in Dutch New Guinea*), London, 1912, pp. 53 *et seq.*
[2] Westervelt, *Legends of Old Honolulu*, pp. 97 *et seq.*

The existence of these boats on the Nile at a time when great race migrations were in progress may well account for the early appearance of dug-outs in Northern Europe. One of the Clyde canoes, found embedded in Clyde silt twenty-five feet above the present sea-level, was found to have a plug of cork which could only have come from the area in which cork trees grow—Spain,

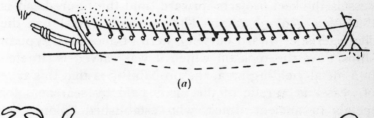

(a)

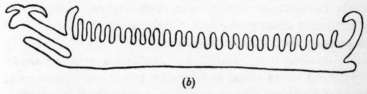

(b)

(a) Sketch of a boat from Victoria Nyanza, after the drawing in Sir Henry Stanley's *Darkest Africa*. Only the handles of the oars are shown. In outline the positions of some of the oarsmen are roughly represented.

(b) Crude drawing of a similar boat carved upon the rocks in Sweden during the Early Bronze Age, after Montelius. By comparison with (a) it will be seen that the vertical projections were probably intended to represent the oarsmen.

The upturned hook-like appendage at the stern is found in ancient Egyptian and Mediterranean ships, but is absent in the modern African vessel shown in (a).

These figures are taken from Elliot Smith's *Ancient Mariners* (1918).

Southern France, or Italy.[1] It may have been manned by the Azilians of Spain whose rock paintings date from the Transition period. Similar striking evidence of the drift of culture from the Mediterranean area towards Northern Europe is obtained from some of the rock paintings and carvings of Sweden. Among the canoes depicted are some with distinct Mediterranean characteristics. One at Tegneby in Bohuslän bears a striking resemblance to a boat seen by Sir Henry Stanley on

[1] Lyell, *Antiquity of Man*, p. 48.

Lake Victoria Nyanza. It seems undoubted that the designs are of common origin, although separated not only by centuries but by barriers of mountain, desert, and sea extending many hundreds of miles. From the Maglemosian boat the Viking ship was ultimately developed; the unprogressive Victoria Nyanza boat-builders continued through the Ages repeating the design adopted by their remote ancestors. In both vessels the keel projects forward, and the figure-head is that of a goat or ram. The northern vessel has the characteristic inward curving stern of ancient Egyptian ships. As the rock on which it was carved is situated in a metal-yielding area, the probability is that this type of vessel is a relic of the visits paid by searchers for metals in ancient times, who established colonies of dark miners among the fair Northerners and introduced the elements of southern culture.

The ancient boats found in Scotland are of a variety of types. One of those at Glasgow lay, when discovered, nearly vertical, with prow uppermost as if it had foundered; it had been built " of several pieces of oak, though without ribs". Another had the remains of an outrigger attached to it: beside another, which had been partly hollowed by fire, lay two planks that appear to have been wash-boards like those on a Sussex dug-out. A Clyde clinker-built boat, eighteen feet long, had a keel and a base of oak to which ribs had been attached. An interesting find at Kinaven in Aberdeenshire, several miles distant from the Ythan, a famous pearling river, was a dug-out eleven feet long, and about four feet broad. It lay embedded at the head of a small ravine in five feet of peat which appears to have been the bed of an ancient lake. Near it were the stumps of big oaks, apparently of the Upper Forestian period.

Among the longest of the ancient boats that have been discovered are one forty-two feet long, with an animal head on the prow, from Loch Arthur, near Dumfries, one thirty-five long from near the River Arun in Sussex, one sixty-three feet long excavated near the Rother in Kent, one forty - eight feet six inches long, found at Brigg, Lincolnshire, with wooden patches where she had sprung a leak, and signs of the caulking of cracks and small holes with moss.

These vessels do not all belong to the same period. The date of the Brigg boat is, judging from the geological strata, between 1100 and 700 B.C. It would appear that some of the Clyde vessels found at twenty-five feet above the present sea-level are even older. Beside one Clyde boat was found an axe of polished greenstone similar to the axes used by Polynesians and others in shaping dug-outs. This axe may, however, have been a religious object. To the low bases of some vessels were fixed ribs on which skins were stretched. These boats were eminently suitable for rough seas, being more buoyant than dug-outs. According to Himilco the inhabitants of the Œstrymnides, the islands "rich in tin and lead", had most sea-worthy skiffs. "These people do not make pine keels, nor", he says, "do they know how to fashion them; nor do they make fir barks, but, with wonderful skill, fashion skiffs with sewn skins. In these hide-bound vessels, they skim across the ocean." Apparently they were as daring mariners as the Oregon Islanders of whom Washington Irving has written:

"It is surprising to see with what fearless unconcern these savages venture in their light barks upon the roughest and most tempestuous seas. They seem to ride upon the wave like sea-fowl. Should a surge throw the canoe upon its side, and endanger its over turn, those to the windward lean over the upper gunwale, thrust their paddles deep into the wave, and by this action not merely regain an equilibrium, but give their bark a vigorous impulse forward."

The ancient mariners whose rude vessels have been excavated around our coasts were the forerunners of the Celtic sea-traders, who, as the Gaelic evidence shows, had names not only for the North Sea and the English Channel but also for the Mediterranean Sea.   They cultivated what is known as the "sea sense", and developed shipbuilding and the art of navigation in accordance with local needs.   When Julius Cæsar came into conflict with the Veneti of Brittany he tells that their vessels were greatly superior to those of the Romans. "The bodies of the ships", he says, "were built entirely of oak, stout enough to withstand any shock or violence. . . . Instead of cables for their anchors they used iron chains. . . . The encounter of our fleet with these ships was of such a nature that our fleet excelled in speed alone, and the plying of oars; for neither could our ships injure theirs with their rams, so great was their strength, nor was a weapon easily cast up to them owing to their height. . . . About 220 of their ships . . . sailed forth from the harbour."   In this great allied fleet were vessels from our own country.[1]

It must not be imagined that the "sea sense" was cultivated because man took pleasure in risking the perils of the deep.   It was stern necessity that at the beginning compelled him to venture on long voyages. After England was cut off from France the peoples who had adopted the Neolithic industry must have either found it absolutely necessary to seek refuge in Britain, or were attracted towards it by reports of prospectors who found it to be suitable for residence and trade.

[1] Cæsar's *Gallic War*, Book III, c. 13-15.

CHAPTER VIII

Neolithic Trade and Industries

Attractions of Ancient Britain—Romans search for Gold, Silver, Pearls, &c.—The Lure of Precious Stones and Metals—Distribution of Ancient British Population—Neolithic Settlements in Flint-yielding Areas —Trade in Flint—Settlements on Lias Formation—Implements from Basic Rocks—Trade in Body-painting Materials—Search for Pearls— Gold in Britain and Ireland—Agriculture—The Story of Barley—Neolithic Settlers in Ireland—Scottish Neolithic Traders—Neolithic Peoples not Wanderers—Trained Neolithic Craftsmen.

The "drift" of peoples into Britain which began in Aurignacian times continued until the Roman period. There were definite reasons for early intrusions as there were for the Roman invasion. "Britain contains to reward the conqueror", Tacitus wrote,[1] "mines of gold and silver and other metals. The sea produces pearls." According to Suetonius, who at the end of the first century of our era wrote the *Lives of the Cæsars*, Julius Cæsar invaded Britain with the desire to enrich himself with the pearls found on different parts of the coast. On his return to Rome he presented a corselet of British pearls to the goddess Venus. He was in need of money to further his political ambitions. He found what he required elsewhere, however. After the death of Queen Cleopatra sufficient gold and silver flowed to Rome from Egypt to reduce the loan rate of interest from 12 to 4 per cent. Spain likewise contributed its share to enrich the great predatory state of Rome.[2]

Long ages before the Roman period the early peoples

---

[1] *Agricola*, Chap. XII. [2] Smith, *Roman Empire*.

entered Britain in search of pearls, precious stones, and
precious metals because these had a religious value.
The Celts of Gaul offered great quantities of gold to
their deities, depositing the precious metals in their
temples and in their sacred lakes.   Poseidonius of
Apamea tells that after conquering Gaul "the Romans
put up these sacred lakes to public sale, and many of
the purchasers found quantities of solid silver in them".
He also says that gold was similarly placed in these
lakes.[1]   Apparently the Celts believed, as did the Aryo-
Indians, that gold was "a form of the gods" and "fire,
light, and immortality", and that it was a "life giver".[2]
Personal ornaments continued to have a religious value
until Christian times.

As we have seen when dealing with the "Red Man
of Paviland", the earliest ornaments were shells, teeth
of wild animals, coloured stones, ivory, &c.   Shells
were carried great distances.   Then arose the habit of
producing substitutes which were regarded as of great
potency as the originals.   The ancient Egyptians made
use of gold to manufacture imitation shells, and before
they worked copper they wore charms of malachite,
which is an ore of copper.   They probably used copper
first for magical purposes just as they used gold.   Pearls
found in shells were regarded as depositories of supernatural influence, and so were coral and amber (see
Chapter XIII).   Like the Aryo-Indians, the Egyptians,
Phœnicians, Greeks, and others connected precious
metals, stones, pearls, &c., with their deities, and believed that these contained the influence of their deities,
and were therefore "lucky".   These and similar beliefs
are of great antiquity in Europe and Asia and North
Africa.   It would be rash to assume that they were not

---

[1] *Strabo*—IV, c. 1-13.
[2] *Satapatha-Brahmana*, Pt. V, "Sacred Books of the East", XLIV, pp. 187, 203, 236, 239, 348-50.

FLINT LANCE-HEADS FROM IRELAND (British Museum)

Photo. Oxford University Press

CHIPPED AND POLISHED ARTIFACTS FROM SOUTHERN
ENGLAND (British Museum)

known to the ancient mariners who reached our shores in vessels of Mediterranean type.

The colonists who were attracted to Britain at various periods settled in those districts most suitable for their modes of life. It was necessary that they should obtain an adequate supply of the materials from which their implements and weapons were manufactured. The distribution of the population must have been determined by the resources of the various districts.

At the present day the population of Britain is most dense in those areas in which coal and iron are found and where commerce is concentrated. In ancient times, before metals were used, it must have been densest in those areas where flint was found—that is, on the upper chalk formations. If worked flints are discovered in areas which do not have deposits of flint, the only conclusion that can be drawn is that the flint was obtained by means of trade, just as Mediterranean shells were in Aurignacian and Magdalenian times obtained by hunters who settled in Central Europe. In Devon and Cornwall, for instance, large numbers of flint implements have been found, yet in these counties suitable flint was exceedingly scarce in ancient times, except in East Devon, where, however, the surface flint is of inferior character. In Wilts and Dorset, however, the finest quality of flint was found, and it was no doubt from these areas that the early settlers in Cornwall and Devon received their chief supplies of the raw material, if not of the manufactured articles.

In England, as on the Continent, the most abundant finds of the earliest flint implements have been made in those areas where the early hunters and fishermen could obtain their raw materials. River drift implements are discovered in largest numbers on the chalk formations of south-eastern England between the Wash and the estuary of the Thames.

The Neolithic peoples, who made less use of horn and bone than did the Azilians and Maglemosians, had many village settlements on the upper chalk in Dorset and Wiltshire, and especially at Avebury where there were veritable flint factories, and near the famous flint mines at Grimes Graves in the vicinity of Weeting in Norfolk and at Cissbury Camp not far from Worthing in Sussex. Implements were likewise made of basic rocks, including quartzite, ironstone, greenstone, hornblende schist, granite, mica-schist, &c.; while ornaments were made of jet, a hydrocarbon compound allied to cannel coal, which takes on a fine polish, Kimeridge shale and ivory. Withal, like the Aurignacians and Magdalenians, the Neolithic-industry people used body paint, which was made with pigments of ochre, hæmatite, an ore of iron, and ruddle, an earthy variety of iron ore.

In those districts, where the raw materials for stone implements, ornaments, and body paint were found, traces survive of the activities of the Neolithic peoples. Their graves of long-barrow type are found not only in the chalk areas but on the margins of the lias formations. Hæmatite is found in large quantities in West Cumberland and north Lancashire and in south-western England, while the chief source of jet is Whitby in Yorkshire, where it occurs in large quantities in beds of the Upper Lias shale.

Mr. W. J. Perry, of Manchester University, who has devoted special attention to the study of the distribution of megalithic monuments, has been drawing attention to the interesting association of these monuments with geological formations.[1] In the Avebury district stone circles, dolmens, chambered barrows, long barrows, and Neolithic settlements are numerous; another group of megalithic monuments occurs in Oxford on the margin

---

[1] *Proceedings of the Manchester Literary and Philosophical Society,* 1921.

ENGLAND & WALES
showing distribution of
Megalithic Monuments
and deposits of metals and minerals

English Miles
0 10 20 30 40 50   100

Areas in which Megalithic Monuments
are situated...................................

of the lias formation, and at the south-end of the great iron field extending as far as the Clevelands. According to the memoir of the geological survey, there are traces of ancient surface iron-workings in the Middle Lias formation of Oxfordshire, where red and brown hæmatite were found. Mr. Perry notes that there are megalithic monuments in the vicinity of all these surface workings, as at Fawler, Adderbury, Hook Norton, Woodstock, Steeple Aston, and Hanbury. Apparently the Neolithic peoples were attracted to the lias formation because it contains hæmatite, ochre, shale, &c. There are significant megaliths in the Whitby region where the jet is so plentiful. Amber was obtained from the east coast of England and from the Baltic.

The Neolithic peoples appear to have searched for pearls, which are found in a number of English, Welsh, Scottish, and Irish rivers, and in the vicinity of most, if not all, of these megaliths occur. Gold was the first metal worked by man, and it appears to have attracted some of the early peoples who settled in Britain. The ancient seafarers who found their way northward may have included searchers for gold and silver. The latter metal was at one time found in great abundance in Spain, while gold was at one time fairly plentiful in south-western England, in North Wales, in various parts of Scotland and especially in Lanarkshire, and in north-eastern, eastern, and western Ireland. That there was a "drift" of civilized peoples into Britain and Ireland during the period of the Neolithic industry is made evident by the fact that the agricultural mode of life was introduced. Barley does not grow wild in Europe. The nearest area in which it grew wild and was earliest cultivated was the delta area of Egypt, the region from which the earliest vessels set out to explore the shores of the Mediterranean. It may be that the barley seeds were carried to Britain not by the overland routes alone to Channel ports, but also by the seafarers whose boats, like the Glasgow one with the cork plug, coasted round by Spain and Brittany, and crossed the Channel to south-western England and thence went northward to Scotland. As Irish flints and ground axe-heads occur chiefly in Ulster, it may be that the drift of early Neolithic settlers into County Antrim, in which gold was also found, was from south-western Scotland. The Neolithic settlement at Whitepark Bay, five miles from the Giant's Causeway, was embedded at a considerable depth, showing that there has been a sinking of the land in this area since the Neolithic industry was introduced.

Neolithic remains are widely distributed over Scotland, but these have not received the intensive study devoted to similar relics in England. Mr. Ludovic Mann, the Glasgow archæologist, has, however, compiled interesting data regarding one of the local industries that bring out the resource and activities of early man. On the island of Arran is a workable variety of the natural volcanic glass, called pitch-stone, that of other parts of Scotland and of Ireland being "too much cracked into small pieces to be of use". It was used by the Neolithic settlers in Arran for manufacturing arrow-heads, and as it was imported into Bute, Ayrshire, and Wigtownshire, a trade in this material must have existed. "If", writes Mr. Mann, "the stone was not locally worked up into implements in Bute, it was so manipulated on the mainland, where workshops of the Neolithic period and the immediately succeeding overlap period yielded long fine flakes, testifying to greater expertness in manufacturing there than is shown by the remains in the domestic sites yet awaiting adequate exploration in Arran. The explanation may be that the Wigtownshire flint knappers, accustomed to handle an abundance of flint, were more proficient than in most other places, and that the pitch-stone was brought to them as experts, because the material required even more skilful hand-ling than flint ".[1]   In like manner obsidian, as has been noted, was imported into Crete from the island of Melos by seafarers, long before the introduction of metal working.[2]

It will be seen that the Neolithic peoples were no mere wandering hunters, as some have represented them to have been, but they had their social organiza-tion, their industries, and their system of trading by land and sea.   They settled not only in those areas where they could procure a regular food supply, but those also in which they obtained the raw materials for implements, weapons, and the colouring material which they used for religious purposes.   They made pottery for grave offerings and domestic use, and wooden imple-ments regarding which, however, little is known. Withal, they had their spinners and weavers.   The conditions prevailing in Neolithic settlements must have been similar to those of later times.   There must have been systems of laws to make trade and peaceful social intercourse possible, and no doubt these had, as else-where, a religious basis.   Burial customs indicate a uniformity of beliefs over wide areas.   The skill dis-played in working stone was so great that it cannot now be emulated.   Ripple-flaking has long been a lost art. Craftsmen must have undergone a prolonged period of training which was intelligently controlled under settled conditions of life.   It is possible that the so-called Neo-lithic folk were chiefly foreigners who exploited the riches of the country.   The evidence in this connection will be found in the next chapter.

[1] *Proceedings of the Society of Antiquaries of Scotland*, 1917–18, pp. 149 *et seq.*
[2] See my *Myths of Crete and pre-Hellenic Europe* under "Obsidian" in Index.

CHAPTER IX

Metal Workers and Megalithic Monuments

"Broad-heads" of Bronze Age—The Irish Evidence—Bronze Introduced by Traders—How Metals were Traced—A Metal Working Tribe—
Damnonii in England, Scotland, and Ireland—Miners as Slaves—The Lot
of Women Workers—Megalithic Monuments in English Metal-yielding
Areas—Stone Circles in Barren Localities—Early Colonies of Easterners
in Spain—Egyptian and Babylonian Relics associated with British Jet and
Baltic Amber—A New Flint Industry of Eastern Origin—British Bronze
identical with Continental—Ancient Furnaces of Common Origin—
"Stones of Worship" adorned with Metals—The "Maggot God" of Stone
Circles—Ancient Egyptian Beads at Stonehenge—Earliest Authentic Date
in British History—The Aim of Conquests.

It used to be thought that the introduction of metal
working into Britain was the result of an invasion of
alien peoples, who partly exterminated and partly en-
slaved the long-headed Neolithic inhabitants. This view
was based on the evidence afforded by a new type of
grave known as the "Round Barrow". In graves of
this class have been found Bronze Age relics, a distinctive kind of pottery, and skulls of broad-heads. The
invasion of broad-heads undoubtedly took place, and
their burial customs suggest that their religious beliefs
were not identical with those of the long-heads.
But it remains to be proved that they were the actual
introducers of the bronze industry. They do not appear
to have reached Ireland, where bronze relics are associated with a long-headed people of comparatively low
stature.

The early Irish bronze forms were obviously obtained from Spain, while early English bronze forms resemble those of France and Italy. Cutting implements were the first to be introduced. This fact does not suggest

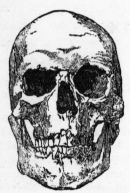 

Long-head (Dolichocephalic) Skull

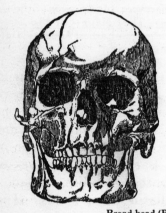 

Broad-head (Brachycephalic) Skull

Both these specimens were found in "Round" Barrows in the East Riding of Yorkshire

that a conquest took place. The implements may have been obtained by traders. Britain apparently had in those ancient times its trading colonies, and was visited by active and enterprising seafarers.

The discovery of metals in Britain and Ireland was,

no doubt, first made by prospectors who had obtained experience in working them elsewhere. They may have simply come to exploit the country. How these men conducted their investigations is indicated by the report found in a British Museum manuscript, dating from about 1603, in which the prospector gives his reason for believing that gold was to be found on Crawford Moor in Lanarkshire. He tells that he saw among the rocks what Scottish miners call "mothers" and English miners "leaders" or "metalline fumes". It was believed that the "fumes" arose from veins of metal and coloured the rocks as smoke passing upward through a tunnel blackens it, and leaves traces on the outside. He professed to be able to distinguish between the colours left by "fumes" of iron, lead, tin, copper, or silver. On Crawford Moor he found "sparr, keel, and brimstone" between rocks, and regarded this discovery as a sure indication that gold was *in situ*. The "mothers" or "leaders" were more pronounced than any he had ever seen in Cornwall, Somersetshire, about Keswick, or "any other mineral parts wheresoever I have travelled".[1] Gold was found in this area of Lanarkshire in considerable quantities, and was no doubt worked in ancient times. Of special interest in this connection is the fact that it was part of the territory occupied by Damnonians,[2] who appear to have been a metal-working people. Besides occupying the richest metal-yielding area in Scotland, the Damnonians were located in Devon and Cornwall, and in the east-midland and western parts of Ireland, in which gold, copper, and tin-stone were found as in south-western England. The Welsh *Dyfneint* (Devon) is supposed by some to be connected with a form of this tribal name. Another form in a Yarrow inscription is Dumnogeni. In Ireland Inber Domnann is the

---

[1] R. W. Cochrane Patrick, *Early Records relating to Mining in Scotland*, Edinburgh, 1878, p. xxviii.　　[2] The *Damnonii* or *Dumnonii*.

old name of Malahide Bay north of Dublin. Domnu, the genitive of which is Domnann, was the name of an ancient goddess. In the Irish manuscripts these people are referred to as Fir-domnann,[1] and associated with the Fir-bolg (the men with sacks). A sack-carrying people are represented in Spanish rock paintings that date from the Azilian till early "Bronze Age" times. In an Irish manuscript which praises the fair and tall people, the Fir-bolg and Fir-domnann are included among the black-eyed and black-haired people, the descendants of slaves and churls, and "the promoters of discord among the people".

The reference to "slaves" is of special interest because the lot of the working miners was in ancient days an extremely arduous one. In one of his collected records which describes the method "of the greatest antiquity" Diodorus Siculus (A.D. first century) tells how gold-miners, with lights bound on their foreheads, drove galleries into the rocks, the fragments of which were carried out by frail old men and boys. These were broken small by men in the prime of life. The pounded stone was then ground in handmills by women: three women to a mill and "to each of those who bear this lot, death is better than life". Afterwards the milled quartz was spread out on an inclined table. Men threw water on it, work it through their fingers, and dabbed it with sponges until the lighter matter was removed and the gold was left behind. The precious metal was placed in a clay crucible, which was kept heated for five days and five nights. It may be that the Scandinavian references to the nine maidens who turn the handle of the "world mill" which grinds out metal and soil, and the Celtic references to the nine maidens who are associ-

---

[1] The Fir-domnann were known as "the men who used to deepen the earth", or "dig pits". Professor J. MacNeil in *Labor Gabula*, p. 119. They were thus called "Diggers" like the modern Australians. The name of the goddess referred to the depths (the Under-world). It is probable she was the personification of the metal-yielding earth.

ated with the Celtic cauldron, survive from beliefs that reflected the habits and methods of the ancient metal workers.

It is difficult now to trace the various areas in which gold was anciently found in our islands. But this is not to be wondered at. In Egypt there were once rich goldfields, especially in the Eastern Desert, where about 100 square miles were so thoroughly worked in ancient times that "only the merest traces of gold remain".[1] Gold, as has been stated, was formerly found in south-western England, North Wales, and, as historical records, archæological data, and place names indicate, in various parts of Scotland and Ireland. During the period of the "Great Thaw" a great deal of alluvial gold must have distributed throughout the country. Silver was found in various parts. In Sutherland it is mixed with gold as it is elsewhere with lead. Copper was worked in a number of districts where the veins cannot in modern times be economically worked, and tin was found in Ireland and Scotland as well as in south-western England, where mining operations do not seem to have been begun, as Principal Sir John Rhys has shown,[2] until after the supplies of surface tin were exhausted. Of special interest in connection with this problem is the association of megalithic monuments with ancient mine workings. An interesting fact to be borne in mind in connection with these relics of the activities and beliefs of the early peoples is that they represent a distinct culture of complex character. Mr. T. Eric Peet[3] shows that the megalithic buildings "occupy a very remarkable position along a vast seaboard which includes the Mediterranean coast of Africa and the Atlantic coast of Europe. In other words, they lie entirely along a

---

[1] Alford, *A Report on Ancient and Prospective Gold Mining in Egypt*, 1900, and *Mining in Egypt* (by Egyptologist).

[2] *Celtic Britain*, pp. 44 *et seq.* (4th edition).

[3] *Rough Stone Monuments*, London, 1912, pp. 147-8.

natural sea route." He gives forcible reasons for arriving at the conclusion that "it is impossible to consider megalithic building as a mere phase through which many nations passed, and it must therefore have been a system originating with one race, and spreading far and wide, owing either to trade influence or migration". He adds:

"Great movements of races by sea were not by any means unusual in primitive days. In fact, the sea has always been less of an obstacle to early man than the land with its deserts, mountains, and unfordable rivers. There is nothing inherently impossible or even improbable in the suggestion that a great immigration brought the megalithic monuments from Sweden to India or vice versa. History is full of instances of such migrations."

But there must have been a definite reason for these race movements. It cannot be that in all cases they were forced merely by natural causes, such as changes of climate, invasions of the sea, and the drying up of once fertile districts, or by the propelling influences of stronger races in every country from the British Isles to Japan—that is, in all countries in which megalithic monuments of similar type are found. The fact that the megalithic monuments are distributed along "a vast seaboard" suggests that they were the work of people who had acquired a culture of common origin, and were attracted to different countries for the same reason. What that attraction was is indicated by studying the elements of the megalithic culture. In a lecture delivered before the British Association in Manchester in 1915, Mr. W. J. Perry threw much light on the problem by showing that the carriers of the culture practised weaving linen, and in some cases the use of Tyrian purple, pearls, precious stones, metals, and conch-shell trumpets, as well as curious beliefs and superstitions attached to the latter, while they "adopted certain definite metallurgical methods, as well as mining". Mr. Perry's paper was subsequently published by the Manchester Literary and Philosophical Society. It shows that in Western Europe the megalithic monuments are distributed in those areas in which ancient pre-Roman and pre-Greek mine workings and metal washings have been traced. "The same correspondence", he writes, "seems to hold in the case of England and Wales. In the latter country the counties where megalithic structures abound are precisely those where mineral deposits and ancient mine-workings occur. In England the grouping in Cumberland, Westmorland, Northumberland, Durham, and Derbyshire is precisely that of old mines; in Cornwall the megalithic structures are mainly grouped west of Falmouth, precisely in that district where mining has always been most active."

Pearls, amber, coral, jet, &c., were searched for as well as metals. The megalithic monuments near pearling rivers, in the vicinity of Whitby, the main source of jet, and in Denmark and the Baltic area where amber was found were, in all likelihood, erected by people who had come under the spell of the same ancient culture.

When, therefore, we come to deal with groups of monuments in areas which were unsuitable for agriculture and unable to sustain large populations, a reasonable conclusion to draw is that precious metals, precious stones, or pearls were once found near them. The pearling beds may have been destroyed or greatly reduced in value,[1] or the metals may have been worked out, leaving but slight if any indication that they were ever *in situ*. Reference has been made to the traces left by ancient miners in Egypt where no gold is now

---

[1] The Scottish pearling beds have suffered great injury in historic times. They are the property of the "Crown", and no one takes any interest in them except the "pearl poachers".

found.   In our own day rich goldfields in Australia and
North America have been exhausted.   It would be
unreasonable for us to suppose that the same thing did
not happen in our country, even although but slight
traces of the precious metal can now be obtained in areas
which were thoroughly explored by ancient miners.

When early man reached Scotland in search of suitable districts in which to settle, he was not likely to be
attracted by the barren or semi-barren areas in which
nature grudged soil for cultivation, where pasture lands
were poor and the coasts were lashed by great billows
for the greater part of the year, and the tempests of winter
and spring were particularly severe.   Yet in such places
as Carloway, fronting the Atlantic on the west coast of
Lewis, and at Stennis in Orkney, across the dangerous
Pentland Firth, are found the most imposing stone
circles north of Stonehenge and Avebury.   Traces of
tin have been found in Lewis, and Orkney has yielded
traces of lead, including silver-lead, copper and zinc, and
has flint in glacial drift.   Traces of tin have likewise
been found on the mainlands of Ross-shire and Argyllshire, in various islands of the Hebrides and in Stirling-
shire.   The great Stonehenge circle is like the Callernish
and Stennis circles situated in a semi-barren area, but it
is an area where surface tin and gold were anciently
obtained.   One cannot help concluding that the early
people, who populated the wastes of ancient Britain and
erected megalithic monuments, were attracted by something more tangible than the charms of solitude and
wild scenery.   They searched for and found the things
they required.   If they found gold, it must be recognized
that there was a psychological motive for the search for
this precious metal.   They valued gold, or whatever
other metal they worked in bleak and isolated places,
because they had learned to value it elsewhere.

Who were the people that first searched for, found,

and used metals in Western Europe? Some have assumed that the natives themselves did so "as a matter of course". Such a theory is, however, difficult to maintain. Gold is a useless metal for all practical purposes. It is too soft for implements. Besides, it cannot be found or worked except by those who have acquired a great deal of knowledge and skill. The men who first "washed" it from the soil in Britain must have obtained the necessary knowledge and skill in a country where it was more plentiful and much easier to work, and where—and this point is a most important one—the magical and religious beliefs connected with gold have a very definite history. Copper, tin, and silver were even more difficult to find and work in Britain. The ancient people who reached Britain and first worked metals or collected ores were not the people who were accustomed to use implements of bone, horn, and flint, and had been attracted to its shores merely because fish, fowl, deer, and cows, were numerous. The searchers for metals must have come from centres of Eastern civilization, or from colonies of highly skilled peoples that had been established in Western Europe. They did not necessarily come to settle permanently in Britain, but rather to exploit its natural riches.

This conclusion is no mere hypothesis. Siret,[1] the Belgian archæologist, has discovered in southern Spain and Portugal traces of numerous settlements of Easterners who searched for minerals, &c., long before the introduction of bronze working in Western Europe. They came during the archæological "Stone Age"; they even introduced some of the flint implements classed as Neolithic by the archæologists of a past generation.

These Eastern colonists do not appear to have been an organized people. Siret considers that they were merely groups of people from Asia—probably the Syrian coast

[1] *L'Anthropologie*, 1921, contains a long account of his discoveries.

—who were in contact with Egypt. During the Empire period of Egypt, the Egyptian sphere of influence extended to the borders of Asia Minor. At an earlier period Babylonian influence permeated the Syrian coast and part of Asia Minor. The religious beliefs of seafarers from Syria were likely therefore to bear traces of the Egyptian and Babylonian religious systems. Evidence that this was the case has been forthcoming in Spain.

These Eastern colonists not only operated in Spain and Portugal, but established contact with Northern Europe. They exported what they had searched for and found to their Eastern markets. No doubt, they employed native labour, but they do not appear to have instructed the natives how to make use of the ores they themselves valued so highly. In time they were expelled from Spain and Portugal by the people or mixed peoples who introduced the working of bronze and made use of bronze weapons. These bronze carriers and workers came from Central Europe, where colonies of peoples skilled in the arts of mining and metal working had been established. In the Central European colonies Ægean and Danubian influences have been detected.

Among the archæological finds, which prove that the Easterners settled in Iberia before bronze working was introduced among the natives, are idol-like objects made of hippopotamus ivory from Egypt, a shell (*Dentalium elephantum*) from the Red Sea, objects made from ostrich eggs which must have been carried to Spain from Africa, alabaster perfume flasks, cups of marble and alabaster of Egyptian character which had been shaped with copper implements, Oriental painted vases with decorations in red, black, blue, and green,[1] mural paintings on layers of plaster, feminine statuettes in alabaster which Siret considers to be of Babylonian type,

---

[1] The colours blue and green were obtained from copper.

Valentine

THE RING OF STENNIS, ORKNEY (see page 94)

for they differ from Ægean and Egyptian statuettes, a cult object (found in graves) resembling the Egyptian *ded* amulet, &c. The Iberian burial places of these Eastern colonists have arched cupolas and entrance corridors of Egyptian-Mycenæan character.

Of special interest are the beautifully worked flints associated with these Eastern remains in Spain and Portugal. Siret draws attention to the fact that no trace has been found of "flint factories". This particular flint industry was an entirely new one. It was not a development of earlier flint-working in Iberia. Apparently the new industry, which suddenly appears in full perfection, was introduced by the Eastern colonists. It afterwards spread over the whole maritime west, including Scandinavia where the metal implements of more advanced countries were imitated in flint. This important fact emphasizes the need for caution in making use of such a term as "Neolithic Age". Siret's view in this connection is that the Easterners, who established trading colonies in Spain and elsewhere, prevented the local use of metals which they had come to search for and export. It was part of their policy to keep the natives in ignorance of the uses to which metals could be put.

Evidence has been forthcoming that the operations of the Eastern colonies in Spain and Portugal were extended towards the maritime north. Associated with the Oriental relics already referred to, Siret has discovered amber from the Baltic, jet from Britain (apparently from Whitby in Yorkshire) and the green-stone called "callais" usually found in beds of tin. The Eastern seafarers must have visited Northern Europe to exploit its virgin riches. A green-stone axe was found, as has been stated, near the boat with the cork plug, which lay embedded in Clyde silt at Glasgow. Artifacts of callais have been discovered in Brittany, in the south of France, in Portugal, and in south-eastern Spain. In the latter area, as Siret has proved, the Easterners worked silver-bearing lead and copper.

The colonists appear to have likewise searched for and found gold. A diadem of gold was discovered in a necropolis in the south of Spain, where some eminent ancient had been interred. This find is, however, an exception. Precious metals do not as a rule appear in the graves of the period under consideration.

As has been suggested, the Easterners who exploited the wealth of ancient Iberia kept the natives in ignorance. " This ignorance ", Siret says, "was the guarantee of the prosperity of the commerce carried on by the strangers. . . . The first action of the East on the West was the exploitation for its exclusive and personal profit of the virgin riches of the latter." These early Westerners had no idea of the use and value of the metals lying on the surface of their native land, while the Orientals valued them, were in need of them, and were anxious to obtain them. As Siret puts it:

" The West was a cow to be milked, a sheep to be fleeced, a field to be cultivated, a mine to be exploited."

In the traditions preserved by classical writers, there are references to the skill and cunning of the Phœnicians in commerce, and in the exploitation of colonies founded among the ignorant Iberians. They did not inform rival traders where they found metals. " Formerly ", as Strabo says, " the Phœnicians monopolized the trade from Gades (Cadiz) with the islanders (of the Cassiterides); and they kept the route a close secret." A vague ancient tradition is preserved by Pliny, who tells that " tin was first fetched from Cassiteris (the tin island) by Midacritus ".[1] We owe it to the secretive Phœnicians that the problem of the Cassiterides still remains a difficult one to solve.

[1] *Nat. Hist.*, VII, 56 (57), § 197.

To keep the native people ignorant the Easterners, Siret believes, forbade the use of metals in their own colonies. A direct result of this policy was the great development which took place in the manufacture of the beautiful flint implements already referred to. These the natives imitated, never dreaming that they were imitating some forms that had been developed by a people who used copper in their own country. When, therefore, we pick up beautiful Neolithic flints, we cannot be too sure that the skill displayed belongs entirely to the "Stone Age", or that the flints "evolved" from earlier native forms in those areas in which they are found.

The Easterners do not appear to have extracted the metals from their ores either in Iberia or in Northern Europe. Tin-stone and silver-bearing lead were used for ballast for their ships, and they made anchors of lead. Gold washed from river beds could be easily packed in small bulk. A people who lived by hunting and fishing were not likely to be greatly interested in the laborious process of gold-washing. Nor were they likely to attach to gold a magical and religious value as did the ancient Egyptians and Sumerians.

So far as can be gathered from the Iberian evidence, the period of exploitation by the colonists from the East was a somewhat prolonged one. How many centuries it covered we can only guess. It is of interest to find, in this connection, however, that something was known in Mesopotamia before 2000 B.C. regarding the natural riches of Western Europe. Tablets have recently been found on the site of Asshur, the ancient capital of Assyria, which was originally a Sumerian settlement. These make reference to the Empire of Sargon of Akkad (*c.* 2600 B.C.), which, according to tradition, extended from the Persian Gulf to the Syrian coast. Sargon was a great conqueror. "He poured out his glory over the world", declares a tablet found a good many years ago.

It was believed, too, that Sargon embarked on the Mediterranean and occupied Cyprus. The fresh evidence from the site of Asshur is to the effect that he conquered Kaptara (? Crete) and "the Tin Land beyond the Upper Sea" (the Mediterranean). The explanation may be that he obtained control of the markets to which the Easterners carried from Spain and the coasts of Northern Europe the ores, pearls, &c., they had searched for and found. It may be, therefore, that Britain was visited by Easterners even before Sargon's time, and that the Glasgow boat with the plug of cork was manned by dark Orientals who were prospecting the Scottish coast before the last land movement had ceased—that is, some time after 3000 B.C.

When the Easterners were expelled from Spain by a people from Central Europe who used weapons of bronze, some of them appear to have found refuge in Gaul. Siret is of opinion that others withdrew from Brittany, where subsidences were taking place along the coast, leaving their megalithic monuments below high-water mark, and even under several feet of water as at Morbraz. He thinks that the settlements of Easterners in Brittany were invaded at one and the same time by the enemy and the ocean. Other refugees from the colonies may have settled in Etruria, and founded the Etruscan civilization. Etruscan menhirs resemble those of the south of France, while the Etruscan crozier or wand, used in the art of augury, resembles the croziers of the megaliths, &c., of France, Spain, and Portugal. There are references in Scottish Gaelic stories to "magic wands" possessed by "wise women", and by the mothers of Cyclopean one-eyed giants. Ammianus Marcellinus, quoting Timagenes,[1] attributes to the

---

[1] Timagenes (c. 85-5 B.C.), an Alexandrian historian, wrote a history of the Gauls which was made use of by Ammianus Marcellinus (A.D. fourth century), a Greek of Antioch, and the author of a history of the Roman Emperors.

MEGALITHS

Upper: Kit's Coty House, Kent.   Lower: Trethevy Stone, Cornwall.

Druids the statement that part of the inhabitants of Gaul were indigenous, but that some had come from the farthest shores and districts across the Rhine, "having been expelled from their own lands by frequent wars and the encroachments of the ocean".

The bronze-using peoples who established overland trade routes in Europe, displacing in some localities the colonies of Easterners and isolating others, must have instructed the natives of Western Europe how to mine and use metals. Bronze appears to have been introduced into Britain by traders. That the ancient Britons did not begin quite spontaneously to work copper and tin and manufacture bronze is quite evident, because the earliest specimens of British bronze which have been found are made of ninety per cent of copper and ten per cent of tin as on the Continent. "Now, since a knowledge of the compound", wrote Dr. Robert Munro, "implies a previous acquaintance with its component elements, it follows that progress in metallurgy had already reached the stage of knowing the best combination of these metals for the manufacture of cutting tools before bronze was practically known in Britain."[1]

The furnaces used were not invented in Britain. Professor Gowland has shown that in Europe and Asia the system of working mines and melting metals was identical in ancient times. Summarizing Professor Gowland's articles in *Archæologia* and the *Journal of the Royal Anthropological Institute*, Mr. W. J. Perry writes in this connection:[2] "The furnaces employed were similar; the crucibles were of the same material, and generally of the same form; the process of smelting, first on the surface and then in the crucibles was found everywhere, even persisting down to present times in

---

[1] *Prehistoric Britain*, p. 145.
[2] *The Relationship between the Geographical Distribution of Megalithic Monuments and Ancient Mines*, pp. 21 *et seq.*

the absence of any fresh cultural influence. The study of the technique of mining and smelting has served to consolidate the floating mass of facts which we have accumulated, and to add support for the contention that one cultural influence is responsible for the earliest mining and smelting and washing of metals and the getting of precious stones and metals. The cause of the distribution of the megalithic culture was the search for certain forms of material wealth."

That certain of the megalithic monuments were intimately connected with the people who attached a religious value to metals is brought out very forcibly in the references to pagan customs and beliefs in early Christian Gaelic literature. There are statements in the Lives of St. Patrick regarding a pagan god called "Cenn Cruach" and "Crom Cruach" whose stone statue was "adorned with gold and silver, and surrounded by twelve other statues with bronze ornaments". The "statue" is called "the king idol of Erin", and it is stated that "the twelve idols were made of stone, but he ('Crom Cruach') was of gold". To this god of a stone circle were offered up "the firstlings of every issue and the chief scions of every clan". Another idol was called Crom Dubh ("Black Crom"), and his name "is still connected", O'Curry has written, "with the first Sunday of August in Munster and Connaught". An Ulster idol was called Crom Chonnaill, which was either a living animal or a tree, or was "believed to have been such", O'Curry says. De Jubainville translates *Cenn Cruach* as "Bloody Head" and *Crom Cruach* as "Bloody Curb" or "Bloody Crescent". O'Curry, on the other hand, translates *Crom Cruach* as "Bloody Maggot" and *Crom Dubh* as "Black Maggot". In Gaelic legends "maggots" or "worms" are referred to as forms of supernatural beings. The maggot which appeared on the flesh of a slain animal was apparently

regarded as a new form assumed by the indestructible
soul, just as in the Egyptian story of Bata the germ of
life passes from his bull form in a drop of blood from
which two trees spring up, and then in a chip from one
of the trees from which the man is restored in his
original form.[1] A similar belief, which is widespread,
is that bees have their origin as maggots placed in trees.
One form of the story was taken over by the early
Christians, which tells that Jesus was travelling with
Peter and Paul and asked hospitality from an old
woman. The woman refused it and struck Paul on the
head. When the wound putrified maggots were produced. Jesus took the maggots from the wound and
placed them in the hollow of a tree. When next they
passed that way, " Jesus directed Paul to look in the
tree hollow where, to his surprise, he found bees and
honey sprung from his own head ".[2] The custom of
placing crape on hives and "telling the bees " when a
death takes place, which still survives in the south of
England and in the north of Scotland, appears to be
connected with the ancient belief that the maggot, bee,
and tree were connected with the sacred animal and the
sacred stone in which was the spirit of a deity. Sacred
trees and sacred stones were intimately connected.
Tacitus tells us that the Romans invaded Mona (Anglesea), they destroyed the sacred groves in which the
Druids and black-robed priestesses covered the altars
with the blood of captives.[3] There are a number of
dolmens on this island and traces of ancient mine-
workings, indicating that it had been occupied by the
early seafarers who colonized Britain and Ireland and
worked metals. A connection between the tree cult of
the Druids and the cult of the builders of megaliths is

[1] A worm crept from the heart of a dead Phœnix, and gave origin to a new Phœnix.—
Herodotus, II, 73.

[2] Rendel Harris, *The Ascent of Olympus*, p. 2.

[3] *Annals of Tacitus*, Book XIV, Chapter 29-30.

thus suggested by Tacitus, as well as by the Irish evidence regarding the Ulster idol Crom Chonnaill, referred to above (see also Chapter XII).

Who were the people that followed the earliest Easterners and visited our shores to search like them for metals and erect megalithic monuments? It is impossible to answer that question with certainty. There were after the introduction of bronze working, as has been indicated, intrusions of aliens. These included the introducers of the short-barrow method of burial and the later introducers of burial by cremation. It does not follow that all intrusions were those of conquerors. Traders and artisans may have come with their families in large numbers and mingled with the earlier peoples. Some intruders appear to have come by overland routes from southern and central France and from Central Europe and the Danube valley, while others came across the sea from Spain. That a regular over-seas trade-route was in existence is indicated by the references made by classical writers to the Cassiterides (Tin Islands). Strabo tells that the natives "bartered tin and hides with merchants for pottery, salt, and articles of bronze". The Phœnicians, as has been noted, "monopolized the trade from Gades (Cadiz) with the islanders and kept the route a close secret". It was probably along this sea-route that Egyptian blue beads reached Britain. Professor Sayce has identified a number of these in Devizes Museum, and writes:

"They are met with plentifully in the Early Bronze Age tumuli of Wiltshire in association with amber beads and barrel-shaped beads of jet or lignite. Three of them come from Stonehenge itself. Similar beads of ivory have been found in a Bronze Age cist near Warminster: if the material is really ivory it must have been derived from the East. The cylindrical faience beads, it may be added, have been discovered in Dorsetshire as well as in Wiltshire."

Professor Sayce emphasizes that these blue beads "belong to one particular period in Egyptian history, the latter part of the Eighteenth Dynasty and the earlier part of the Nineteenth Dynasty. . . . The period to which they belong may be dated 1450–1250 B.C., and as

Beads from Bronze Age Barrows on Salisbury Plain

The large central bead and the small round ones are of amber; the long plain ones are of jet; and the long segmented or notched beads are of an opaque blue substance (faience).

we must allow some time for their passage across the trade routes to Wiltshire an approximate date for their presence in the British barrows will be 1300 B.C."

Dr. H. R. Hall, of the British Museum, who discovered, at Deir el-Bahari in Egypt, "thousands of blue glaze beads of the exact particular type of those found in Britain", says that they date back till "about 1500 B.C.". He noted the resemblance before Professor

Sayce had written. "It is gratifying", he comments, "that the Professor agrees that the Devizes beads are undoubtedly Egyptian, as an important voice is thereby added to the consensus of opinion on the subject." Similar beads have been found in the "Middle Bronze Age in Crete and in Western Europe". Dr. Hall thinks the Egyptian beads may have reached Britain as early as "about 1400 B.C. ".[1] We have thus provided for us an early date in British history, based on the well authenticated chronology of the Empire period of Ancient Egypt. Easterners, or traders in touch with Easterners, reached our shores carrying Egyptian beads shortly before or early in the fourteenth century B.C. At this time amber was being imported into the south of England from the Baltic, while jet was being carried from Whitby in Yorkshire.

After the introduction of bronze working in Western Europe the natives began to work and use metals. These could not have been Celts, for in the fourteenth century B.C. the Celts had not yet reached Western Europe.[2] The earliest searchers for metals who visited Britain must therefore have been the congeners of those who erected the megalithic monuments in the metal-yielding areas of Spain and Portugal and north-western France.

It would appear that the early Easterners exploited the virgin riches of Western Europe for a long period— perhaps for over a thousand years—and that, after their Spanish colonies were broken up by a bronze-using people from Central Europe, the knowledge of how to work metals spread among the natives. Overland trade routes were then opened up. At first these were controlled in Western Europe by the Iberians. In time the Celts

---

[1] *The Journal of Egyptian Archæology*, Vol. I, part I, pp. 18-19.
[2] It may be that Celtic chronology will have to be readjusted in the light of recent discoveries.

swept westward and formed with the natives mixed communities of Celtiberians. The Easterners appear to have inaugurated a new era in Western European commerce after the introduction of iron working. They had colonies in the south and west of Europe and on the North African coast, and obtained supplies of metals, &c., by sea. They kept the sea-routes secret. British ores, &c., were carried to Spain and Carthage. After Pytheas visited Britain (see next chapter) the overland trade-route to Marseilles was opened up. Supplies of surface tin having become exhausted, tin-mines were opened in Cornwall. The trade of Britain then came under the control of Celtiberian and Celtic peoples, who had acquired their knowledge of shipbuilding and navigation from the Easterners and the mixed descendants of Eastern and Iberian peoples.

It does not follow that the early and later Easterners were all of one physical type. They, no doubt, brought with them their slaves, including miners and seamen, drawn from various countries where they had been purchased or abducted.

The men who controlled the ancient trade were not necessarily permanent settlers in Western Europe. When the carriers of bronze from Central Europe obtained control of the Iberian colonies, many traders may have fled to other countries, but many colonists, and especially the workers, may have become the slaves of the intruders, as did the Firbolgs of Ireland who were subdued by the Celts. The Damnonians of Britain and Ireland who occupied mineral areas may have been a "wave" of early Celtic or Celtiberian people. Ultimately the Celts came, as did the later Normans, and formed military aristocracies over peoples of mixed descent. The idea that each intrusion involved the extermination of earlier peoples is a theory which does not accord with the evidence of the ancient Gaelic manu-

scripts, of classical writers, of folk tradition, and of existing race types in different areas in Britain and Ireland.

A people who exterminated those they conquered
would have robbed themselves of the chief fruits of
conquest.   In ancient as in later times the aim of
conquest was to obtain the services of a subject people
and the control of trade.

CHAPTER X

Celts and Iberians as Intruders and Traders

Few Invasions in 1000 Years — Broad-heads — The Cremating People—A New Religion—Celtic People in Britain—The Continental Celts—Were Celts Dark or Fair?—Fair Types in Britain and Ireland—Celts as Pork Traders—The Ancient Tin Trade—Early Explorers—Pytheas and Himilco—The Cassiterides—Tin Mines and Surface Tin—Cornish Tin—Metals in Hebrides and Ireland—Lead in Orkney—Dark People in Hebrides and Orkney—Celtic Art—Homeric Civilization in Britain and Ireland—Why Romans were Conquerors.

The beginnings of the Bronze and Iron Ages in Britain are, according to the chronology favoured by archæologists, separated by about a thousand years. During this long period only two or three invasions appear to have taken place, but it is uncertain, as has been indicated, whether these came as sudden outbursts from the Continent or were simply gradual and peaceful infiltrations of traders and settlers. We really know nothing about the broad-headed people who introduced the round-barrow system of burial, or of the people who cremated their dead. The latter became predominant in south-western England and part of Wales. In the north of England the cremating people were less numerous. If they were conquerors they may have, as has been suggested, represented military aristocracies. It may be, however, on the other hand, that the cremation custom had in some areas more a religious than a racial signifi-

cance.   The beliefs associated with cremation of the
dead may have spread farther than the people who introduced the new religion.   It would appear that the habit
of burning the dead was an expresssion of the beliefs
that souls were transported by means of fire to the Otherworld paradise.   As much is indicated by Greek evidence.
Homer's heroes burned their dead, and when the ghost
of Patroklos appeared to his friend Achilles in a dream,
he said: "Thou sleepest, and hast forgotten me, O
Achilles.   Not in my life wast thou unmindful of me,
but in my death.   Bury me with all speed, that I may
pass the gates of Hades.   Far off the spirits banish me,
the phantoms of men outworn, nor suffer me to mingle
with them beyond the River, but vainly I wander along
the wide-gated dwelling of Hades.   Now give me, I pray
pitifully of thee, thy hand, for never more again shall
I come back from Hades, when ye have given me my
due of fire."[1]   The Arab traveller Ibn Haukal, who
describes a tenth-century cremation ceremony at Kieff,
was addressed by a Russ, who said: "As for you Arabs
you are mad, for those who are the most dear to you,
and whom you honour most, you place in the ground,
where they will become a prey to worms, whereas with
us they are burned in an instant and go straight to
Paradise."[2]

The cremating people, who swept into Greece and
became the over-lords of the earlier settlers, were represented in the western movement of tribes towards Gaul
and Britain.   It is uncertain where the cremation
custom had origin.   Apparently it entered Europe from
Asia.   The Vedic Aryans who invaded Northern India
worshipped the fire-god Agni, who was believed to carry
souls to Paradise; they cremated their dead and com-

---

[1] *Iliad*, XXIII, 75 (Lang, Leaf, and Myers' translation, p. 452).
[2] *The Mythology of the Eddas*, pp. 538-9 (*Transactions of the Royal Society of Literature*, second series, Vol. XII).

bined with it the practice of *suttee*, that is, of burning
the widows of the dead. In Gaul, however, as we
gather from Julius Cæsar, only those widows suspected of
being concerned in the death of their husbands were
burned.   The Norsemen, however, were acquainted
with *suttee*.   In one of the Volsung lays Brynhild rides
towards the pyre on which Sigurd is being burned, and
casts herself into the flames.   The Russians strangled
and burned widows when great men were cremated.

The cremating people erected megalithic monuments,
some of which cover their graves in Britain and elsewhere.

In some districts the intruders of the Bronze Age
were the earliest settlers.   The evidence of the graves in
Buchan, Aberdeenshire, for instance, shows that the
broad-heads colonized that area.   It may be that, like
the later Norsemen, bands of people sought for new
homes in countries where the struggle for existence
would be less arduous than in their own, which suffered
from over population, and did not land at points where
resistance was offered to them.   Agriculturists would, no
doubt, select areas suitable for their mode of life and
favour river valleys, while seafarers and fishermen
would cling to the coasts.   The tendency of fishermen
and agriculturists to live apart in separate communities
has persisted till our own time.   There are fishing
villages along the east coast of Scotland the inhabitants
of which rarely intermarry with those who draw their
means of sustenance from the land.

During the Bronze Age Celtic peoples were filter-
ing into Britain from Gaul.   They appear to have come
originally from the Danube area as conquerors who
imposed their rule on the people they subjected.   Like
the Achæans who overran Greece they seem to have
originally been a vigorous pastoral people who had
herds of pigs, were "horse-tamers", used chariots, and

were fierce and impetuous in battle. In time they crossed the Rhine and occupied Gaul. They overcame the Etruscans. In 390 B.C. they sacked Rome. Their invasion of Greece occurred in the third century, but their attempt to reach Delphi was frustrated. Crossing into Asia Minor they secured a footing in the area subsequently known as Galatia, and their descendants there were addressed in an epistle by St. Paul.

Like the Achæans, the Celts appear to have absorbed the culture of the Ægean area and that of the Ægean colony at Hallstatt in Austria. They were withal the "carriers" of the La Tène Iron Age culture to Britain and Ireland. The potter's wheel was introduced by them into Britain during the archæological early Iron Age. It is possible that the cremating people of the Bronze Age were a Celtic people. But later "waves" of the fighting charioteers did not cremate their dead.

Sharp difference of opinion exists between scholars regarding the Celts. Some identify them with the dark-haired, broad-headed Armenoids, and others with the tall and fair long-headed people of Northern Europe. It is possible that the Celts were not a pure race, but rather a confederacy of peoples who were influenced at different periods by different cultures. That some sections were confederacies or small nations of blended people is made evident by classic references to the Celtiberians, the Celto-Scythians, the Celto-Ligyes, the Celto-Thracians, and the Celtillyrians. On reaching Britain they mingled with the earlier settlers, forming military aristocracies, and dominating large areas. The fair Caledonians of Scotland had a Celtic tribal name, and used chariots in battle like the Continental Celts. Two Caledonian personal names are known—Calgacus ("swordsman") and Argentocoxus ("white foot"). In Ireland the predominant tribes before and during the early Roman period were of similar type. Queen Meave

Weapons and Religious Objects (British Museum)

Bronze socketed celts, bronze dagger, sword and spear-heads from Thames; two bronze boars with "sun-disc" ears, which were worn on armour; bronze "sun-disc" from Ireland; "chalk drum" from grave (Yorkshire), with ornamentation showing butterfly and St. Andrew's Cross symbols; warrior with shield, from rock carving (Denmark).

of Connaught was like Queen Boadicea[1] of the Iceni, a fair-haired woman who rode to battle in a chariot.

The Continental trade routes up the Danube and Rhone valleys leading towards Britain were for some centuries under the control of the Celts. It was no doubt to obtain a control over trade that they entered Britain and Ireland. On the Continent they engaged in pork curing, and supplied Rome and indeed the whole of Italy with smoked and salted bacon. Dr. Sullivan tells that among the ancient Irish the general name for bacon was *tini*. Smoke-cured hams and flitches were called *tineiccas*, which "is almost identical in form with the Gallo-Roman word *taniaccae* or *tanacae* used by Varro for hams imported from Transalpine Gaul into Rome and other parts of Italy". Puddings prepared from the blood of pigs—now known as "black puddings"—were, we learn from Varro, likewise exported from Gaul to Italy. The ancient Irish were partial to "black puddings".[2] It would appear, therefore, that the so-called dreamy Celt was a greasy pork merchant.

According to Strabo the exports from Britain in the early part of the first century consisted of gold, silver, and iron, wheat, cattle, skins, slaves, and dogs; while the imports included ivory ornaments, such as bracelets, amber beads, and glass. Tin was exported from Cornwall to Gaul, and carried overland to Marseilles, but this does not appear to have been the earliest route. As has been indicated, tin appears to have been carried, before the Celts obtained control of British trade, by the sea route to the Carthaginian colonies in Spain.

The Carthaginians had long kept secret the sources of their supplies of tin from the group of islands known

---

[1] *Boudicca* was her real name.
[2] Introduction to O'Curry's *Manners and Customs of the Ancient Irish*, Vol. I, pp. ccclxix *et seq.*

as the Cassiterides. About 322 B.C., however, the Greek merchants at Marseilles fitted out an expedition which was placed in charge of Pytheas, a mathematician, for the purpose of exploring the northern area. This scholar wrote an account of his voyage, but only fragments of it quoted by different ancient authors have come down to us. He appears to have coasted round Spain and Brittany, and to have sailed up the English Channel to Kent, to have reached as far north as Orkney and Shetland, and perhaps, as some think, Iceland, to have crossed the North Sea towards the mouth of the Baltic, and explored a part of the coast of Norway. He returned to Britain, which he appears to have partly explored before crossing over to Gaul. In an extract from his diary, quoted by Strabo, he tells that the Britons in certain districts not detailed grew corn, millet, and vegetables. Such of them as had corn and honey made a beverage from these materials. They brought the corn ears into great houses (barns) and threshed them there, for on account of the rain and lack of sunshine out-door threshing floors were of little use to them. Pytheas noted that in Britain the days were longer and the nights brighter than in the Mediterranean area. In the northern parts he visited the nights were so short that the interval between sunset and sunrise was scarcely perceptible. The farthest north headland of Britain was Cape Orcas.[1] Six days sail north of Britain lay Thule, which was situated near the frozen sea. There a day lasted six months and a night for the same space of time.

Another extract refers to hot springs in Britain, and a presiding deity identified with Minerva, in whose temple "the fires never go out, yet never whiten into ashes; when the fire has got dull it turns into round lumps like stones". Apparently coal was in use at a temple situated

---

[1] *Orcas* is a Celtic word signifying "young boar".

at Bath.   Timæus, a contemporary of Pytheas, quoting
from the lost diary of the explorer, states that tin was
found on an island called Mictis, lying inwards (northward) at a distance of six days' sail from Britain.   The
natives made voyages to and from the island in their
canoes of wickerwork covered with hides.   Mictis could
not have been Cornwall or an island in the English
Channel.   Strabo states that Crassus, who succeeded in
reaching the Cassiterides, announced that the distance
to them was greater than that from the Continent to
Britain, and he found that the tin ore lay on the surface.
Evidently tin was not mined on the island of Mictis as
it was in Cornwall in later times.

An earlier explorer than Pytheas was Himilco, the
Carthaginian.   He reached Britain about 500 B.C.   A
Latin metrical rendering of his lost work was made by
Rufus Festus Avienus in the fourth century of our era.
Reference is made to the islands called the Œstrymnides
that "raise their heads, lie scattered, and are rich in tin
and lead".   These islands were visited by Himilco, and
were distant "two days voyage from the Sacred Island
(Ireland) and near the broad Isle of the Albiones".   As
Rufus Festus Avienus refers to "the hardy folk of
Britain", his Albiones may have been the people of
Scotland.   The name Albion was originally applied to
England and Scotland.   In the first century, however,
Latin writers never used "Albion" except as a curiosity,
and knew England as Britain.   According to Himilco,
the Tartessi of Spain were wont to trade with the natives
of the northern tin islands.   Even the Carthaginians
"were accustomed to visit these seas".   From other
sources we learn that the Phœnicians carried tin from the
Cassiterides direct to the Spanish port of Corbilo, the
exact location of which is uncertain.

It is of special importance to note that the tin-stone
was collected on the surface of the islands before mining

ENAMELLED BRONZE SHIELD (from the Thames near Battersea)
(British Museum)

operations were conducted elsewhere.   In all probability
the laborious work of digging mines was not commenced
before the available surface supplies became scanty.
According to Sir John Rhys[1] the districts in southern
England, where surface tin was first obtained, were
"chiefly Dartmoor, with the country round Tavistock
and that around St. Austell, including several valleys
looking towards the southern coast of Cornwall.   In
most of the old districts where tin existed, it is supposed
to have lain too deep to have been worked in early
times."   When, however, Poseidonius visited Cornwall
in the first century of our era, he found that a beginning
had been made in skilful mining operations.   It may be
that the trade with the Cassiterides was already languish-
ing on account of changed political conditions and the
shortage of supplies.

Where then were the Cassiterides?   M. Reinach
struck at the heart of the problem when he asked, "In
what western European island is tin found?"   Those
writers who have favoured the group of islands off the
north-western coast of Spain are confronted by the difficulty that these have failed to yield traces of tin, while
those writers who favour Cornwall and the Scilly Islands
cannot ignore the precise statements that the "tin
islands" were farther distant from the Continent than
Britain, and that in the time of Pytheas tin was carried
from Mictis, which was six days' sail from Britain.   The
fact that traces of tin, copper, and lead have been found
in the Hebrides is therefore of special interest.   Copper,
too, has been found in Shetland, and lead and zinc in
Orkney.   Withal there are Gaelic place-names in which
staoin (tin) is referred to, in Islay, Jura (where there are
traces of old mine-workings), in Iona, and on the mainland of Ross-shire.   Traces of tin are said to have been
found in Lewis where the great stone circle of Callernish

[1] *Celtic Britain*, p. 44.

in a semi-barren area indicates the presence at one time in its area of a considerable population. The Hebrides may well have been the Œstrymnides of Himilco and the Cassiterides of classical writers. Jura or Iona may have been the Mictis of Pytheas. Tin-stone has been found in Ireland too, near Dublin, in Wicklow, and in Killarney.

The short dark people in the Hebrides and Orkney may well be, like the Silurians of Wales, the descendants of the ancient mine workers. They have been referred to by some as descendants of the crews of wrecked ships of the Spanish Armada, and by others as remnants of the Lost Ten Tribes.

In Irish Gaelic literature, however, there is evidence that the dark people were in ancient times believed to be the descendants of the Fir-bolgs (men with sacks), the Fir-domnann (the men who dug the ground), and the Galioin (Gauls). Campbell in his *West Highland Tales* has in a note referred to the dark Hebrideans. "Behind the fire", he wrote, "sat a girl with one of those strange faces which are occasionally to be seen in the Western Isles, a face which reminded me of the Nineveh sculptures, and of faces seen in San Sebastian. Her hair was black as night, and her clear dark eyes glittered through the peat smoke. Her complexion was dark, and her features so unlike those who sat about her that I asked if she were a native of the island (of Barra), and learned that she was a Highland girl." It may be that the dark Eastern people were those who introduced the Eastern and non-Celtic, non-Teutonic prejudice against pork as food into Scotland. In Ireland the Celtic people apparently obliterated the "taboo" at an early period.

It was during the Archæological Late Bronze and Early Iron Ages that the Celtic artistic patterns reached England. These betray affinities with Ægean motifs, and they were afterwards developed in Ireland and

Scotland. In both countries they were fused with symbols of Egyptian and Anatolian origin.

Like the Celts and the pre-Hellenic people of Greece and Crete, the Britons and the Irish wore breeches. The Roman poet, Martial,[1] satirizes a *life* "as loose as the old breeches of a British pauper". Claudian, the poet, pictures Britannia with her cheeks tattooed and wearing a sea-coloured cloak and a cap of bear-skin. The fact that the Caledonians fought with scanty clothing, as did the Greeks, and as did the Highlanders in historic times, must not be taken as proof that they could not manufacture cloth. According to Rhys, Briton means a "cloth clad"[2] person. The bronze fibulæ found at Bronze Age sites could not have been used to fasten heavy skins.

When the Romans reached Britain, the natives, like the heroes of Homer, used chariots, and had weapons of bronze and iron. The archæology of the ancient Irish stories is of similar character.

In the Bronze Age the swords were pointed and apparently used chiefly for thrusting. The conquerors who introduced the unpointed iron swords were able to shatter the brittle bronze weapons. These iron swords were in turn superseded by the pointed and well-tempered swords of the Romans. But it was not only their superior weapons, their discipline, and their knowledge of military strategy that brought the Romans success. England was broken up into a number of petty kingdoms. "Our greatest advantage", Tacitus confessed, "in dealing with such powerful people is that they cannot act in concert; it is seldom that even two or three tribes will join in meeting a common danger; and so while each fights for himself they are all conquered together."[3]

[1] *Ep.* x, 22.   [2] *Celtic Britain* (4th edition), p. 212.
[3] Tacitus, *Agricola*, Chap. XII.

When the Britons, under Agricola, began to adopt Roman civilization they "rose superior", Tacitus says, "by the forces of their natural genius, to the attainments of the Gauls". In time they adopted the Roman dress,[1] which may have been the prototype of the kilt. The Roman language supplanted the Celtic dialects in certain parts of England.

[1] *Agricola*, Chap. XXI.

CHAPTER XI

Races of Britain and Ireland

Colours of Ancient Races and Mythical Ages—Caucasian Race Theory—The Aryan or Indo-European Theory—Races and Languages —Celts and Teutons—Fair and Dark Palæolithic Peoples in Modern Britain—Mediterranean Man—The Armenoid or Alpine Broad-heads —Ancient British Tribes — Cruithne and Picts — The Picts of the " Brochs " as Pirates and Traders—Picts and Fairies—Scottish Types— Racial " Pockets ".

The race problem has ever been one of engrossing interest to civilized peoples. In almost every old mythology we meet with theories that were formulated to account for the existence of the different races living in the world, and for the races that were supposed to have existed for a time and became extinct. An outstanding feature of each racial myth is that the people among whom it grew up are invariably represented to be the finest type of humanity.

A widespread habit, and one of great antiquity, was to divide the races, as the world was divided, into four sections, and to distinguish them by their colours. The colours were those of the cardinal points and chiefly Black, White, Red, and Yellow. The same system was adopted in dealing with extinct races. Each of these were coloured according to the Age in which they had existence, and the colours were connected with metals. In Greece and India, for instance, the " Yellow Age " was a " Golden Age ", the " White Age " a " Silver

Age", the "Red Age" a "Bronze Age", and the "Black Age" an "Iron Age".

Although the old theories regarding the mythical ages and mythical races have long been discarded, the habit of dividing mankind and their history into four sections, according to colours and the metals chiefly used by them, is not yet extinct. We still speak of the "Black man", the "Yellow man", the "Red man", and the "White man". Archæologists have divided what they call the "pre-history of mankind" into the two "Stone Ages", the "Bronze Age" and the "Iron Age". The belief that certain races have become extinct as the result of conquest by invaders is still traceable in those histories that refer, for instance, to the disappearance of "Stone Age man" or "Bronze Age man", or of the British Celts, or of the Picts of Scotland.

That some races have completely disappeared there can be no shadow of a doubt. As we have seen, Neanderthal man entirely vanished from the face of the globe, and has not left a single descendant among the races of mankind. In our own day the Tasmanians have become extinct. These cases, however, are exceptional. The complete extinction of a race is an unusual thing in the history of mankind. A section may vanish in one particular area and yet persist in another. As a rule, in those districts where races are supposed to have perished, it is found that they have been absorbed by intruders. In some cases the chief change has been one of racial designation and nationality.

Crô-Magnon man, who entered Europe when the Neanderthals were hunting the reindeer and other animals, is still represented in our midst. Dr. Collignon, the French ethnologist, who has found many representatives of this type in the Dordogne valley where their ancestors lived in the decorated cave-dwellings before their organization was broken up by the Azilian and other intruders, shows that the intrusion of minorities of males rarely leaves a permanent change in a racial type. The alien element tends to disappear. "When", he writes, "a race is well seated in a region, fixed to the soil by agriculture, acclimatized by natural selection and sufficiently dense, it opposes, for the most precise observations confirm it, an enormous resistance to newcomers, whoever they may be." Intruders of the male sex only may be bred out in time.

Our interest here is with the races of Britain and Ireland, but, as our native islands were peopled from the Continent, we cannot ignore the evidence afforded by Western and Northern Europe when dealing with our own particular phase of the racial problem.

It is necessary in the first place to get rid of certain old theories that were based on imperfect knowledge or wrong foundations. One theory applies the term "Caucasian Man" to either a considerable section or the majority of European peoples. "The utter absurdity of the misnomer Caucasian, as applied to the blue-eyed and fair-haired Aryan (?) race of Western Europe, is revealed", says Ripley,[1] "by two indisputable facts. In the first place, this ideal blond type does not occur within many hundred miles of Caucasia; and, secondly, nowhere along the great Caucasian chain is there a single native tribe making use of a purely inflectional or Aryan language."

The term "Aryan" is similarly a misleading one. It was invented by Professor Max Müller and applied by him chiefly to a group of languages at a time when races were being identified by the languages they spoke. These peoples—with as different physical

[1] *Races of Europe*, p. 436.

characteristics as have Indians and Norseman, or Russians and Spaniards, who spoke Indo-European, or, as German scholars have patriotically adapted the term, Indo-Germanic languages—were regarded by ethnologists of the "philological school" as members of the one Indo-European or Aryan race or "family". Language, however, is no sure indication of race. The spread of a language over wide areas may be accounted for by trade or political influence or cultural contact. In our own day the English language is spoken by "Black", "Yellow", and "Red", as well as by "White" peoples.

A safer system is to distinguish racial types by their physical peculiarities. When, however, this system is applied in Europe, as elsewhere, we shall still find differences between peoples. Habits of thought and habits of life exercise a stronger influence over individuals, and groups of individuals, than do, for instance, the shape of their heads, the colours of their hair, eyes, and skin, or the length and strength of their limbs. Two particular individuals may be typical representatives of a distinct race and yet not only speak different languages, but have a different outlook on life, and different ideas as to what is right and what is wrong. Different types of people are in different parts of the world united by their sense of nationality. They are united by language, traditions, and beliefs, and by their love of a particular locality in which they reside or in which their ancestors were wont to reside. A sense of nationality, such as unites the British Empire, may extend to far-distant parts of the world.

But, while conscious of the uniting sense of nationality, our people are at the same time conscious of and interested in their physical differences and the histories of different sections of our countrymen. The problem as

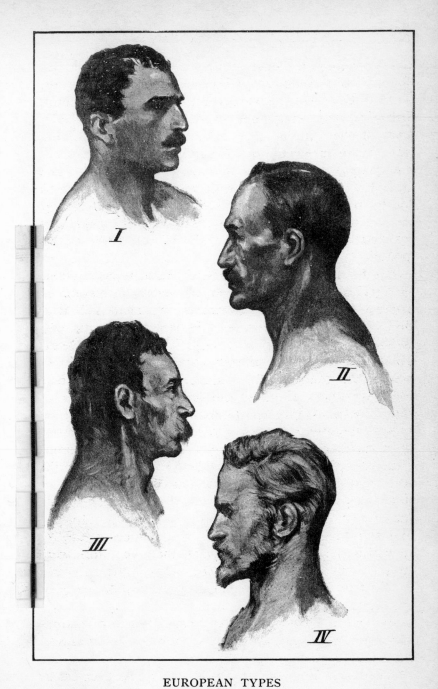

EUROPEAN TYPES

I, Mediterranean. II, Crô-Magnon. III, Armenoid (Alpine).
IV, Northern.

to whether we are mainly Celtic or mainly Teutonic is one of perennial interest.

Here again, when dealing with the past, we meet with the same condition of things that prevail at the present day. Both the ancient Celts and the people they called Teutons ("strangers") were mixed peoples with different physical peculiarities. The Celts known to the Greeks were a tall, fair-haired people. In Western Europe, as has been indicated, they mingled with the dark Iberians, and a section of the mingled races was known to the Romans as Celtiberians. The Teutons included the tall, fair, long-headed Northerners, and the dark, medium-sized, broad-headed Central Europeans. Both the fair Celts and the fair Teutons appear to have been sections of the northern race known to antiquaries as the "Baltic people", or "Maglemosians", who entered Europe from Siberia and "drifted" along the northern and southern shores of the Baltic Sea—the ancient "White Sea" of the "White people" of the "White North". As we have seen, other types of humanity were "drifting" towards Britain at the same time—that is, before the system of polishing stone implements and weapons inaugurated what has been called the "Neolithic Age".

As modern-day ethnologists have found that the masses of the population in Great Britain and Ireland are of the early types known to archæologists as Palæolithic, Neolithic, and Bronze Age men, the race history of our people may be formulated as follows:

The earliest inhabitants of our islands whose physical characteristics can be traced among the living population were the Crô-Magnon peoples. These were followed by the fair Northerners, the "carriers" of Maglemosian culture, and the dark, medium-sized Iberians, who were the "carriers" of Azilian-Tardenoisian culture. There were thus fair people in England, Scotland, and Ireland thousands of years before the invasions of Celts, Angles, Saxons, Jutes, Norsemen, or Danes.

For a long period, extending over many centuries, the migration "stream" from the Continent appears to have been continuously flowing. The carriers of Neolithic culture were in the main Iberians of Mediterranean racial type—the descendants of the Azilian-Tardenoisian peoples who used bows and arrows, and broke up the Magdalenian civilization of Crô-Magnon man in western and central Europe. This race appears to have been characterized in north and north-east Africa. "So striking", writes Professor Elliot Smith, "is the family likeness between the early Neolithic peoples of the British Isles and the Mediterranean and the bulk of the population, both ancient and modern, of Egypt and East Africa, that a description of the bones of an Early Briton of that remote epoch might apply in all essential details to an inhabitant of Somaliland."[1]

This proto-Egyptian (Iberian) people were of medium stature, had long skulls and short narrow faces, and skeletons of slight and mild build; their complexions were as dark as those of the southern Italians in our own day, and they had dark-brown or black hair with a tendency to curl; the men had scanty facial hair, except for a chin-tuft beard.

These brunets introduced the agricultural mode of life, and, as they settled on the granite in south-western England, appear to have searched for gold there, and imported flint from the settlers on the upper chalk formation.

In time Europe was invaded from Asia Minor by increasing numbers of an Asiatic, broad-headed, long-bearded people of similar type to those who had filtered into Central Europe and reached Belgium and

[1] *The Ancient Egyptians*, p. 58.

Denmark before Neolithic times. This type is known as the "Armenoid race" (the "Alpine race" of some writers). It was quite different from the long-headed and fair Northern type and the short, brunet Mediterranean (proto-Egyptian and Iberian) type. The Armenoid skeletons found in the early graves indicate that the Asiatics were a medium-sized, heavily-built people, capable, as the large bosses on their bones indicate, of considerable muscular development.

During the archæological Bronze Age these Armenoids reached Britain in considerable numbers, and introduced the round-barrow method of burial. They do not appear, however, as has been indicated, to have settled in Ireland.

At a later period Britain was invaded by a people who cremated their dead. As they thus destroyed the evidence that would have afforded us an indication of their racial affinities, their origin is obscure.

While these overland migrations were in progress, considerable numbers of peoples appear to have reached Britain and Ireland by sea from northern and north-western France, Portugal, and Spain. They settled chiefly in the areas where metals and pearls were once found or are still found. "Kitchen middens" and megalithic remains are in Ireland mainly associated with pearl-yielding rivers.

The fair Celts and the darker Celtiberians were invading and settling in Britain before and after the Romans first reached its southern shores. During the Roman period, the ruling caste was mainly of south-European type, but the Roman legions were composed of Gauls, Germans, and Iberians, as well as Italians. No permanent change took place in the ethnics of Britain during the four centuries of Roman occupation. The Armenoid broad-heads, however, became fewer: "the disappearance", as Ripley puts it, "of the round-barrow men is the last event of the prehistoric period which we are able to distinguish ". The inhabitants of the British Isles are, on the whole, long-headed. "Highland and lowland, city or country, peasant or philosopher, all are", says Ripley, "practically alike in respect to this fundamental racial characteristic." Broad-headed types are, of course, to be found, but they are in the minority.

The chief source of our knowledge regarding the early tribes or little nations of Britain and Ireland is the work of Ptolemy, the geographer, who lived between A.D. 50 and 150, from which the earliest maps were compiled in the fourth century. He shows that England, Wales, Scotland, and Ireland were divided among a number of peoples. The Dumnonii,[1] as has been stated, were in possession of Devon and Cornwall, as well as of a large area in the south-western and central lowlands of Scotland. Near them were the Durotriges, who were also in Ireland. Sussex was occupied by the Regni and Kent by the Cantion. The Atrebates, the Belgæ, and the Parisii were invaders from Gaul during the century that followed Cæsar's invasion. The Belgæ lay across the neck of the land between the Bristol Channel and the Isle of Wight; the Atrebates clung to the River Thames, while the Parisii, who gave their name to Paris, occupied the east coast between the Wash and the Humber. Essex was the land of the Iceni or Eceni, the tribe of Boadicea (Boudicca). Near them were the Catuvellauni (men who rejoiced in battle) who were probably rulers of a league, and the Trinovantes, whose name is said to signify "very vigorous". The most important tribe of the north and midlands of England was the Brigantes,[2] whose sphere of influence extended to the Firth of Forth,

---

[1] Englished "Damnonians" (Chapter IX).

[2] Tacitus says that the Brigantes were in point of numbers the most considerable folk in Britain (*Agricola*, Chapter XVII).

Valentine

RUINS OF PICTISH TOWER AT CARLOWAY, LEWIS

Modern "black house" in the foreground.

where they met the Votadini, who were probably kins-
men or allies. On the north-west were the Setantii,
who appear to have been connected with the Brigantes
in England and Ireland. Cuchullin, the hero of the Red
Branch of Ulster, was originally named Setanta.[1] In
south Wales the chief tribe was the Silures, whose
racial name is believed to cling to the Scilly (Silura)
Islands. They were evidently like the Dumnonii a
metal-working people. South-western Wales was
occupied by the Demetæ (the "firm folk"). In south-
western Scotland, the Selgovæ ("hunters") occupied
Galloway, their nearest neighbours being the Novantæ
of Wigtownshire. The Selgovæ may have been those
peoples known later as the Atecotti. From Fife to
southern Aberdeenshire the predominant people on the
east were the Vernicones. In north-east Aberdeenshire
were the Tæxali. To the west of these were the Vaco-
magi. The Caledonians occupied the Central Highlands from Inverness southward to Loch Lomond.
In Ross-shire were the Decantæ, a name resembling
Novantæ and Setantii. The Lugi and Smertæ (smeared
people) were farther north. The Cornavii of Caithness
and North Wales were those who occupied the "horns"
or "capes". Along the west of Scotland were peoples
called the Cerones, Creones, and Carnonacæ, or Carini,
perhaps a sheep-rearing people. The Epidii were an
Argyll tribe, whose name is connected with that of the
horse—perhaps a horse-god.[2] Orkney enshrines the
tribal name of the boar—perhaps that of the ancient
boar-god represented on a standing stone near Inverness
with the sun symbol above its head. The Gaelic name

---

[1] Evidently Cuchullin and other heroes of the "Red Branch" in Ireland were descended
from peoples who had migrated into Ireland from Britain. Their warriors in the old
manuscript tales receive their higher military training in Alba. It is unlikely they would
have been trained in a colony.

[2] Ancient sacred stones with horses depicted on them survive in Scotland. In Harris
one horse-stone remains in an old church tower.

of the Shetlanders is "Cat". Caithness is the county
of the "Cat" people, too. Professor Watson reminds
us that the people of Sutherland are still "Cats" in
Gaelic, and that the Duke of Sutherland is referred to as
"Duke of the Cats".

The Picts are not mentioned by Ptolemy. They
appear to have been an agricultural and sea-faring
people who (c. A.D. 300) engaged in trade and piracy.
A flood of light has been thrown on the Pictish problem
by Professor W. J. Watson, Edinburgh.[1] He shows
that when Agricola invaded Scotland (A.D. 85) the predominant people were the Caledonians. Early in the
third century the Caledonians and Mæatæ — names
which included all the tribes north of Hadrian's
Wall—were so aggressive that Emperor Septimus
Severus organized a great expedition against them.
He pressed northward as far as the southern shore of
the Moray Firth, and, although he fought no battle, lost
50,000 men in skirmishes, &c. The Caledonians and
Mæatæ rose again, and Severus was preparing a second
expedition when he died at York in A.D. 211. His son,
Caracalla, withdrew from Scotland altogether. The
Emperor Constantius, who died at York in A.D. 306,
had returned from an expedition, not against the Caledonians, but against the Picts. The Picts were beginning to become prominent. In 360 they had again to
be driven back. They had then become allies of the
Scots from Ulster, who were mentioned in A.D. 297
by the orator Eumenius, as enemies of the Britons
in association with the Picti. Professor Watson, drawing on Gaelic evidence, dates the first settlement of the
Scots in Argyll "about A.D. 180".

In 368 the Caledonians were, like the Verturiones, a
division of the Picts. Afterwards their tribal name dis-

---

[1] *The Picts*, Inverness, 1921 (lecture delivered to the Gaelic Society of Inverness and
reprinted from *The Inverness Courier*).

appeared. That the Picts and Caledonians were originally separate peoples is made clear by the statement of a Roman orator who said: "I do not mention the woods and marshes of the Caledonians, the Picts, and others". In 365 the Pecti, Saxons, Scots, and Atecotti harassed the Britons. Thus by the fourth century the Picts had taken the place of the Caledonians as the leading tribe, or as the military aristocrats of a great part of Scotland, the name of which, formerly Caledonia, came to be Pictland, Pictavia.

Who then were the Picts? Professor Watson shows that the racial name is in old Norse "Pettr", in Old English "Peohta", and in old Scots "Pecht".[1] These forms suggest that the original name was "Pect". Ammianus refers to the "Pecti". In old Welsh "Peith-wyr" means "Pict-men" and "Peith" comes from "Pect". The derivation from the Latin "pictus" (painted) must therefore be rejected. It should be borne in mind in this connection that the Ancient Britons stained their bodies with woad. The application of the term "painted" to only one section of them seems improbable. "Pecti", says Professor Watson, "cannot be separated etymologically from Pictones, the name of a Gaulish tribe on the Bay of Biscay south of the Loire, near neighbours of the Veneti. Their name

[1] The fact that in the Scottish Lowlands the fairies were sometimes called "Pechts" has been made much of by those who contend that the prototypes of the fairies were the original inhabitants of Western Europe. This theory ignores the well-established custom of giving human names to supernatural beings. In Scotland the hill-giants (Fomorians) have been re-named after Arthur (as in Arthur's Seat, Edinburgh), Patrick (Inverness), Wallace (Eildon Hills), Samson (Ben Ledi), &c. In like manner fairies were referred to as Pechts. The Irish evidence is of similar character. The Danann deities were consigned to fairyland. Donald Gorm, a West Highland chief, gave his name to an Irish fairy. Fairyland was the old Paradise. Arthur, Thomas the Rhymer, Finn-mac-Coul, &c., became "fairymen" after death. A good deal of confusion has been caused by mistranslating the Scottish Gaelic word *sith* (Irish *sidhe*) as "fairy". The word *sith* (pronounced *shee*) means anything unearthly or supernatural, and the "peace" of supernatural life—of death after life, as well as the silence of the movements of supernatural beings. The cuckoo was supposed to dwell for a part of the year in the underworld, and was called *eun sith* ("supernatural bird"). Mysterious epidemics were *sith* diseases. There were *sith* (supernatural) dogs, cats, mice, cows, &c., as well as *sith* men and *sith* women.

shows the same variation between Pictones and Pectones. We may therefore claim Pecti as a genuine Celtic word. It is of the Cymric or Old British and Gaulish type, not of the Gaelic type, for Gaelic has no initial P, while those others have." Gildas (*c.* A.D. 570), Bede (*c.* A.D. 730), and Nennius (*c.* A.D. 800) refer to the Picts as a people from the north of Scotland. Nennius says they occupied Orkney first. The legends which connect the Picts with Scythia and Hercules were based on Virgil's mention of " picti Agathyrsi " and "picti Geloni " (*Æneid* IV, 146, *Georgics*, II, 115) combined with the account by Herodotus (IV, 10) of the descent of Gelonus and Agathyrsus from Hercules. Of late origin therefore was the Irish myth that the Picts from Scythia were called Agathyrsi and were descended from Gelon, son of Hercules.

There never were Picts in Ireland, except as visitors. The theory about the Irish Picts arose by mistranslating the racial name "Cruithne" as "Picts". Communities of Cruithne were anciently settled in the four provinces of Ireland, but Cruithne means Britons not Picts.

The ancient name of Great Britain was Albion, while Ireland was in Greek " Ierne ", and in Latin " Iubernia " (later "Hibernia"). The racial name was applied by Pliny to Albion and Hibernia when he referred to the island group as "Britanniæ". Ptolemy says that Albion is "a Britannic isle " and further that Albion (England and Scotland) was an island "belonging to the Britannic Isles ". Ireland was also a Britannic isle. It is therefore quite clear that the Britons were regarded as the predominant people in England, Wales, Scotland, and Ireland, and that the verdict of history includes Ireland in the British Isles. The Britons were P-Celts, and their racial name " Pretan-Pritan " became in the Gaelic language of the Q-Celts "Cruithen", plural "Cruithne".

In Latin the British Isles are called after their inhabi-

Valentine

A SCOTTISH "BROCH" (Mousa, Shetland Isles)

Compare with Sardinian *Nuraghe*, page 136.

tants, the rendering being "Britanni", while in Greek it is "Pretannoi" or "Pretanoi". As Professor W. J. Watson and Professor Sir J. Morris Jones, two able and reliable philologists, have insisted, the Greek form is the older and more correct, and the Latin form is merely an adaptation of the Greek form.

In the early centuries of our era the term "Britannus" was shortened in Latin to "Britto" plural "Brittones". This diminutive form, which may be compared with "Scotty" for Scotsman, became popular. In Gaelic it originated the form "Breatain", representing "Brittones" (Britons), which was applied to the Britons of Strathclyde, Wales, and Cornwall, who retained their native speech under Roman rule; in Welsh, the rendering was "Brython". The Welsh name for Scotland became "Prydyn". The northern people of Scotland, having come under the sway of the Picts, were referred to as Picts just as they became "Scots" after the tribe of Scots rose into prominence. In this sense the Scottish Cruithne were Picts. But the Cruithne (Britons) of Ireland were never referred to as Picts. Modern scholars who have mixed up Cruithne and Picts are the inventors of the term "Irish Picts".

The Picts of Scotland have been traditionally associated with the round buildings known as "brochs", which are all built on the same plan. "Of 490 known brochs", says Professor W. J. Watson, "Orkney and Shetland possess 145, Caithness has 150, and Sutherland 67—a total of 362. On the mainland south of Sutherland there are 10 in Ross, 6 Inverness-shire, 2 in Forfar, 1 in Stirling, Midlothian, Selkirk, and Berwick-shires, 3 in Wigtownshire. In the Isles there are 28 in Lewis, 10 in Harris, 30 in Skye, 1 in Raasay, and at least 5 in the isles of Argyll. The inference is that the original seat of the broch builders must have been in the far north, and that their influence proceeded southwards. The masonry and contents of the brochs prove them to be the work of a most capable people, who lived partly at least by agriculture and had a fairly high standard of civilization. . . . The distribution of the brochs also indicate that their occupants combined agriculture with seafaring. . . . The Wigtown brochs, like the west coast ones generally, are all close to the sea, and in exceedingly strong positions."

These Scottish brochs bear a striking resemblance to the *nuraghi* of the island of Sardinia. Both the broch and the *nuraghe* have low doorways which "would at once put an enemy at a disadvantage in attempting to enter".

Describing the Sardinian structures, Mr. T. Eric Peet writes:[1] "All the *nuraghi* stand in commanding situations overlooking large tracts of country, and the more important a position is from a strategical point of view the stronger will be the *nuraghe* which defends it". Ruins of villages surround these structures. "There cannot be the least doubt", says Peet, "that in time of danger the inhabitants drove their cattle into the fortified enclosure, entered it themselves, and then closed the gates."

In the Balearic Islands are towers called *talayots* which "resemble rather closely", in Peet's opinion, the *nuraghi* of Sardinia. The architecture of the *talayots*, the *nuraghi*, and the brochs resembles that of the bee-hive tombs of Mycenæ (pre-Hellenic Greece). There are no brochs in Ireland. The "round towers" are of Christian origin (between ninth and thirteenth centuries A.D.). A tomb at Labbamologa, County Cork, however, resembles the tombs of the Balearic Isles and Sardinia (Peet, *Rough Stone Monuments*, pp. 43-4).

The Picts appear to have come to Scotland from the country of the ancient Pictones, whose name survives in

[1] *Rough Stone Monuments*, pp. 82 *et seq.*

Poitiers (Poictiers) and the province of Poitou in France. These Pictones were anciently rivals of the Veneti, the chief sea-traders in Western and Northern Europe during the pre-Roman period. We gather from Cæsar that the Pictones espoused the cause of the Romans when the Veneti and their allies revolted. They and their near neighbours, the Santoni, supplied Cæsar with ships.[1] These were apparently skiffs which were much lighter and smaller than the imposing vessels of the Veneti. As the big vessels of the Armada were no match for the smaller English vessels, so were the Veneti ships no match for the skiffs of the Pictones.

The Picts who settled in Orkney appear to have dominated the eastern and western Scottish sea-routes. It is possible that they traded with Scandinavia and imported Baltic amber. Tacitus states that the Baltic people, who engaged in the amber trade, spoke a dialect similar to that of Britain, worshipped the mother-goddess, and regarded the boar as the symbol of their deity.[2] Orkney, as has been noted, is derived from the old Celtic word for boar. The boar-people of Orkney who came under the sway of the Picts may have been related to the amber traders.

The Scottish broch-people, associated in tradition with the Picts, were notorious for their piratic habits. In those ancient days, however, piracy was a common occupation. The later Vikings, who seized the naval base of Orkney for the same reason we may conclude as did the Picts, occupied the brochs. Viking means "pirate", as York Powell has shown. In *Egil's Saga* (Chapter XXXII) the hero Bjorn "was sometimes in Viking but sometimes on trading voyages".[3]

It may be that the term *pictus* was confused with the

[1] *De Bello Gallico*, Book III, Chapter II.
[2] *Manners of the Germans*, Chapter XLV. The boar was the son of a sow-goddess. Demeter had originally a sow form.
[3] *Scandinavian Britain* (London, 1908), pp. 61-3.

racial name Pecti, because the Picts had adopted the sailor-like habit of tattoing their skins—a habit which probably had a religious significance. Claudian, the fourth-century Roman poet, refers to "the fading steel-wrought figures on the dying Pict". Like the seafaring Scots of northern Ireland who harried the Welsh coast between the second and fifth centuries of our era, the Picts of Scotland had skiffs (scaphæ) with sails and twenty oars a side. Vessels, masts, ropes, and sails were painted a neutral tint, and the crews were attired in the same colour. Thus "camouflaged", the Picts and Scots were able to harry the coasts of Romanized Britain. They appear to have turned Hadrian's wall from the sea. The Pictish seafaring tribes, the Keiths or Cats and the Mæatæ, have left their names in Caithness, Inchkeith, Dalkeith, &c., and in the Isle of May, &c.[1]

A glimpse of piratical operations in the first century before the Christian era is obtained in an Irish manuscript account of certain happenings in the reign of King Conaire the Great of Ireland. So strict was this monarch's rule that several lawless and discontented persons were forced into exile.

"Among the most desperate of the outlaws were the monarch's own foster brothers, the four sons of Dond Dess, an important chieftain of Leinster. These refractory youths, with a large party of followers, took to their boats and ships and scoured the coasts of Britain and Scotland, as well as of their own country. Having met on the sea with Ingcel, the son of the King of Britain, who, for his misdeeds, had been likewise banished by his own father, both parties entered into a league, the first fruits of which were the plunder and devastation of a great part of the British coast."

They afterwards made a descent on the coast of Ireland, and when King Conaire returned from a visit to

---

[1] Rhys, *Celtic Britain* (4th ed.), pp. 152, 317.

By courtesy of the Director of The British School of Rome

A SARDINIAN *NURAGHE* (page 134)

Compare with the Scottish "Broch", page 132.

Clare, "he found the whole country before him one sheet of fire, the plunderers having landed in his absence and carried fire and sword wherever they went".[1]

In his description of Britain, Tacitus says that the inhabitants varied in their physical traits. Different conclusions were drawn concerning their origin. He thought the Caledonians were, because of their ruddy hair and muscular limbs, of German descent, and that the dark Silures of Wales were descendants of Iberian colonists. He noted that the inhabitants of southern England resembled those of Gaul.[2]

Later writers have expressed divergent views regarding the ethnics of the British Isles. One theory is that the fair Teutonic peoples, who invaded Britain during the post-Roman period, drove the "dark Celts" westward, and that that is the reason why in England and Scotland the inhabitants of western areas are darker than those in the eastern. As we have seen, however, the early metal workers settled in the western areas for the reason that the minerals they sought for were located there. In south-western Scotland the inhabitants are darker than those on the east, except in Aberdeenshire, where there are distinctive megalithic remains and two famous pearling rivers, the Ythan and Ugie, as well as deposits of flint and traces of gold.

The people of Scotland are, on the whole, the tallest and heaviest people in Europe. It has been suggested that their great average stature is due to the settlement in their country of the hardy Norsemen of the Viking period, but this is improbable, because the average stature of Norway, Sweden, and Denmark is lower than that of Scotland. A distinctive feature of the Scottish face is the high cheek-bone. The Norse cheek-bone is distinctly flatter. It may be that the

---

[1] O'Curry, *Manners and Customs of the Ancient Irish*, Vol. III, p. 136.
[2] *Agricola*, Chap. XI.

tall Crô-Magnons, who had high cheek-bones, have contributed to Scottish physical traits. That all the fair peoples of Britain and Ireland are, as has been indicated, not necessarily descendants of the fair Celts and Anglo-Saxons is evident from the traces that have been found of the early settlement in these islands of the proto-Scandinavians, who introduced the Maglemosian culture long before the introduction of the Neolithic industry. Modern ethnologists lean to the view that the masses of the present-day population of Europe betray Palæolithic racial affinities. In no country in Europe, other than our own, have there been fewer ethnic changes. As we have seen, there were only two or three intrusions from the Continent between the periods when the bronze and iron industries were introduced—that is, during about a thousand years. The latter invasions were those of types already settled in Britain. As in other countries, the tendency to revert to the early types represented by the masses of the people has not been absent in our native land. The intrusions of energetic minorities may have caused changes of languages and habits of life, but in time the alien element has been absorbed.[1] Withal, the influences of climate and of the diseases associated with localities have ever been at work in eliminating the physically unfit—that is, those individuals who cannot live in a climate too severe for their constitutions. In large industrial cities the short, dark types are more numerous than the tall, fair, and large-lunged types. The latter appear to be more suited for an open-air life.

"Pockets" of peoples of distinctive type are to be found in different parts of the British Isles. In Barvas, Lewis, and elsewhere in the Hebrides, pockets of dark peoples of foreign appearance are reputed by theorists,

---

[1] "The rule is", writes Beddoe in this connection (*The Anthropological History of Europe*, p. 53), "that an anthropological type is never wholly dispossessed or extirpated".

as has been indicated, to be descendants of the sailors of the Spanish Armada. They resemble, however, the Firbolgs of Ireland and the Silures of Wales. Hertfordshire has a dark, short people too. Galloway, the country of the ancient Selgovæ (hunters), is noted for its tall people. It may be that there is a Crô-Magnon strain in Galloway, and that among the short, dark peoples are descendants of the ancient metal workers, including the Easterners who settled in Spain. (See Chaps. IX and XII.) Beddoe thinks that the Phœnician type "occasionally crops up" in Cornwall.[1]

[1] *The Anthropological History of Europe* (new edition, Paisley, 1912), p. 50.

CHAPTER XII

Druidism in Britain and Gaul

Culture Mixing—Classical Evidence regarding Druids—Doctrine of Transmigration of Souls—Celtic Paradises: Isles of the Blest, Land-under-waves, Fairyland, and "Loveless Land"—Paradise as Apple-land—Apples, Nuts, and Pork of Longevity—Mistletoe connected with the Oak, Apple, and Other Trees—Druids and Oracular Birds—Druids as Soothsayers—Thomas the Rhymer as "True Thomas"—Christ as the Druid of St. Columba—Stones of Worship—Druid Groves and Dolmens in Anglesea—Early Christians denounce Worship of Stones, Trees, Wells, and Heavenly Bodies—Vows over Holy Objects—Bull Sacrifices, Stone Worship, &c., in Highlands—"Cup-marked" Stones—Origin of Druidism — Milk-Goddesses and Milk-yielding Trees — European and Oriental Milk Myths—Tree Cults and Megalithic Monuments.

When the question is asked "What was the religion of the ancient Britons?" the answer generally given is "Druidism". But such a term means little more than "Priestism". It would perhaps be better not to assume that the religious beliefs of our remote ancestors were either indigenous or homogeneous, or that they were ever completely systematized at any period or in any district. Although certain fundamental beliefs may have been widespread, it is clear that there existed not a few local or tribal cults. "I swear by the gods of my people" one hero may declare in a story, while of another it may be told that "Coll" (the hazel) or "Fire" was his god. Certain animals were sacred in some districts and not in others, or were sacred to some individuals only in a single tribe.

In a country like Britain, subjected in early times

to periodic intrusions of peoples from different areas, the process of "culture mixing" must have been active and constant. Imported beliefs were fused with native beliefs, or beliefs that had assumed local features, while local pantheons no doubt reflected local politics—the gods of a military aristocracy being placed over the gods of the subject people. At the same time, it does not follow that when we find a chief deity bearing a certain name in one district, and a different name in another, that the religious rites and practices differed greatly. Nor does it follow that all peoples who gave recognition to a political deity performed the same ceremonies or attached the same importance to all festivals. Hunters, seafarers, and agriculturists had their own peculiar rites, as surviving superstitions (the beliefs of other days) clearly indicate, while the workers in metals clung to ceremonial practices that differed from those performed by representatives of a military aristocracy served by the artisans.

Much has been written about the Druids, but it must be confessed that our knowledge regarding them is somewhat scanty. Classical writers have made contradictory statements about their beliefs and ceremonies. Pliny alone tells that they showed special reverence for the mistletoe growing on the oak, and suggests that the name Druid was connected with the Greek word *drus* (an oak). Others tell that there were Druids, Seers, and Bards in the Celtic priesthood. In his book on divination, Cicero indicates that the Druids had embraced the doctrines of Pythagoras, the Greek philosopher, who was born about 586 B.C., including that of the transmigration of souls.[1] Julius Cæsar tells that the special province of the Druids in Gaulish society was religion in all its aspects; they read oracles,

---

[1] Cæsar (*De Bello Gallico*, VI, XIV, 4) says the Druids believed the soul passed from one individual to another.

and instructed large numbers of the nation's youth. Pomponius Mela[1] says the instruction was given in caves and in secluded groves. Cæsar records that once a year the Druids presided over a general assembly of the Gauls at a sacred spot in the country of the Carnutes, which was supposed to be the centre of Gaul. It is not known whether this holy place was marked by a mound, a grove, a stone circle, or a dolmen. The Archdruid was chief of the priesthood. Cæsar notes that the Germans had no Druids and paid no attention to sacrifices.

Of special interest is the statement that the Druids believed in the doctrine of Transmigration of Souls— that is, they believed that after death the soul passed from one individual to another, or into plants or animals before again passing into a human being at birth. According to Diodorus Siculus, who lived in the latter part of the first century A.D., the Gauls took little account of the end of life, believing they would come to life after a certain term of years, entering other bodies. He also refers to the custom of throwing letters on the funeral pyre, so that the dead might read them.[2] This suggests a belief in residence for a period in a Hades.

The doctrine of Transmigration of Souls did not, however, prevail among all Celtic peoples even in Gaul. Valerius Maximus, writing about A.D. 30, says that the Gauls were in the habit of lending sums of money on the promise that they would be repaid in the next world. Gaelic and Welsh literature contains little evidence of the doctrine of Transmigration of Souls. A few myths suggest that re-birth was a privilege of certain specially famous individuals. Mongan, King of Dalriada in Ulster, and the Welsh Taliessin, for instance, were supposed to have lived for periods in

---

[1] A Spaniard of the first century A.D. [2] Book V, Chap. XXVIII.

various forms, including animal, plant, and human forms, while other heroes were incarnations of deities. The most persistent British belief, however, was that after death the soul passed to an Otherworld.

Julius Cæsar says that Druidism was believed to have originated in Britain.[1] This cannot apply, however, to the belief in transmigration of souls, which was shared in common by Celts, Greeks, and Indians. According to Herodotus, "the Egyptians are the first who have affirmed that the soul is immortal, and that when the body decays the soul invariably enters another body on the point of death". The story of "The Two Brothers" (Anpu and Bata) indicates that the doctrine was known in Egypt. There are references in the "Book of the Dead" to a soul becoming a lily, a golden falcon, a ram, a crocodile, &c., but this doctrine was connected, according to Egyptologists, with the belief that souls could assume different shapes in the Otherworld. In India souls are supposed to pass through animal or reptile forms only. The Greek doctrine, like the Celtic, includes plant forms. Certain African tribes believe in the transmigration of souls.

In ancient Britain and Ireland the belief obtained, as in Greece and elsewhere, that there was an Underworld Paradise and certain Islands of the Blest (in Gaelic called "The Land of Youth", "The Plain of Bliss", &c.) The Underworld was entered through caves, wells, rivers or lakes, or through the ocean cavern from which the moon arose. There are references in Scottish folk-tales to "The Land-Under-Waves", and to men and women entering the Underworld through a "fairy" mound, and seeing the dead plucking fruit and reaping grain as in the Paradise of the Egyptian god Osiris. It

---

[1] Pliny (Book XXX) says Britain seems to have taught Druidism to the Persians. Siret's view, given in the concluding part of this chapter, that Druidism was of Eastern origin, is of special interest in this connection.

is evident that Fairyland was originally a Paradise, and the fairy queen an old mother goddess. There are references in Welsh to as gloomy an Underworld as the Babylonian one. "In addition to *Annwfn*, a term which", according to the late Professor Anwyl, "seems to mean the 'Not-world', we have other names for the world below, such as *anghar*, 'the loveless place'; *difant*, the unrimmed place (whence the modern Welsh word *difancoll*, 'lost for ever'); *affwys*, the abyss; *affan*, 'the land invisible'." In a Welsh poem a bard speaks of the Otherworld as "the cruel prison of earth, the abode of death, the loveless land".[1]

The Border Ballads of Scotland contain references to the Fairyland Paradise of the Underworld, to the islands or continent of Paradise, and to the dark Otherworld of the grave in which the dead lie among devouring worms.

In one Celtic Elysium, known to the Welsh and Irish, the dead feast on pork as do the heroes in the Paradise of the Scandinavian god Odin. There is no trace in Scotland of a belief or desire to reach a Paradise in which the pig was eaten. The popularity of the apple as the fruit of longevity was, however, widespread. It is uncertain when the beliefs connected with it were introduced into England, Wales, Scotland, and Ireland. As they were similar to those connected with the hazel-nut, the acorn, the rowan, &c., there may have simply been a change of fruit rather than a religious change, except in so far as new ceremonies may have been associated with the cultivated apple tree.

A Gaelic story tells of a youth who in Paradise held a fragrant golden apple in his right hand. "A third part of it he would eat and still, for all he consumed, never a whit would it be diminished." As long as he ate the apple "nor age nor dimness could affect him". Paradise was in Welsh and Gaelic called "Apple land".[2]

[1] *Celtic Religion*, p. 62.   [2] Avalon, Emain Ablach, &c.

Its "tree of life" always bore ripe fruit and fresh blossoms. One of the Irish St. Patrick legends pictures a fair youth coming from the south [1] clad in crimson mantle and yellow shirt, carrying a "double armful of round yellow-headed nuts and of most beautiful golden-yellow apples". There are stories, too, about the hazel with its "good fruit", and of holy fire being taken from this tree, and withal a number of hazel place-names that probably indicate where sacred hazel groves once existed. Hallowe'en customs connected with apples and nuts are evidently relics of ancient religious beliefs and ceremonies.

The Druids are reported by Pliny (as has been stated) to have venerated the mistletoe, especially when it was found growing on an oak. But the popular parasitic plant is very rarely found associated with this tree. In France and England it grows chiefly on firs and pines or on apple trees, but never on the plane, beech, or birch.[2] It is therefore doubtful if the name Druid was derived from the root *dru* which is found in the Greek word *drus* (oak). In Gaelic the Druids are "wise men" who read oracles, worked spells, controlled the weather, and acted as intercessors between the gods and men. Like the dragon-slayers of romance, they understood "the language of birds", and especially that of the particular bird associated with the holy tree of a cult. One sacred bird was the wren. According to Dr. Whitley Stokes the old Celtic names of wren and Druid were derived from the root *dreo*, which is cognate with the German word *treu* and the English *true*. The Druid was therefore, as one who understood the language of the wren, a soothsayer, a truth-sayer—a revealer of

[1] The south was on the right and signified heaven, while the north was on the left and signified hell.
[2] Bacon wrote: "Mistletoe groweth chiefly upon crab trees, apple trees, sometimes upon hazels, and rarely upon oaks; the mistletoe whereof is counted very medicinal. It is evergreen in winter and summer, and beareth a white glistening berry; and it is a plant utterly differing from the plant on which it groweth."

divine truth. A judgment pronounced by Druid or king was supposed to be inspired by the deity. It was essentially a divine decree. The judge wore round his neck the symbol of the deity. "When what he said was true, it was roomy for his neck; when false, it was narrow." This symbol according to *Cormac's Glossary* was called *sin* (sheen). Some seers derived their power to reveal the truth by tasting the blood or juice of a holy animal or reptile, or, like Thomas the Rhymer, by eating of an apple plucked from the tree of life in the Paradise of Fairyland. In an old ballad it is told that when Thomas was carried off to the Underworld by the fairy queen he was given an inspiring apple that made him a "truth-sayer" (a prophet).

> Syne they came to a garden green
>   And she pu'd an apple frae a tree;
> "Take this for thy wages, True Thomas;
>   It will give thee the tongue that can never lee (lie)."

"True Thomas" was "Druid Thomas".

An interesting reference to Druidism is found in a Gaelic poem supposed to have been written by St. Columba, in which the missionary says:

> The voices of birds I do not reverence,
> Nor sneezing, nor any charm in this wide world.
> Christ, the Son of God, is my Druid.

There are Gaelic stories about Druids who read the omens of the air and foretell the fates of individuals at birth, fix the days on which young warriors should take arms, &c.

In England, Scotland, Ireland, and Wales not only trees and birds were reverenced, but also standing stones, which are sometimes referred to even in modern Gaelic as "stones of worship". Some stories tell of standing stones being transformed into human beings when struck

by a magician's wand. The wand in one story is possessed by a "wise woman". Other traditions relate
that once a year the stones become maidens who visit a
neighbouring stream and bathe in it. A version of this
myth survives in Oxfordshire. According to Tacitus
there were on the island of Mona (Anglesea), which was
a centre of religious influence, not only Druids, but
"women in black attire like Furies"—apparently priestesses. As has been noted, a large number of dolmens
existed on Mona, in which there were also "groves
devoted to inhuman superstitions".[1]

The early Christian writers refer to the "worship of
stones" in Ireland. In the seventh century the Council
at Rouen denounced all those who offer vows to trees,
or wells, or stones, as they would at altars, or offer
candles or gifts, as if any divinity resided there capable
of conferring good or evil. The Council at Arles (A.D.
452) and the Council at Toledo (A.D. 681) dealt with
similar pagan practices. That sacred stones were associated with sacred trees is indicated in a decree of an
early Christian Council held at Nantes which exhorts
"bishops and their servants to dig up and remove and
hide in places where they cannot be found those stones
which in remote and woody places are still worshipped
and where vows are still made". This worship of stones
was in Britain, or at any rate in part of England, connected with the worship of the heavenly bodies. A
statute of the time of King Canute forbids the barbarous
adoration of the sun and moon, fire, fountains, stones,
and all kinds of trees and wood. In the Confession
attributed to St. Patrick, the Irish are warned that all
those who adore the sun shall perish eternally. *Cormac's*

---

[1] *The Annals of Tacitus*, XIV, 30. The theory that mediæval witches were the
priestesses of a secret cult that perpetuated pre-Roman British religion is not supported
by Gaelic evidence. The Gaelic "witches" had no meetings with the devil, and never
rode on broomsticks. The Gaelic name for witchcraft is derived from English and is
not old.

Glossary explains that *Indelba* signified *Images* and that this name was applied to the altars of certain idols. "They (the pagans) were wont to carve on them the forms of the elements they adored: for example, the figure of the sun." Irish Gaels swore by "the sun, moon, water, and air, day and night, sea and land". In a Scottish story some warriors lift up a portion of earth and swear on it. The custom of swearing on weapons was widespread in these islands. In ancient times people swore by what was holiest to them.[1]

One of the latest references to pagan religious customs is found in the records of Dingwall Presbytery dating from 1649 to 1678. In the Parish of Gairloch, Ross-shire, bulls were sacrificed, oblations of milk were poured on the hills, wells were adored, and chapels were "circulated"—the worshippers walked round them sun-wise. Those who intended to set out on journeys thrust their heads into a hole in a stone.[2] If a head entered the hole, it was believed the man would return; if it did not, his luck was doubtful. The reference to "oblations of milk" is of special interest, because milk was offered to the fairies. A milk offering was likewise poured daily into the "cup" of a stone known as Clach-na-Gruagach (the stone of the long-haired one). A bowl of milk was, in the Highlands, placed beside a corpse, and, after burial took place, either outside the house door or at the grave. The conventionalized Azilian human form is sometimes found to be depicted by small "cups" on boulders or rocks. Some "cups" were formed by "knocking" with a small stone for purposes of divination. The "cradle stone" at Burghead is a case in point. It is dealt with by Sir Arthur Mitchell (*The Past in the Present*, pp. 263-5), who refers to other "cup-stones"

---

[1] "Every weapon has its demon" is an old Gaelic saying.

[2] According to the Dingwall records knowledge of "future events in reference especialle to lyfe and death" was obtained by performing a ceremony in connection with the hollowed stone.

that were regarded as being "efficacious in cases of barrenness". In some hollowed stones Highland parents immersed children suspected of being changelings.

A flood of light has been thrown on the origin of Druidism by Siret,[1] the discoverer of the settlements of Easterners in Spain which have been dealt with in an earlier chapter. He shows that the colonists were an intensely religious people, who introduced the Eastern Palm-tree cult and worshipped a goddess similar to the Egyptian Hathor, a form of whom was Nut. After they were expelled from Spain by a bronze-using people, the refugees settled in Gaul and Italy, carrying with them the science and religious beliefs and practices associated with Druidism. Commercial relations were established between the Etruscans, the peoples of Gaul and the south of Spain, and with the Phœnicians of Tyre and Carthage during the archæological Early Iron Age. Some of the megalithic monuments of North Africa were connected with this later drift.

The goddess Hathor of Egypt was associated with the sycamore fig which exudes a milk-like fluid, with a sea-shell, with the sky (as Nut she was depicted as a star-spangled woman), and with the primeval cow. The tree cult was introduced into Rome. The legend of the foundation of that city is closely associated with the "milk"-yielding fig tree, under which the twins Romulus and Remus were nourished by the wolf. The fig-milk was regarded as an elixir and was given by the Greeks to newly born children.

Siret shows that the ancient name of the Tiber was Rumon, which was derived from the root signifying milk. It was supposed to nourish the earth with terrestrial milk. From the same root came the name of Rome. The ancient milk-providing goddess of Rome

[1] *L'Anthropologie*, 1921, Tome XXX, pp. 235 *et seq.*

was Deva Rumina.   Offerings of milk instead of wine
were made to her.   The starry heavens were called
"Juno's milk" by the Romans, and "Hera's milk" by
the Greeks, and the name "Milky Way" is still retained.

The milk tree of the British Isles is the hazel.   It
contains a milky fluid in the green nut, which Highland
children of a past generation regarded as a fluid that
gave them strength.   Nut-milk was evidently regarded in
ancient times as an elixir like fig-milk.[1]   There is a great
deal of Gaelic lore connected with the hazel.   In Keat-
ing's *History of Ireland* (Vol. I, section 12) appears the
significant statement, "Coll (the hazel) indeed was god
to MacCuil".   "Coll" is the old Gaelic word for hazel;
the modern word is "Call".   "Calltuinn" (Englished
"Calton") is a "hazel grove".   There are Caltons in
Edinburgh and Glasgow and well-worn forms of the
ancient name elsewhere.   In the legends associated with
the Irish Saint Maedóg is one regarding a dried-up
stick of hazel which "sprouted into leaf and blossom
and good fruit".   It is added that this hazel "endures
yet (A.D. 624), a fresh tree, undecayed, unwithered, nut-
laden yearly".[2]   The sacred hazel was supposed to be
impregnated with the substance of life.   Another reference is made to *Coll na nothar* ("hazel of the wounded").
Hazel-nuts of longevity, as well as apples of longevity,
were supposed to grow in the Gaelic Paradise.   In a St.
Patrick legend a youth comes from the south ("south"
is Paradise and "north" is hell) carrying "a double armful of round yellow-headed nuts and of beautiful golden-
yellow apples".   Dr. Joyce states that the ancient Irish
"attributed certain druidical or fairy virtues to the yew,
the hazel, and the quicken or rowan tree", and refers to
"innumerable instances in tales, poems, and other old

---

[1] "Comb of the honey and milk of the nut" (in Gaelic *cìr na meala 'is bainne nan cnò*)
was given as a tonic to weakly children, and is still remembered, the Rev. Kenneth
MacLeod, Colonsay, informs me.

[2] Standish H. O'Grady, *Silva Gadelica*, p. 505.

records, in such expressions as 'Cruachan of the fair hazels', 'Derry-na-nath, on which fair-nutted hazels are constantly found'. . . . Among the blessings a good king brought on the land was plenty of hazel-nuts:— 'O'Berga (the chief) for whom the hazels stoop', 'Each hazel is rich from the hero'." Hazel-nuts were like the figs and dates of the Easterners, largely used for food.[1]

Important evidence regarding the milk elixir and the associated myths and doctrines is preserved in the ancient religious literature of India and especially in the *Mahá-bhárata*. The Indian Hathor is the cow-mother Surabhi, who sprang from Amrita (Soma) in the mouth of the Grandfather (Brahma). A single jet of her milk gave origin to "Milky Ocean". The milk "mixing with the water" appeared as foam, and was the only nourishment of the holy men called "Foam drinkers". Divine milk was also obtained from "milk-yielding trees", which were the "children" of one of her daughters. These trees included nut trees. Another daughter was the mother of birds of the parrot species (oracular birds). In the Vedic poems *soma*, a drink prepared from a plant, is said to have been mixed with milk and honey, and mention is made of "*Su-soma*" ("river of Soma"). *Madhu* (mead) was a drink identified with *soma*, or milk and honey.[2]

There are rivers of mead in the Celtic Paradise. Certain trees are in Irish lore associated with rivers that were regarded as sacred. These were not necessarily milk-yielding trees. In Gaul the plane tree took the place of the southern fig tree. The elm tree in Ireland and Scotland was similarly connected with the ancient milk cult. One of the old names for new milk, found in "Cormac's Glossary", is *lemlacht*, the later form of which is *leamhnacht*. From the same root (*lem*) comes

---

[1] *A Smaller Social History of Ancient Ireland*, pp. 100–2 and 367–8.
[2] Macdonell and Keith, *Vedic Index*, under *Soma* and *Madhu*.

leamh, the name of the elm. The River Laune in Killarney is a rendering of the Gaelic name *leamhain*, which in Scotland is found as Leven, the river that gave its name to the area known as Lennox (ancient *Leamhna*). Milk place-names in Ireland include "new milk lake" (Lough Alewnaghta) in Galway, "which", Joyce suggests, "may have been so called from the softness of its water". A mythological origin of the name is more probable. Wounds received in battle were supposed to be healed in baths of the milk of white hornless cows.[1] In Irish blood-covenant ceremonies new milk, blood, and wine were mixed and drunk by warriors.[2] As late as the twelfth century a rich man's child was in Ireland immersed immediately after birth in new milk.[3] In Rome, in the ninth century, at the Easter-eve baptism the chalice was filled "not with wine but with milk and honey, that they may understand . . . that they have entered already upon the promised land".[4]

The beliefs associated with the apple, rowan, hazel, and oak trees were essentially the same. These trees provided the fruits of longevity and knowledge, or the wine which was originally regarded as an elixir that imparted new life and inspired those who drank it to prophecy[5]. The oak provided acorns which were eaten. Although it does not bear red berries like the rowan, a variety of the oak is greatly favoured by the insect *Kermes*, "which yields a scarlet dye nearly equal to cochineal, and is the 'scarlet' mentioned in Scripture". This fact is of importance as the early peoples attached

---

[1] Joyce, *Irish Names of Places*, Vol. I, pp. 507-9, Vol. II, pp. 206-7 and 345. Marsh mallows (*leamh*) appear to have been included among the herbals of the milk-cult as the soma-plant was in India.

[2] *Revue Celtique*, Vol. XIII, p. 75.

[3] Warren, *Liturgy and Ritual of the Celtic Church*, p. 67.

[4] Henderson's *Survivals*, p. 218.

[5] Rowan-berry wine was greatly favoured. There are Gaelic references to "the wine of the apple (cider)".

much value to colour and especially to red, the colour of
life blood. Withal, acorn-cups "are largely imported
from the Levant for the purposes of tanning, dyeing,
and making ink".[1] A seafaring people like the ancient
Britons must have tanned the skins used for boats so as
to prevent them rotting on coming into contact with
water. Dr. Joyce writes of the ancient Irish in this
connection, "Curraghs[2] or wicker-boats were often
covered with leather. A jacket of hard, tough, tanned
leather was sometimes worn in battle as a protecting
corslet. Bags made of leather, and often of undressed
skins, were pretty generally used to hold liquids. There
was a sort of leather wallet or bag called *crioll*, used like
a modern travelling bag, to hold clothes and other soft
articles. The art of tanning was well understood in
ancient Ireland. The name for a tanner was *sudaire*,
which is still a living word. Oak bark was employed,
and in connection with this use was called *coirteach*
(Latin, *cortex*)." The oak-god protected seafarers by
making their vessels sea-worthy.

Mistletoe berries may have been regarded as milk-
berries because of their colour, and the ceremonial cutting of the mistletoe with the golden sickle may well
have been a ceremony connected with the fertilization
of trees practised in the East. The mistletoe was reputed
to be an "all-heal", although really it is useless for
medicinal purposes.

That complex ideas were associated with deities imported into this country, the history of which must be
sought for elsewhere, is made manifest when we find
that, in the treeless Outer Hebrides, the goddess known
as the "maiden queen" has her dwelling in a tree and
provides the "milk of knowledge" from a sea-shell. She
could not possibly have had independent origin in Scot-

---

[1] George Nicholson, *Encyclopædia of Horticulture*, under "Oak".
[2] Curragh is connected with the Latin *corium*, a hide.

land. Her history is rooted in ancient Egypt, where
Hathor, the provider of the milk of knowledge and
longevity, was, as has been indicated, connected with
the starry sky (the Milky Way), a sea-shell, the milk-
yielding sycamore fig, and the primeval cow.

The cult animal of the goddess was in Egypt the star-
spangled cow; in Troy it was a star-spangled sow[1].
The cult animal of Rome was the wolf which suckled
Romulus and Remus. In Crete the local Zeus was
suckled, according to the belief of one cult, by a horned
sheep[2], and according to another cult by a sow. There
were various cult animals in ancient Scotland, including
the tabooed pig, the red deer milked by the fairies, the
wolf, and the cat of the "Cat" tribes in Shetland, Caithness, &c. The cow appears to have been sacred to
certain peoples in ancient Britain and Ireland. It would
appear, too, that there was a sacred dog in Ireland.[3]

It is evident that among the Eastern beliefs anciently
imported into the British Isles were some which still
bear traces of the influence of cults and of culture
mixing. That religious ideas of Egyptian and Babylonian origin were blended in this country there can
be little doubt, for the Gaelic-speaking peoples, who
revered the hazel as the Egyptians revered the sycamore,
regarded the liver as the seat of life, as did the Babylonians, and not the heart, as did the Egyptians. In
translations of ancient Gaelic literature "liver" is always
rendered as "vitals".

It is of special interest to note that Siret has found
evidence to show that the Tree Cult of the Easterners
was connected with the early megalithic monuments.
The testimony of tradition associates the stone circles,

---

[1] Schliemann, *Troy and Its Remains*, p. 232.

[2] *Journal of Hellenic Studies*, Vol. XXI, p. 129.

[3] It was because Zeus had been suckled by a sow that the Cretans, as Athenæus records,
"will not taste its flesh" (Farnell, *Cults of the Greek States*, Vol. I, p. 37). In Ireland
the dog was taboo to Cuchullin. There is a good deal of Gaelic lore about the sacred
cow.

Cult Animals and "Wonder Beasts" (dragons or makaras) on Scottish Sculptured Stones

&c., with the Druids. "We are now obliged", he writes[1], "to go back to the theory of the archæologists of a hundred years ago who attributed the megalithic monuments to the Druids. The instinct of our predecessors has been more penetrating than the scientific analysis which has taken its place." In Gaelic, as will be shown, the words for a sacred grove and the shrine within a grove are derived from the same root *nem*. (See also Chapter IX in this connection.)

[1] *L'Anthropologie* (1921), pp. 268 *et seq.*

CHAPTER XIII
The Lore of Charms

Our ancestors were greatly concerned about their
luck. They consulted oracles to discover what luck
was in store for them. To them luck meant everything
they most desired—good health, good fortune, an
abundant food supply, and protection against drowning,
wounds in battle, accidents, and so on. Luck was
ensured by performing ceremonies and wearing charms.
Some ceremonies were performed round sacred bon-
fires (bone fires), when sacrifices were made, at holy
wells, in groves, or in stone circles. Charms included
precious stones, coloured stones, pearls, and articles
of silver, gold, or copper of symbolic shape, or bearing
an image or inscription. Mascots, "lucky pigs", &c.,
are relics of the ancient custom of wearing charms.

The colour as well as the shape of a charm revealed
its particular influence. Certain colours are still regarded as being lucky or unlucky ("yellow is forsaken"
some say). In ancient times colours meant much to
the Britons, as they did to other peoples. This fact

is brought out in many tales and customs. A Welsh story, for instance, which refers to the appearance of supernatural beings attired in red and blue, says, "The red on the one part signifies burning, and the blue on the other signifies coldness".[1]

On their persisting belief in luck were based the religious ideas and practices of the ancient Britons. Their chief concern was to protect and prolong life in this world and in the next. When death came it was regarded as "a change". The individual was supposed either to fall asleep, or to be transported in the body to Paradise, or to assume a new form. In Scottish Gaelic one can still hear the phrase *chaochail e* ("he changed") used to signify that "he died".[2] But after death charms were as necessary as during life. As in Aurignacian times, luck-charms in the form of necklaces, armlets, &c., were placed in the graves of the dead by those who used flint, or bronze, or iron to shape implements and weapons. The dead had to receive nourishment, and clay vessels are invariably found in ancient graves, some of which contain dusty deposits. The writer has seen at Fortrose a deposit in one of these grave urns, which a medical man identified as part of the skeleton of a bird.

Necklaces of shells, of wild animals' teeth, and ornaments of ivory found in Palæolithic graves or burial caves were connected with the belief that they contained the animating influence or "life substance" of the mother goddess. In later times the pearl found in the shell was regarded as being specially sacred.

Venus (Aphrodite) is, in one of her phases, the personification of a pearl, and is lifted from the sea seated on a shell. As a sky deity she was connected with

---

[1] Lady Charlotte Guest, *The Mabinogion* (Story of "Kilwch and Olwen" and note on "Gwyn the son of Nudd").

[2] Also *shiubhail e* which signifies "he went off" (as when walking).

the planet that bears her name[1] and also with the moon.
The ancients connected the moon with the pearl. In
some languages the moon is the "pearl of heaven".
Dante, in his *Inferno*, refers to the moon as "the
eternal pearl". One of the Gaelic names for a pearl
is *neamhnuid*. The root is *nem* of *neamh*, and *neamh*
is "heaven", so that the pearl is "a heavenly thing"
in Gaelic, as in other ancient languages. It was associated not only with the sky goddess but with the
sacred grove in which the goddess was worshipped.
The Gaulish name *nemeton*, of which the root is likewise *nem*, means "shrine in a grove". In early Christian times in Ireland the name was applied as *nemed*
to a chapel, and in Scottish place-names[2] it survives
in the form of *neimhidh*, "church-land", the Englished
forms of which are *Navity*, near Cromarty, *Navaty* in
Fife, "Rosneath", formerly Rosneveth (the promon-
tory of the *nemed*), "Dalnavie" (dale of the *nemed*),
"Cnocnavie" (hillock of the *nemed*), Inchnavie (island
of the *nemed*), &c. The Gauls had a *nemetomarus*
("great shrine"), and when in Roman times a shrine
was dedicated to Augustus it was called *Augustonemeton*.
The root *nem* is in the Latin word *nemus* (a grove).
It was apparently because the goddess of the grove
was the goddess of the sky and of the pearl, and the
goddess of battle as well as the goddess of love, that
Julius Cæsar made a thanksgiving offering to Venus
in her temple at Rome of a corslet of British pearls.

The Irish goddess Nemon was the spouse of the war
god Neit. A Roman inscription at Bath refers to the
British goddess Němětŏna. The Gauls had a goddess
of similar name. In Galatia, Asia Minor, the particular
tree connected with the sky goddess was the oak, as is

---

[1] When depicted with star-spangled garments she was the goddess of the starry sky
("Milky Way") like the Egyptian Hathor or Nut.

[2] Professor W. J. Watson, *Place-names of Ross and Cromarty*, pp. 62-3.

shown by the name of their religious centre which
was *Dru-nemeton* ("Oak-grove"). It will be shown
in a later chapter that the sacred tree was connected
with the sky and the deities of the sky, with the sacred
wells and rivers, with the sacred fish, and with the fire,
the sun, and lightning. Here it may be noted that the
sacred well is connected with the holy grove, the sky, the
pearl, and the mother goddess in the Irish place-name
Neamhnach (Navnagh),[1] applied to the well from which
flows the stream of the Nith. The well is thus, like the
pearl, "the heavenly one". The root *nem* of *neamh*
(heaven) is found in the name of St. Brendan's mother,
who was called *Neamhnat* (Navnat), which means
"little" or "dear heavenly one". In *neamhan* ("raven"
and "crow") the bird form of the deity is enshrined.

Owing to its connection with the moon, the pearl
was supposed to shine by night. The same peculiarity
was attributed to certain sacred stones, to coral, jade,
&c., and to ivory. Munster people perpetuate the
belief that "at the bottom of the lower lake of Killarney
there is a diamond of priceless value, which sometimes
shines so brightly that on certain nights the light bursts
forth with dazzling brilliancy through the dark waters".[2]
Night-shining jewels are known in Scotland. One is
suppose to shine on Arthur's Seat, Edinburgh, and
another on the north "souter" of the Cromarty Firth.[3]
Another sacred stone connected with the goddess was
the onyx, which in ancient Gaelic is called *nem*.
Night-shining jewels are referred to in the myths of
Greece, Arabia, Persia, India, China, Japan, &c.
Laufer has shown that the Chinese received their lore
about the night-shining diamond from "Fu-lin" (the
Byzantine Empire).[4]

---

[1] Dr. Joyce, *Irish Names of Places*, Vol. I, p. 375.   [2] *Ibid*, Vol. II. p. 378.
[3] The two headlands, the "souters" or "sutors", are supposed to have been so called
because they were sites of tanneries.   [4] *The Diamond* (Chicago, 1915).

Upper picture by courtesy of Director, British School of Rome

MEGALITHS

Upper: Dolmen near Birori, Sardinia.   Lower: Tynewydd Dolmen.

The ancient pearl-fishers spread their pearl-lore far and wide. It is told in more than one land that pearls are formed by dew-drops from the sky. Pliny says the dew- or rain-drops fall into the shells of the pearl-oyster when it gapes.[1] In modern times the belief is that pearls are the congealed tears of the angels. In Greece the pearl was called *margaritoe*, a name which survives in Margaret, anciently the name of a goddess. The old Persian name for pearl is *margan*, which signifies "life giver". It is possible that this is the original meaning of the name of Morgan le Fay (Morgan the Fairy), who is remembered as the sister of King Arthur, and of the Irish goddess Morrigan, usually Englished as "Sea-queen" (the sea as the source of life), or "great queen". At any rate, Morgan le fay and the Morrigan closely resemble one another. In Italian we meet with Fata Morgana.

The old Persian word for coral is likewise *margan*. Coral was supposed to be a tree, and it was regarded as the sea-tree of the sea and sky goddess. Amber was connected, too, with the goddess. In northern mythology, amber, pearls, precious stones, and precious metals were supposed to be congealed forms of the tears of the goddess Freyja, the Venus of the Scandinavians.

Amber, like pearls, was sacred to the mother goddess because her life substance (the animating principle) was supposed to be concentrated in it. The connection between the precious or sacred amber and the goddess and her cult animal is brought out in a reference made by Tacitus to the amber collectors and traders on the southern shore of the Baltic. These are the Æstyans, who, according to Tacitus, were costumed like the Swedes, but spoke a language resembling the dialect of the Britons. "They worship", the historian records, "the mother of the gods. The figure of a wild boar

---

[1] *Natural History*, Book IX, Chap. LIV.

is the symbol of their superstition; and he who has
that emblem about him thinks himself secure even in
the thickest ranks of the enemy without any need of
arms or any other mode of defence."[1]   The animal of
the amber goddess was thus the boar, which was the
sacred animal of the Celtic tribe, the Iceni of ancient
Britain, which under Boadicea revolted against Roman
rule.   The symbol of the boar (remembered as the
"lucky pig") is found on ancient British armour.   On
the famous Witham shield there are coral and enamel.
Three bronze boar symbols found in a field at Hounslow
are preserved in the British Museum.   In the same
field was found a solar-wheel symbol.   "The boar
frequently occurs in British and Gaulish coins of the
period, and examples have been found as far off as
Gurina and Transylvania."[2]   Other sacred cult animals
were connected with the goddess by those people who
fished for pearls and coral or searched for sacred
precious stones or precious metals.

At the basis of the ancient religious system that connected coral, shells, and pearls with the mother goddess
of the sea, wells, rivers, and lakes, was the belief that all
life had its origin in water.   Pearls, amber, marsh plants,
and animals connected with water were supposed to
be closely associated with the goddess who herself had
had her origin in water.   Tacitus tells that the Baltic
worshippers of the mother goddess called amber *glesse*.
According to Pliny[3] it was called *glessum* by the Germans, and he tells that one of the Baltic islands famous
for its amber was named *Glessaria*.   The root is the
Celtic word *glas*, which originally meant "water" and
especially life-giving water.   Boece (*Cosmographie*,
Chapter XV) tells that in Scotland the belief prevailed

[1] Tacitus, *Manners of the Germans*, Chap. XLV.
[2] *British Museum Guide to the Antiquities of the Early Iron Age*, pp. 135-6.
[3] *Natural History*, Book XXXVIII, Chapter III.

that amber was generated of sea-froth. It thus had its origin like Aphrodite. *Glas* is now a colour term in Welsh and Gaelic, signifying green or grey, or even a shade of blue. It was anciently used to denote vigour, as in the term *Gaidheal glas* ("the vigorous Gael" or "the ambered Gael", the vigour being derived from the goddess of amber and the sea); and in the Latinized form of the old British name Cuneglasos, which like the Irish Conglas signified "vigorous hound".[1] Here the sacred hound figures in place of the sacred boar.

From the root *glas* comes also *glaisin*, the Gaelic name for woad, the blue dyestuff with which ancient Britons and Gaels stained or tattooed their bodies with figures of sacred animals or symbols,[2] apparently to secure protection as did those who had the boar symbol on their armour. For the same reason Cuchullin, the Irish Achilles, wore pearls in his hair, and the Roman Emperor Caligula had a pearl collar on his favourite horse. Ice being a form of water is in French *glacé*, which also means "glass". When glass beads were first manufactured they were regarded, like amber, as depositories of "life substance" from the water goddess who, as sky goddess, was connected with sun and fire. Her fire melted the constituents of glass into liquid form, and it hardened like jewels and amber. These beads were called "adder stones" (Welsh *glain neidre* and "Druid's gem" or "glass"—in Welsh *Gleini na Droedh* and in Gaelic *Glaine nan Druidhe*).

A special peculiarity about amber is that when rubbed vigorously it attracts or lifts light articles. That is why it is called in Persian Kahruba (*Kah*, straw; *ruba*, to lift). This name appears in modern French as *carabé*

---

[1] Rhys rejects the view of Gildas that "Cuneglasos" meant "tawny butcher".

[2] Herodian, Lib. III, says of the inhabitants of Caledonia, "They mark their bodies with various pictures of all manner of animals".

(yellow amber). In Italian, Spanish, and Portugese it is *carabe*. No doubt the early peoples, who gathered Adriatic and Baltic amber and distributed it and its lore far and wide, discovered this peculiar quality in the sacred substance. In Britain, jet was used in the same way as amber for luck charms and ornaments. Like amber it becomes negatively electric by friction. Bede appears to have believed that jet was possessed of special virture. "When heated", he says, "it drives away serpents."[1] The Romans regarded jet as a depository of supernatural power[2] and used it for ornaments. Until comparatively recently jet was used in Scotland as a charm against witchcraft, the evil eye, &c. "A ring of hard black schistus found in a cairn in the parish of Inchinan", writes a local Scottish historian, "has performed, if we believe report, many astonishing cures."[3] Albertite, which, like jet and amber, attracts light articles when vigorously rubbed, was made into ornaments. It takes on a finer lustre than jet but loses it sooner.

The fact that jet, albertite, and other black substances were supposed to be specially efficacious for protecting black horses and cattle is of peculiar interest. Hathor, the cow goddess of Egypt, had a black as well as a white form as goddess of the night sky and death. She was the prototype of the black Aphrodite (Venus). In Scotland a black goddess (the *nigra dea* in Adamnan's *Life of Columba*) was associated with Loch Lochy.

The use of coral as a sacred substance did not begin in Britain until the knowledge of iron working was introduced. Coral is not found nearer than the Mediterranean. The people who first brought it to Britain must have received it and the beliefs attached to it from the Mediterranean area. Before reaching Britain they

---

[1] Book I. Chapter I.   [2] Pliny, Lib. XXXVI, cap. 34.
[3] Ure's *History of Rutherglen and Kilbride*, p. 219.

had begun to make imitation coral. The substitute was enamel, which required for its manufacture great skill and considerable knowledge, furnaces capable of generating an intense heat being necessary. It is inconceivable that so expensive a material could have been produced except for religious purposes. The warriors apparently believed that coral and its substitutes protected them as did amber and the boar symbol of the mother goddess.

At first red enamel was used as a substitute for red coral, but ultimately blue, yellow, and white enamels were produced. Sometimes we find, as at Traprain in Scotland, that silver took the place of white enamel. It is possible that blue enamel was a substitute for turquoise and lapis lazuli, the precious stones associated with the mother goddesses of Hathor type, and that yellow and white enamels were substitutes for yellow and white amber. The Greeks called white amber "electrum". The symbolism of gold and silver links closely with that of amber. Possibly the various sacred substances and their substitutes were supposed to protect different parts of the body. As much is suggested, for instance, by the lingering belief that amber protects and strengthens the eyes. The solar cult connected the ear and the ear-ring with the sun, which was one of the "eyes" of the world-deity, the other "eye" being the moon. When human ears were pierced, the blood drops were offered to the sun-god. Sailors of a past generation clung to the ancient notion that gold ear-rings exercised a beneficial influence on their eyes. Not only the colours of luck objects, but their shapes were supposed to ensure luck. The Swashtika symbol, the U-form, the S-form, and 8-form symbols, the spiral, the leaf-shaped and equal-limbed crosses, &c., were supposed to "attract" and "radiate" the influence of the deity. Thus Buddhists accumulate religious "merit" not only by fasting and praying, but by making collections of jewels and symbols.

In Britain, as in other countries, the deity was closely associated as an influence with law. A Roman inscription on a slab found at Carvoran refers to the mother goddess "poising life and laws in a balance". This was Ceres, whose worship had been introduced during the Roman period, but similar beliefs were attached to the ancient goddesses of Britain. Vows were taken over objects sacred to her, and sacred objects were used as mediums of exchange. In old Gaelic, for instance, a jewel or pearl was called a *set*; in modern Gaelic it is *sed* (pronounced *shade*). A *set* (pearl) was equal in value to an ounce of gold and to a cow. An ounce of gold was therefore a *set* and a cow was a *set*, too. Three *sets* was the value of a bondmaid. The value of three sets was one *cumal*. Another standard of value was a sack of corn (*miach*).[1]

The value attached to gold and pearls was originally magical. Jewels and precious metals were searched for for to bring wearers "luck"—that is, everything their hearts desired. The search for these promoted trade, and the *sets* were used as a standard of value between traders. Thus not only religious systems, but even the early systems of trade were closely connected with the persistent belief in luck and the deity who was the source of luck.[2]

---

[1] Joyce, *A Smaller Social History of Ancient Ireland*, p. 478.

[2] Professor W. J. Watson has drawn my attention to an interesting reference to amber. In the *Proceedings of the British Academy*, Vol. II, p. 18, under "Celtic Inscriptions of France and Italy", Sir John Rhys deals with Vebrumaros, a man's name. The second element in this name is *māros* (great); the first, *uebru*, "is perhaps to be explained by reference to the Welsh word *gwefr* (amber)". Rhys thought the name meant that the man was distinguished for his display of amber "in the adornment of his person". The name had probably a deeper significance. Amber was closely associated with the mother goddess. One of her names may have been "Uebru". She personified amber.

CHAPTER XIV

The World of Our Ancestors

"All Heals"—Influences of Cardinal Points—The Four Red Divisions of the World—The Black North, White South, Purple East, and Dun or Pale East—Good and Bad Words connected with South and North—North the left, South the right, East in front, and West behind—Cardinal Points Doctrine in Burial Customs—Stone Circle Burials—Christian and Pagan Burial Rites—Sunwise Customs—Raising the Devil in Stone Circle—Coloured Winds—Coloured Stones raise Winds—The "God Body" and "Spirit Husk"—Deities and Cardinal Points—Axis of Stonehenge Avenue—God and Goddesses of Circle—Well Worship—Lore of Druids.

The ancient superstitions dealt with in the previous chapter afford us glimpses of the world in which our ancestors lived, and some idea of the incentives that caused them to undertake long and perilous journeys in search of articles of religious value. They were as greatly concerned as are their descendants about their health and their fate. Everything connected with the deity, or possessing, as was believed, the influence of the deity, was valuable as a charm or as medicine. The mistletoe berry was a famous medicine because it was the fruit of a parasite supposed to contain the "life substance" of a powerful deity. It was an "All Heal" or "Cure All",[1] yet it was a quack medicine and quite useless. Red earth was "blood earth"; it contained the animating principle too. Certain herbs were supposed to be curative. Some herbs were, and in the

[1] Richard of Cirencester (fourteenth century) says the mistletoe increased the number of animals, and was considered as a specific against all poisons (Book I, Chap. 1V).

course of time their precise qualities were identified. But many of them continued in use, although quite useless, because of the colour of their berries, the shape of their leaves, or the position in which they grew. If one red-berried plant was "lucky" or curative, all red-berried plants shared in its reputation. It was because of the lore attached to colours that dusky pearls were preferred to white pearls, just as in Ceylon yellow pearls are chiefly favoured because yellow is the sacred colour of the Buddhists. Richard of Cirencester,[1] referring to Bede, says that British pearls are "often of the best kind and of every colour: that is, red, purple, violet, green, but principally white".

In the lore of plants, in religious customs, including burial customs, and in beliefs connected with the seasons, weather, and sacred sites, there are traces of a doctrine based on the belief that good or bad influences "flowed" from the cardinal points, just as good or bad influences "flowed" from gems, metals, wood, and water. When, for instance, certain herbs were pulled from the ground, it was important that one should at the time of the operation be facing the south. A love-enticing plant had to be plucked in this way, and immediately before sunrise.

There was much superstition in weather lore, as the beliefs connected with St. Swithin's Day indicate. Certain days were lucky for removals in certain directions. Saturday was the day for flitting northward, and Monday for flitting southward. Monday was "the key of the week". An old Gaelic saying, repeated in various forms in folk stories, runs:

> Shut the north window,
>   And quickly close the window to the south;
> And shut the window facing west,
>   Evil never came from the east.

[1] Book I, Chap. V.

South-running water was "powerful" for working protective charms; north-running water brought evil.

The idea behind these and other similar beliefs was that "the four red divisions" or the "four brown divisions" of the world were controlled by deities or groups of deities, whose influences for good or evil were continually "flowing", and especially when winds were

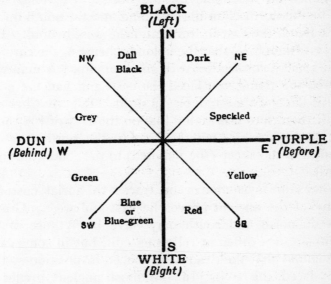

Diagram of the Gaelic Airts (Cardinal Points) and their Associated Colours
referred to in the text
Spring was connected with the east, summer with the south, autumn with the west, and winter with the north.

blowing. A good deity sent a good wind, and a bad deity sent a bad wind. Each wind was coloured. The north was the airt[1] (cardinal point) of evil, misfortune, and bad luck, and was coloured black; the south was the source of good luck, good fortune, summer, and longevity, and was coloured white; the east was a specially sacred airt, and was coloured purple-red, while

[1] This excellent Gaelic word is current in Scotland. Burns uses it in the line, "O' a' the airts the wind can blaw".

the west was the airt of death, and was coloured dun or
pale.   East and south and north and west were connected.   There were various colours for the subsidiary
points of the compass.

This doctrine was a very ancient one, because we find
that in the Gaelic language the specially good words
are based on the word for the south, and the specially
bad ones on the name for the north.   In Welsh and
Gaelic the north is on the left hand and the south on the
right hand, the east in front, and the west behind.   It is
evident, therefore, that the colour scheme of the cardinal
points had a connection with sun worship.   A man who
adored the rising sun faced the east, and had the north
on his left and the south on his right.   In early Christian
Gaelic literature it is stated that on the Day of Judgment
the goats (sinners) will be sent to the north (the left
hand) and the sheep (the justified) to the south (the right
hand).

The same system can be traced in burial customs.
Many of the ancient graves lie east and west.   Graves
that lie north and south may have been those of the
members of a different religious cult, but in some cases
it is found that the dead were placed in position so that
they faced the east.   In the most ancient graves in
Egypt men were laid on their right sides with their feet
directed towards the "red north" and their faces towards
the golden east.   Women were laid on the left sides
facing the east.   Red was in ancient Egypt the male
colour, and white and yellow the female colours; the
feet of the men were towards the red north and those of
women towards the white or yellow south.

All ancient British burials were not made in accordance with solar-cult customs.   It can be shown, however,
in some cases that, although a burial custom may appear
to be either of local or of independent origin, the fundamental doctrine of which it was an expression was the

same as that behind other burial customs. Reference
may be made, by way of illustration, to the graves at
the stone circle of Hakpen Hill in the Avebury area.
In the seventeenth century a large number of skeletons
were here unearthed. Dr. Toope of Oxford, writing in
1685, has recorded in this connection:[1]

"About 80 yards from where the bones were found is a
temple,[2] 40 yards diameter, with another 15 yards; round
about bones layd so close that scul (skull) toucheth scul.
Their feet all round turned towards the temple, one foot
below the surface of the ground. At the feet of the first
order lay the head of the next row, the feet always tending
towards the temple."

Here the stone circle is apparently the symbol of the
sun and the "Mecca" from which the good influence
or "luck" of the sun emanated and gave protection.
One seems to come into touch with the influence of
an organized priesthood in this stone circle burial
custom.

The more ancient custom of burying the dead so that
the influences of the airts might be exercised upon them
according to their deserts seems, however, to have been
deep-rooted and persistent. In England, Wales, Scotland, and Ireland the custom obtained until recently of
reserving the north side of a churchyard for suicides
and murderers; the "black north" was the proper place
for such wrong-doers, who were refused Christian rites
of burial, and were interred according to traditional
pagan customs. The east was reserved chiefly for
ecclesiastics, the south for the upper classes, and the
west for the poorer classes. Funeral processions still
enter the older churchyards from the east, and proceed
in the direction of the sun towards the open graves.
Suicides and murderers were carried in the opposite

---

[1] Quoted by Sir H. Colt Hoare in *Ancient Wiltshire*, II. p. 63.   [2] Stone circle.

direction ("withershins about").[1] The custom of dealing
out cards "sunwise", of stirring food "sunwise", and
other customs in which turning to the right (the south)
is observed, appear to be relics of the ancient belief in
the influences of the airts.   Some fishermen still consider
it unlucky to turn their boats "against the sun".   It
was anciently believed, as references in old ballads indicate, that a tempest-stricken vessel turned round three
times against the sun before it sank.   According to a
belief that has survival in some parts of the north of
Scotland, the devil will appear in the centre of a stone
circle if one walks round it three times "against the sun"
at midnight.   Among the ancient Irish warriors, Professor W. J. Watson tells me, it was a mark of hostile
intent to drive round a fort keeping the left hand towards
it.   The early Christian custom of circulating chapels
and dwelling-houses "sunwise" was based on the
pagan belief that good influences were conjured in this
way.

As the winds were coloured like the airts from which
they blew, it was believed that they could be influenced
by coloured objects.   In his description of the Western
Isles, Martin, a seventeenth century writer, referring to
the Fladda Chuan Island, relates:

"There is a chapel in the isle dedicated to St. Columba.
It has an altar in the east end and therein a blue stone of
a round form on it, which is always moist.   It is an ordinary
custom, when any of the fishermen are detained in the isle by
contrary winds, to wash the blue stone with water all round,
expecting thereby to procure a favourable wind. . . . And so
great is the regard they have for this stone, that they swear
decisive oaths upon it."

The moist stone had an indwelling spirit, and was there-

---

[1] In Gaelic *deis-iùil* means a turning sunwise (by the right or south) from east to west,
and *tual*, i.e. *tuath-iùil*, a turning by the north or left from east to west.   *Deis* is the
genitive of *Deas* (south, right hand), and *Tuath* is north or left hand.

Valentine

ONE OF THE GREAT TRI-LITHONS, STONEHENGE

(see page 174)

fore a holy object which made vows and agreements of binding character. In Japan a stone of this kind is called *shintai* ("god body"). The Gaelic name for a god body is "*cuach anama*" ("soul shrine", or "spirit-case", or "spirit-husk"). *Coich na cno* is the shell of a nut. The Chinese believe that moist and coloured stones are the "eggs" of weather-controlling dragons.

The connection between blue and the mother goddess is of great antiquity. Imitation cowries and other shells in blue enamelled terra-cotta have been found in Egyptian graves. Blue was the colour of the "luck stone" of Hathor, the sky and water goddess whose symbols included the cowrie. The Brigantes of ancient Britain had, according to Seneca, blue shields. Shields were connected with the goddess of war. In Gaelic, blue is the luck colour for womens' clothing.[1] English and Scottish fishermen still use blue as a mourning colour. When a death takes place, a blue line is painted round a fishing-boat. The desire for protection by invoking the blue goddess probably gave origin to this custom.

As influences came from the coloured airts, so did the great deities and the groups of minor deities associated with them. The god Lugh, for instance, always comes in the old stories from the north-east, while the goddess Morrigan comes from the north-west.[2] The fierce wind-raising Scottish goddess of spring comes from the south-west. All over Britain the fairies come from the west and on eddies of wind like the Greek nereids. In Scotland the evil-working giants come from the black north. It was believed that the dead went westward or south-

---

[1] The following stanza is from the "Book of Ballymote":

> Mottled to simpletons; blue to women;
> Crimson to kings of every host;
> Green and black to noble laymen;
> White to clerics of proper devotion.

[2] In the Cuchullin Saga Lugh is "a lone man out of the north-eastern quarter". When the cry of another supernatural being is heard, Cuchullin asks from which direction it came. He is told "from the north-west". The goddess Morrigan then appeared.

westward towards Paradise. The fact that the axis of
Stonehenge circle and avenue points to the north-east is
of special interest when we find that the god Lugh, a
Celtic Apollo, came from that airt. Either Lugh, or a
god like him, may have been invoked to come through
the avenue or to send his influence through it, while the
priests walked in procession round the circle sunwise.
Apparently the south-west part of the circle, with its
great trilithons, resembling the portals of the goddess
Artemis, was specially consecrated to a goddess like the
Scottish Cailleach ("Old Wife") who had herds of wild
animals, protected deer from huntsmen, raised storms,
and transformed herself into a standing stone. The
Gaulish goddess Ro-smerta ("very smeared") is regularly associated with the god identified with Mercury.
The god Smertullis is equated with Essus (the war god)
by d'Arbois de Jubainville.

The differently coloured winds were divine influences
and revealed their characters by their colours. It was
apparently because water was impregnated with the
influences of the deities that wind and water beliefs were
closely associated. Holy and curative wells and sacred
rivers and lakes were numerous in ancient Britain and
Ireland. Offerings made at wells were offerings made
to a deity. These offerings might be gold and silver,
as was the case in Gaul, or simply pins of copper. A
good many wells are still known as "pin wells" and
"penny wells". The metals and pearls and precious
stones supposed to contain vital substance were offered
to the deities so as to animate them. The images of
gods were painted red for the same reason, or sacrifices
were offered and their altars drenched with blood. In
Ireland children were sacrificed to a god called Crom
Cruach and exchanged for milk and corn. As a Gaelic
poem records:

> Great was the horror and the scare of him.

The ancient doctrines of which faint or fragmentary traces survive in Britain and Ireland may have been similar to those taught by the Druids in Gaul. According to Pomponius Mela, these sages professed to know the secrets of the motions of the heavenly bodies and the will of the gods.[1] Strabo's statement that the Druids believed that "human souls and the world were immortal, but that fire and water would sometime prevail" is somewhat obscure. It may be, however, that light is thrown on the underlying doctrine by the evidence given in the next chapter regarding the beliefs that fire, water, and trees were intimately connected with the chief deity.

---

[1] In a Cuchullin saga the hero, addressing the charioteer, says: "Go out, my friend, observe the stars of the air, and ascertain when midnight comes". The Irish Gaelic *grien-tairisem* is given in an eighth- or ninth-century gloss. It means "sun-standing", and refers to the summer solstice.

CHAPTER XV

Why Trees and Wells were Worshipped

Ancient British Idols—Pagan Temples—Animism and Goddess Worship—Trees and Wells connected with Sky—Life Principle in Water—Sacred Berries, Nuts, and Acorns—Parasite as "King of Trees"—Fire-making Beliefs—Tree and Thunder-god—The Sacred Fish—Salmon as form of the Dragon—The Dragon Jewel—Celtic Dragon Myth—The Salmon and the Solar Ring—Polycrates Story—The St. Mungo Legends—Glasgow Coat of Arms—Holy Fire from the Hazel—Hunting the Wren, Robin, and Mouse—Mouse Lore and Mouse Deity—Mouse-Apollo in Britain—Goddess Bride or Brigit—The Brigantian Chief Deity—Goddess of Fire, Healing, Smith-work, and Poetry—Bride's Bird, Tree, and Well—Mythical Serpents—Soul Forms—Souls in Reptiles, Animals, and Trees—Were-animals—The Butterfly Deity—Souls as Butterflies—Souls as Bees—A Hebridean Sea-god.

Gildas, a sixth-century churchman, tells us that the idols in ancient Britain "almost surpassed in number those of Egypt". That he did not refer merely to standing stones, which, as we have seen, were "idols" to the Gaels, is evident from his precise statements that some idols could be seen in his day "mouldering away within or without the deserted temples", and that they had "stiff and deformed features". "Mouldering" suggests wood. Gildas states further that besides worshipping idols the British pagans were wont to pay "divine honour" to hills and wells and rivers. Reference is made in the *Life of Columba* to a well which was worshipped as a god.

The British temples are referred to also by Pope Gregory the Great, who in A.D. 601 addressed a letter to Abbot Mellitus, then on a mission to England, giving him instructions for the guidance of Augustine of Canterbury. The Pope did not wish to have the heathen buildings destroyed, "for", he wrote, "if those are well constructed, it is requisite that they can be converted from the worship of demons to the service of the true God. . . . Let the idols that are in them be destroyed."[1]

The temples in question may have been those erected during the Romano-British period. One which stood at Canterbury was taken possession of by St. Augustine after the conversion of King Ethelbert, who had worshipped idols in it. The Celtic peoples may, however, have had temples before the Roman invasion. At any rate there were temples as well as sacred groves in Gaul. Poseidonius of Apamea refers to a temple at Toulouse which was greatly revered and richly endowed by the gifts of numerous donors. These gifts included "large quantities of gold consecrated to the gods". The Druids crucified human victims who were sacrificed within their temples.

Diodorus Siculus refers as follows to a famous temple in Britain:

"There is in that island a magnificent temple of Apollo and a circular shrine, adorned with votive offerings and tablets with Greek inscriptions suspended by travellers upon the walls. The kings of that city and rulers of the temples are the Boreads who take up the government from each other according to the order of their tribes. The citizens are given up to music, harping and chaunting in honour of the sun."

Some writers have identified this temple with Stonehenge circle. Layamon informs us in his *Brute*, however, that the temple of Apollo was situated in London. Of course there may have been several temples to this god or the British deity identified with him.

---

[1] Bede, *Historia Ecclesiastica*, Lib. I, cap. 30.

It may be that the stone circles were regarded as temples. It may be, too, that temples constructed of wattles and clay were associated with the circles. In Pope Gregory's letter reference is made to the custom of constructing on festival days "tabernacles of branches of trees around those churches which have been changed from heathen temples", and to the pagan custom of slaying "oxen in sacrifices to demons". Pytheas refers to a temple on an island opposite the mouth of the Loire. This island was inhabited by women only, and once a year they unroofed and reroofed their temple. In the Hebrides the annual custom of unroofing and reroofing thatched houses is not yet obsolete; it may originally have had a religious significance.

Gildas's reference to the worship of hills, wells, and rivers is by some writers regarded as evidence of the existence in ancient Britain of the "primitive belief" in spirits. This stage of religious culture is called Animism (Spiritism). The discovery, however, that a goddess was worshipped in Aurignacian times by the Crô-Magnon peoples in Western Europe suggests that Animistic beliefs were not necessarily as ancient as has been assumed. It may be that what we know as Animism was a product of a later period when there arose somewhat complex ideas about the soul or the various souls in man, and the belief became widespread that souls could not only transform themselves into animal shapes, but could enter statues and gravestones. This conception may have been confused with earlier ideas about stones, shells, &c., being impregnated with "life substance" (the animating principle) derived from the mother goddess. Backward peoples, who adopted complex religious beliefs that had grown up in centres of civilization, may not always have had a complete understanding of their significance. It is difficult to believe that even savages, who adopted the boats invented in

Egypt from those peoples that came into touch with them, were always entirely immune to other cultural influences, and retained for thousands of years the beliefs supposed to be appropriate for those who were in the "Stone Age".

Our concern here is with the ancient Britons. It is unnecessary for us to glean evidence from Australia, South America, or Central Africa to ascertain the character of their early religious conceptions and practices. There is sufficient local evidence to show that a definite body of beliefs lay behind their worship of trees, rivers, lakes, wells, standing stones, and of the sun, moon, and stars. Our ancestors do not appear to have worshipped natural objects either because they were beautiful or impressive, but chiefly because they were supposed to contain influences which affected mankind either directly or indirectly. These influences were supposed to be under divine control, and to emanate, in the first place, from one deity or another, or from groups of deities. A god or goddess was worshipped whether his or her influence was good or bad. The deity who sent disease, for instance, was believed to be the controller of disease, and to him or her offerings were made so that a plague might cease. Thus in the *Iliad* offerings are made to the god Mouse-Apollo, who had caused an epidemic of disease.

Trees and wells were connected with the sky and the heavenly bodies. The deity who caused thunder and lightning had his habitation at times in the oak, the fir, the rowan, the hazel, or some other tree. He was the controller of the elements. There are references in Gaelic charms to "the King of the Elements".

The belief in an intimate connection between a well, a tree, and the sky appears to have been a product of a quaint but not unintelligent process of reasoning.[1]

---

[1] Of course it does not follow that the reasoning originally took place in these islands. Complex beliefs were imported at an early period. These were localized.

The early folk were thinkers, but their reasoning was confined within the limits of their knowledge, and biassed by preconceived ideas. To them water was the source of all life. It fell from the sky as rain, or bubbled up from the underworld to form a well from which a stream flowed. The well was the mother of the stream, and the stream was the mother of the lake. It was believed that the well-water was specially impregnated with the influences that sustained life. The tree that grew beside the well was nourished by it. If this tree was a rowan, its red berries were supposed to contain in concentrated form the animating influence of the deity; the berries cured diseases, and thus renewed youth, or protected those who used them as charms against evil influences. They were luck-berries. If the tree was a hazel, its nuts were similarly efficacious; if an oak, its acorns were regarded likewise as luck-bringers. The parasitic plant that grew on the tree was supposed to be stronger and more influential than the tree itself. This belief, which is so contrary to our way of thinking, is accounted for in an old Gaelic story in which a super-natural being says:

"O man that for Fergus of the feasts dost kindle fire . . . never burn the King of the Woods. Monarch of Innisfail's forest the woodbine is, whom none may hold captive; no feeble sovereign's effort it is to hug all tough trees in his embrace."

The weakly parasite was thus regarded as being very powerful. That may be the reason why the mistletoe was reverenced, and why its milk-white berries were supposed to have curative and life-prolonging qualities.

Although the sacred parasite was not used for fire-wood, it served as a fire-producer. Two fire-sticks, one from the soft parasite and one from the hard wood of the tree to which it clung, were rubbed together until sparks issued forth and fell on dry leaves or dry grass. The sparks were blown until a flame sprang up. At this flame of holy fire the people kindled their brands, which they carried to their houses. The house fires were extinguished once a year and relit from the sacred flames. Fire was itself a deity, and the deity was "fed" with fuel. "Need fires" (new fires)[1] were kindled at festivals so that cattle and human beings might be charmed against injury. These festivals were held four times a year, and the "new-fire" custom lingers in those districts where New Year's Day, Midsummer, May Day, and Hallowe'en bonfires are still being regularly kindled.

The fact that fire came from a tree induced the early people to believe that it was connected with lightning, and therefore with the sky god who thundered in the heavens. This god was supposed to wield a thunder-axe or thunder-hammer with which he smote the sky (believed to be solid) or the hills. With his axe or hammer he shaped the "world house".

In Scotland, a goddess, who is remembered as "the old wife",[2] was supposed to wield the hammer, or to ride across the sky on a cloud and throw down "fire-balls" that set the woods in flame. Here we find, probably as a result of culture mixing, a fusion of beliefs connected with the thunder god and the mother goddess.

Rain fell when the sky deity sent thunder and lightning. To early man, who took fire from a tree which was nourished by a well, fire and water seemed to be intimately connected.[3] The red berries on the sacred tree were supposed to contain fire, or the essence of fire. When he made rowan-berry wine, he regarded it as "fire water" or "the water of life". He drank it, and

---

[1] In Gaelic these are called "friction fires".
[2] According to some, Isis is a rendering of a Libyan name meaning "old wife".
[3] This connection can be traced in ancient Egypt. The sun and fire were connected, and the sun originally rose from the primordial waters. The sun's rays were the "tears" of Ra (the sun god). Herbs and trees sprang up where Ra's tears fell.

thus introduced into his blood fire which stimulated him. In his blood was "the vital spark". When he died the blood grew cold, because the "vital spark" had departed from it.

In the water fire lived in another form. Fish were found to be phosphorescent. The fish in the pool was at any rate regarded as a form of the deity who nourished life and was the origin of life. A specially sacred fish was the salmon. It was observed that this fish had red spots, and these were accounted for by the myth that the red berries or nuts from the holy tree dropped into the well and were swallowed by the salmon. The "chief" or "king" of the salmon was called "the salmon of wisdom". If one caught the "salmon of wisdom" and, when roasting it, tasted the first portion of juice that came from its body, one obtained a special instalment of concentrated wisdom, and became a seer, or magician, or Druid.

The salmon was reverenced also because it was a migratory fish. Its comings and goings were regular as the seasons, and seemed to be controlled by the ruler of the elements with whom it was intimately connected. One of its old Gaelic names was *orc* (pig). It was evidently connected with that animal; the sea-pig was possibly a form of the deity. The porpoise was also an *orc*.[1]

Hidden in the well lay a great monster which in Gaelic and Welsh stories is referred to as "the beast", "the serpent", or "the great worm". Ultimately it was identified with the dragon with fiery breath. An Irish story connects the salmon and dragon. It tells that a harper named Cliach, who had the powers of a Druid, kept playing his harp until a lake sprang up.

---

[1] So was a whale. The Latin *orca* is a Celtic loan-word. Milton uses the Celtic whale-name in the line

The haunt of seals, and orcs, and sea-mews' clang.

—*Paradise Lost*, Book XI, line 835.

This lake was visited by a goddess and her attendants, who had assumed the forms of beautiful birds. It was called Loch Bél Seád ("lake of the jewel mouth") because pearls were found in it, and Loch Crotto Cliach ("lake of Cliach's harps"). Another name was Loch Bél Dragain ("dragon-mouth lake"), because Ternog's nurse caught "a fiery dragon in the shape of a salmon" and she was induced to throw this salmon into the loch. The early Christian addition to the legend runs: "And it is that dragon that will come in the festival of St. John, near the end of the world, in the reign of Flann Cinaidh. And it is of it and out of it shall grow the fiery bolt which will kill three-fourth of the people of the world." [1] Here fire is connected with the salmon.

The salmon which could transform itself into a great monster guarded the tree and its life-giving berries and the treasure offered to the deity of the well. Apparently its own strength was supposed to be derived from or concentrated in the berries. The queen of the district obtained the supernatural power she was supposed to possess from the berries too, and stories are told of a hero who was persuaded to enter the pool and pluck the berries for the queen. He was invariably attacked by the "beast", and, after handing the berries to the queen, he fell down and died. There are several versions of this story. In one version a specially valued gold ring, a symbol of authority, is thrown into the pool and swallowed by the salmon. The hero catches and throws the salmon on to the bank. When he plucks the berries, he is attacked by the monster and kills it. Having recovered the ring, he gives it to the princess, who becomes his wife. Apparently she will be chosen as the next queen, because she has eaten the salmon and obtained the gold symbol.

It may be that this story had its origin in the practice

---

[1] O'Curry, *Manuscript Materials*, pp. 426–7.

of offering a human sacrifice to the deity of the pool, so that the youth-renewing red berries might be obtained for the queen, the human representative of the deity. Her fate was connected with the ring of gold in which, as in the berries, the influence of the deity was concentrated.

Polycrates of Samos, a Hellenic sea-king, was similarly supposed to have his "luck" connected with a beautiful seal-stone, the most precious of his jewels. On the advice of Pharaoh Amasis of Egypt he flung it into the sea. According to Herodotus, it was to avert his doom that he disposed of the ring. But he could not escape his fate. The jewel came back; it was found a few days later in the stomach of a big fish.

In India, China, and Japan dragons or sea monsters are supposed to have luck pearls which confer great power on those who obtain possession of them. The famous "jewel that grants all desires" and the jewels that control the ebb and flow of tides are obtained from, and are ultimately returned to, sea-monsters of the dragon order.

The British and Irish myths about sacred gold or jewels obtained from the dragon or one of its forms were taken over with much else by the early Christian missionaries, and given a Christian significance. Among the legends attached to the memory of the Irish Saint Moling is one that tells how he obtained treasure for Christian purposes. His fishermen caught a salmon and found in its stomach an ingot of gold. Moling divided the gold into three parts—"one third for the poor, another for the ornamenting of shrines, a third to provide for labour and work".

The most complete form of the ancient myth is, however, found in the life of Glasgow's patron saint, St. Kentigern (St. Mungo). A queen's gold ring had been thrown into the River Clyde, and, as she was unable, when asked by the king, to produce it, she was condemned to death and cast into a dungeon. The queen appealed to St. Kentigern, who instructed her messenger to catch a fish in the river and bring it to him. A large fish "commonly called a salmon" was caught. In its stomach was found the missing ring. The grateful queen, on her release, confessed her sins to the saint and became a Christian. St. Mungo's seal, now the

Seal of City of Glasgow, 1647-1793, showing Tree, Bird, Salmon, and Bell

coat of arms of Glasgow, shows the salmon with a ring in its mouth, below an oak tree, in the branches of which sits, as the oracle bird, a robin red-breast. A Christian bell dangles from a branch of the tree.

That the Glasgow saint took the place of a Druid,[1] so that the people might say "Kentigern is my Druid" as St. Columba said "Christ is my Druid", is suggested by his intimate connection, as shown in his seal, with the sacred tree of the "King of the Elements", the

---

[1] Professor W. J. Watson says in this connection: "The Celtic clerics stepped in to the shoes of the Druids. The people regarded them as superior Druids."

oracular bird (the thunder bird), the salmon form of the
deity, and the power-conferring ring. As the Druids
produced sacred fire from wood, so did St. Kentigern.
It is told that when a youth his rivals extinguished the
sacred fire under his care. Kentigern went outside the
monastery and obtained "a bough of growing hazel and
prayed to the 'Father of Lights'". Then he made
the sign of the cross, blessed the bough, and breathed
on it.

"A wonderful and remarkable thing followed. Straightway
fire coming forth from heaven, seizing the bough, as if the
boy had exhaled flames for breath, sent forth fire, vomiting
rays, and banished all the surrounding darkness. . . . God
therefore sent forth His light, and led him and brought him
into the monastery. . . . That hazel from which the little
branch was taken received a blessing from St. Kentigern,
and afterwards began to grow into a wood. If from that
grove of hazel, as the country folks say, even the greenest
branch is taken, even at the present day, it catches fire like
the driest material at the touch of fire. . . ."

A redbreast, which was kept as a pet at the monastery,
was hunted by boys, who tore off its head. Kentigern
restored the bird to life. The robin was hunted down
in some districts as was the wren in other districts. An
old rhyme runs:

> A robin and a wren
> Are God's cock and hen.

In Pagan times the oracular bird connected with the
holy tree was sacrificed annually. The robin represented the god and the wren (Kitty or Jenny Wren) the
goddess in some areas. In Gaelic, Spanish, Italian,
and Greek the wren is "the little King" or "the King
of Birds". A Gaelic folk-tale tells that the wren flew
highest in a competition held by the birds for the kingship, by concealing itself on an eagle's back. When

the eagle reached its highest possible altitude, the wren
rose above it and claimed the honour of kingship. In
the Isle of Man the wren used to be hunted on St.
Stephen's Day. Elsewhere it was hunted on Christmas
Eve or Christmas Day. The dead bird was carried on
a pole at the head of a procession and buried with ceremony in a churchyard.

In Scotland the shrew mouse was hunted in like manner, and buried under an apple tree. A standing stone
in Perthshire is called in Gaelic "stone of my little
mouse". As there were mouse feasts in ancient Scotland, it would appear that a mouse god like Smintheus
(Mouse-Apollo) was worshipped in ancient times. Mouse
cures were at one time prevalent. The liver of the
mouse [1] was given to children who were believed to be
on the point of death. They rallied quickly after swal-
lowing it. Roasted mouse was in England and Scotland
a cure for whooping-cough and smallpox. The Boers
in South Africa are perpetuating this ancient folk-cure. [2]
In Gaelic folk-lore the mouse deity is remembered as
lucha sith ("the supernatural mouse").

There still survive traces of the worship of a goddess
who is remembered as Bride in England and Scotland,
and as Brigit in Ireland. A good deal of the lore
connected with her has been attached to the memory
of St. Brigit of Ireland.

February 1st (old style) was known as Bride's Day.
Her birds were the wood linnet, which in Gaelic is called
"Bird of Bride", and the oyster catcher called "Page
of Bride", while her plant was the dandelion (*am bearnan
bride*), the "milk" of which was the salvation of the
early lamb. On Bride's Day the serpent awoke from its
winter sleep and crept from its hole. This serpent is

---

[1] In old Gaelic the liver is the seat of life.

[2] Mrs. E. Tawse Jollie, Hervetia, S. Melsetter, S. Rhodesia, writes me under October
12, 1918, in answer to my query, that the Boers regard *striep muis* (striped mice) as a
cure for "weakness of the bowel" in children, &c.

called in Gaelic "daughter of Ivor", *an ribhinn* ("the damsel"), &c.

The white serpent was, like the salmon, a source of wisdom and magical power. It was evidently a form of the goddess. Brigit was the goddess of the Brigantes, a tribe whose territory extended from the Firth of Forth to the midlands of England.[1] The Brigantes took possession of a part of Ireland where Brigit had three forms as the goddess of healing, the goddess of smith-work, and the goddess of poetry, and therefore of metrical magical charms. Some think her name signifies "fiery arrow". She was the source of fire, and was connected with different trees in different areas. The Bride-wells were taken over by Saint Bride.

The white serpent, referred to in the legends associated with Farquhar, the physician, and Michael Scott, some-times travelled very swiftly by forming itself into a ring with its tail in its mouth. This looks like the old Celtic solar serpent. If the serpent were cut in two, the parts wriggled towards a stream and united as soon as they touched water. If the head were not smashed, it would become a *beithis*, the biggest and most poisonous variety of serpent.[2] The "Deathless snake" of Egypt, referred to in an ancient folk-tale, was similarly able to unite its severed body. Bride's serpent links with the serpent dragons of the Far East, which sleep all winter and emerge in spring, when they cause thunder and send rain, spit pearls, &c. Dr. Alexander Carmichael trans-lates the following Gaelic serpent-charm:

> To-day is the day of Bride,
> The serpent shall come from his hole;

---

[1] In a Roman representation of her at Birrens, in Perthshire, she is shown as a winged figure holding a spear in her right hand and a globe in her left. An altar in Chester is dedicated to "De Nymphæ Brig". Her name is enshrined in Bregentz (anciently Brigantium), a town in Switzerland.

[2] The *beithis* lay hidden in arms of the sea and came ashore to devour animals.

> I will not molest the serpent
> And the serpent will not molest me.

De Visser[1] quotes the following from a Chinese text referring to the dragons:

> If we offer a deprecatory service to them,
> They will leave their abodes;
> If we do not seek the dragons
> They will also not seek us.

The serpent, known in Scotland as *nathair challtuinn* ("snake of the hazel grove"), had evidently a mythological significance. Leviathan is represented by the Gaelic *cirein cròin* (sea-serpent), also called *mial mhòr a chuain* ("the great beast of the sea") and *cuairtag mhòr a chuain* ("the great whirlpool of the sea"); a sea-snake was supposed to be located in Corryvreckan whirlpool. Kelpies and water horses and water bulls are forms assumed by the Scottish dragon. There are Far Eastern horse- and bull-dragons.

In ancient British lore there are references to souls in serpent form. A serpent might be a "double" like the Egyptian "Ka". It was believed in Wales that snake-souls were concealed in every farm-house. When one crept out from its hiding-place and died, the farmer or his wife died soon afterwards. Lizards were supposed to be forms assumed by women after death.[2] The otter, called in Scottish Gaelic *Dobhar-chù* ("water dog") and *Righ nàn Dobhran* ("king of the water" or "river"), appears to have been a soul form. When one was killed a man or a woman died. The king otter was supposed to have a jewel in its head like the Indian *nāga* (serpent deity), the Chinese dragon, the toad, &c. The king otter was invulnerable except on one white

---

[1] *The Dragon in China and Japan* (1913).
[2] Trevelyan, *Folk-lore and Folk-stories of Wales*, p. 165.

spot below its chin. Those who wore a piece of its skin as a charm were supposed to be protected against injury in battle. Evidently, therefore, the otter was originally a god like the boar, the image of which, as Tacitus records, was worn for protection by the Baltic amber searchers of Celtic speech. The *biasd na srogaig* ("the beast of the lowering horn") was a Hebridean loch dragon with a single horn on its head; this unicorn was tall and clumsy.

The "double" or external soul might also exist in a tree. Both in England and Scotland there are stories of trees withering when some one dies, or of some one dying when trees are felled. Aubrey tells that when the Earl of Winchelsea began to cut down an oak grove near his seat at Eastwell in Kent, the Countess died suddenly, and then his eldest son, Lord Maidstone, was killed at sea. Allan Ramsay, the Scottish poet, tells that the Edgewell tree near Dalhousie Castle was fatal to the family from which he was descended, and Sir Walter Scott refers to it in his "Journal", under the date 13th May, 1829. When a branch fell from it in July, 1874, an old forester exclaimed "The laird's deed noo!" and word was received not long afterwards of the death of the eleventh Earl of Dalhousie. Souls of giants were supposed to be hidden in thorns, eggs, fish, swans, &c. At Fasnacloich, in Argyllshire, the visit of swans to a small loch is supposed to herald the death of a Stewart.

"External souls", or souls after death, assumed the forms of cormorants, cuckoos, cranes, eagles, gulls, herons, linnets, magpies, ravens, swans, wrens, &c., or of deer, mice, cats, dogs, &c. Fairies (supernatural beings) appeared as deer or birds. Among the Scottish were-animals are cats, black sheep, mice, hares, gulls, crows, ravens, magpies, foxes, dogs, &c. Children were sometimes transformed by magicians into white dogs, and were restored to human form by striking them with a magic wand or by supplying shirts of bog-cotton. The floating lore regarding were-animals was absorbed in witch-lore after the Continental beliefs regarding witches were imported into this country. In like manner a good deal of floating lore was attached to the devil. In Scotland he is supposed to appear as a goat or pig, as a gentleman with a pig's or horse's foot, or as a black or green man riding a black or green horse followed by black or green dogs. Eels were "devil-fish", and were supposed to originate from the hairs of horses' manes or tails. Men who ate eels became insane, and fought horses.

In Scotland butterflies and bees were not only soul-forms but deities, and there are traces of similar beliefs in England, Wales, and Ireland. Scottish Gaelic names of the butterfly include *dealbhan-dé* ("image" or "form of God"), *dealbh* signifying "image", "form", "picture", "idol", or "statue"; *dearbadan-dé* ("manifestation of God"); *eunan-dé* ("small bird of God"); *teine-dé* ("fire of God"); and *dealan-dé* ("brightness of God"). The word *dealan* refers to (1) lightning, (2) the brightness of the starry sky, (3) burning coal, (4) the wooden bar of a door, and (5) to a wooden peg fastening a cow-halter round the neck. The bar and peg, which gave security, were evidently connected with the deity.

In addition to meaning butterfly, *dealan-dé* ("the *dealan* of God") refers to a burning stick which is shaken to and fro or whirled round about. When "need fires" (new fires) were lit at Beltain festival (1st May) — "Beltain" is supposed to mean "bright fires" or "white fires", that is, luck-bringing or sacred fires—burning brands were carried from them to houses, all domestic fires having previously been extinguished. The "new fire" brought luck, prosperity, health, increase, protection, &c. Until recently Highland boys who perpetuated the custom of lighting bon-fires to celebrate old Celtic festivals were wont to snatch burning sticks from them and run homewards, whirling the *dealan-dé* round about so as to keep it burning.

Souls took the form of a *dealan-dé* (butterfly). Lady Wilde relates in *Ancient Legends* (Vol. I, pp. 66-7) the Irish story of a child who saw the butterfly form of the soul — "a beautiful living creature with four snow-white wings"; it rose from the body of a man who had just died and went "fluttering round his head". The child and others watched the winged soul "until it passed from sight into the clouds". The story continues: "This was the first butterfly that was ever seen in Ireland; and now all men know that the butterflies are the souls of the dead waiting for the moment when they may enter Purgatory, and so pass through torture to purification and peace".

In England and Scotland moths were likewise souls of the dead that entered houses by night or fluttered outside windows, as if attempting to return to former haunts.

The butterfly god or soul-form was known to the Scandinavians. Freyja, the northern goddess, appears to have had a butterfly *avatar*. At any rate, the butterfly was consecrated to her. In Greece the nymph Psyche, beloved by Cupid, was a beautiful maiden with the wings of a butterfly; her name signifies "the soul". Greek artistes frequently depicted the human soul as a butterfly, and especially the particular species called ψυχή ("the soul"). On an ancient tomb in Italy a butterfly is shown issuing from the open mouth of a death-mask. The Serbians believed that the butterfly souls of witches arose from their mouths when they slept. They died if their butterfly souls did not return.[1] Evidence of belief in the butterfly soul has been forth-

---

[1] W. R. S. Ralston, *Songs of the Russian People*, pp. 117 *et seq.*

coming in Burmah, where ceremonies are performed to prevent the baby's butterfly soul following that of a dead mother.[1] The pre-Columbian Americans, and especially the Mexicans, believed in butterfly souls and butterfly deities. In China the butterfly soul was carved in jade and associated with the plum tree;[2] the sacred butterfly was in Scotland associated apparently with the honeysuckle (*deoghalag*), a plant containing "life-substance" in the form of honey (*lus a mheal*: "honey herb") and milk (another name of the plant being *bainne-ghamhnach*: "milk of the heifer"). As we have seen, the honeysuckle was supposed to be more powerful than the tree to which it clung; like the ivy and mistletoe, it was the plant of a powerful deity. Its milk and honey names connect it with the Great Mother goddess who was the source of life and nourishment, and provided the milk-and-honey elixir of life.

Bee-souls figure in Scottish folk-stories. Hugh Miller relates a story of a sleeping man from whose mouth the soul issued in the form of the bee.[3] Another of like character is related by a clergyman.[4] Both are located in the north of Scotland, where, as in the south of England, the custom was prevalent of "telling the bees" when a death took place, and of placing crape on hives. The bee-mandible symbol appears on Scottish sculptured stones. Both the bee and the butterfly were connected with the goddess Artemis. Milk-yielding fig trees were fertilized by bees or wasps, and the goddess, especially in her form as Diana of the Ephesians, was connected with the fig tree, the figs being "teats".

Little is known regarding the Hebridean sea-god *Seonaidh* (pronounced "shony"), who may have been

---

[1] *Journal of the Anthropological Institute*, XXVI (1897), p. 23.
[2] Laufer, *Jade*, p. 310.
[3] *My Schools and Schoolmasters*, Chapter VI.
[4] Rev. W. Forsyth, Dornoch, in *Folk-lore Journal*, VI, 171.

a form of the sea-god known to the Irish as Lir and to the Welsh as Llyr. His name connects him with the word *seonadh*, signifying "augury", "sorcery", "druidism". According to Martin, the inhabitants of Lewis contributed the malt from which ale was brewed for an offering to the gods. At night a man waded into the sea up to his middle and cried out, "Seonaidh! I give thee this cup of ale, hoping that thou wilt be so good as to send us plenty of sea-ware for enriching our ground during the coming year." He then poured the ale into the sea. The people afterwards gathered in the church of St. Mulway, and stood still for a time before the altar on which a candle was burning. When a certain signal was given the candle was extinguished. The people then made merry in the fields, drinking ale.

CHAPTER XVI
Ancient Pagan Deities

Many of the old British and Irish deities had bird forms, and might appear as doves, swallows, swans, cranes, cormorants, scald crows, ravens, &c. The cormorant, for instance, is still in some districts called the *Cailleach dubh* ("the black old wife"). Some deities, like Brigit and Morrigan, had triple forms, and appeared as three old hags or as three beautiful girls, or assumed the forms of women known to those they visited. In the Cuchullin stories the Morrigan appears with a supernatural cow, the milk of which heals wounds and prolongs life. When in conflict with Cuchullin, she takes alternately the forms of an eel, a grey wolf, and a white cow with red ears. On one occasion she changes from human form to that of a dark bird. An old west of England goddess was remembered until recently in Leicestershire as "Black Annis", "Black Anny", or "Cat Anna". She frequented a cave on the Dane

Hills,[1] above which grew an oak tree.   In the branches of
the tree she concealed herself, so that she might pounce
unawares on human beings.   Shepherds attributed to
her the loss of lambs, and mothers their loss of children.
The supernatural monster had one eye in her blue face,
and talons instead of hands.   Round her waist she wore
a girdle of human skins.

A Scottish deity called "Yellow Muilearteach" was
similarly one-eyed and blue-faced, and had tusks pro-
truding from her mouth.   An apple dangled from her
waist girdle.   The Indian goddess Black Kali is depicted
as a ferocious being of like character, with a forehead
eye, in addition to ordinary eyes, and a waist girdle of
human heads.   Greece had its Black Demeter with
animal-head (a horse's or pig's), and snakes in her
hair.   She haunted a cave in Phigalia.   The Egyptian
goddess Hathor in her cat form (Bast) was kindly,
and in her Sekhet form was a fierce slayer of mankind.[2]

Witches assume cat forms in Scottish witch lore,[3] and
appear on the riggings and masts of ships doomed to
destruction.   There are references, too, to cat roasting,
so as to compel the "Big Cat" to appear.   The "Big
Cat" is evidently the deity.   In northern India dogs are
tortured to compel the "Big Dog" (the god Indra) to
send rain.   "Lapus Cati" (the cat stone) is referred to
in early Christian records.   As a mouse was buried
under an apple tree to make it fruitful, a cat was buried
under a pear tree.

The Scottish "Yellow Muilearteach" revels in the
slaughter of human beings, and folk poems, describing
a battle waged against her, have been collected.   In the
end she is slain, and her consort comes from the sea to

---

[1] It has been suggested that "Dane" stands for "Danann".

[2] A text states: "Kindly is she as Bast: terrible is she as Sekhet."

[3] The Gaelic word for "witch" comes from English. Gaelic "witch lore" is distinctive,
having retained more ancient beliefs than those connected with the orthodox witches.

lament her death. A similar hag is remembered as the Cailleach ("the old wife"). She had a "blue-black face" and one eye "on the flat of her forehead", and she carried a magic hammer. During the period of "the little sun" (the winter season) she held sway over the world. Her blanket was washed in the whirlpool of Corryvreckan, which kept boiling vigorously for several days. Ben Nevis was her chief dwelling-place, and in a cave in that mountain she kept as a prisoner all winter a beautiful maiden who was given the task of washing a brown fleece until it became white. When wandering among the mountains or along the sea-shore she is followed, like Artemis, by herds of deer, goats, swine, &c. The venomous black boar is in some of the stories under her special protection. Apparently this animal was her symbol as it was that of the Baltic amber traders. The hero who hunts and slays the boar is himself killed by it, as was the Syrian god Adonis by the boar form of Ares (Mars). In Gaul the boar-god Moccus was identified by the Romans with Mars.

In Gaelic stories the hero who hunts and slays the boar is remembered as Diarmid, the eponymous ancestor of the Campbell clan. Apparently the goddess was the ugly hag to whom he once gave shelter. She transformed herself into a beautiful maiden who touched his forehead and left on it a "love spot".[1]

When she vanished he followed her to the "Land-Under-Waves". There he finds her as a beautiful girl who is suffering from a wasting disease. To cure her he goes on a long journey to obtain a draught of water from a healing well. This water he carries in the "Cup of Healing".

---

[1] The "fairy" Queen (the queen of enchantment), who carried off Thomas the Rhymer, appeared as a beautiful woman, but was afterwards transformed into an ugly hag. Thomas laments:

> How art thou faded thus in the face,
> That shone before as the sun so bricht (bright).

The winter hag has a son who falls in love with the beautiful maiden of Ben Nevis. When he elopes with her, his mother raises storms in the early spring season to keep the couple apart and prevent the grass growing. These storms are named in the Gaelic Calendar as "the Pecker", "the Whistle", "the Sweeper", "the Complaint", &c. In the end her son pursues her on horseback, until she transforms herself into a moist grey stone "looking over the sea". The story tells that the son's horse leapt over arms of the sea. On Loch Etiveside a place-name "Horseshoes" is attached to marks on a rock supposed to have been caused by his great steed. In the Isle of Man the place of the giant son is taken by St. Patrick. He rides from Ireland on horseback like the ancient sea god. He cursed a monster, which was turned into solid rock. St. Patrick's steed left the marks of its hoofs on the cliffs.[1]

In Arthurian romance King Arthur pursues Morgan le Fay, who likewise transforms herself into a stone. A Welsh folk story tells that Arthur's steed leapt across the Bristol Channel, and left the marks of its hoofs on a rock.

It appears that Morgan le Fay is the same deity as the Irish Morrigan. Both appear to link with Anu, or Danu, the Irish mother goddess, and with Black Anna or Annis of Leicestershire. The Irish Danann deities wage war against the Fomorians, who are referred to in one instance as the gods of the Fir Domnann (Dumnonii), the mineral workers or "diggers" of Cornwall and Devon, of the south-western and central lowlands of Scotland, and central and south-western Ireland. In Scotland the Fomorians are numerous; they are hill and cave giants like the giants of Cornwall. But there are no Scottish Dananns and no "war of the gods". The Fomorians of Scotland wage war against the fairies

---

[1] Wm. Cashen, *Manx Folk-lore* (Douglas, 1912), p. 48.

(as in Wester Ross) or engage in duels, throwing great boulders at one another.

The intruding people who in Ireland formulated the Danann mythology do not appear to have reached Scotland before the Christian period.

An outstanding difference between Scottish and Irish beliefs and practices is brought out by the treatment of the pig in both countries. Like the Continental Celts, the Irish Celts, who formed a military aristocracy over the Firbolgs, the Fir Domnann, and the Fir Gailian (Gauls), kept pigs and ate pork. In Scotland the pig was a demon as in ancient Egypt, and pork was tabooed over wide areas. The prejudice against pork in Scotland is not yet extinct. It is referred to by Sir Walter Scott in a footnote in *The Fortunes of Nigel*, which states:

" The Scots (Lowlanders), till within the last generation, disliked swine's flesh as an article of food as much as the Highlanders do at present. Ben Jonson, in drawing James's character,[1] says he loved no part of a swine." [2]

Dr. Johnson wrote in his *A Journey to the Western Highlands in 1773*:

" Of their eels I can give no account, having never tasted them, for I believe they are not considered as wholesome food. . . . The vulgar inhabitants of Skye, I know not whether of the other islands, have not only eels, but pork and bacon in abhorrence; and, accordingly, I never saw a hog in the Hebrides, except one at Dunvegan."

" In the year 1691 a question was put, ' Why do Scotchmen hate swine's flesh?' and ", says J. G. Dalyell,[3] "unsatisfactorily answered, ' They might borrow it of the Jews '." As the early Christians of England and

---

[1] King James VI of Scotland and I of England.
[2] Ben Jonson's reference is in *A Masque of the Metamorphosed Gipsies*.
[3] *The Darker Superstitions of Scotland* (London, 1834), p. 425, and *Athenian Mercury*, V, 1, No. 20, p. 13.

Ireland did not abhor pork, the prejudice could not have been of Christian origin. It was based on superstition, and as the superstitions of to-day were the religious beliefs of yesterday, the prejudice appears to be a survival from pagan times. An ancient religious cult, which may have originally been small, became influential in Scotland, and the taboo spread even after its original significance was forgotten. The Scottish prejudice against pork existed chiefly among "the common people", as Dr. Johnson found when in Skye. Proprietors of alien origin and monks ate pork, but the old taboo persisted. Pig-dealers, &c., in the Highlands in the nineteenth century refused to eat pork. They exported their pigs.[1]

Traces of ancient food taboos, which were connected evidently with religious beliefs, have been obtained by archæologists in England. In some districts pork appears to have been more favoured than the beef or mutton or goat flesh preferred in other districts. Evidence has been forthcoming that horse flesh was eaten in ancient England. A reference in the *Life of St. Columba* to a relapsing Christian returning to horse flesh suggests that it was a favoured food of a Pagan cult.

As the devil is called in Scottish Gaelic the "Big Black Pig" and in Wales is associated with the "Black Sow of All Hallows", it may be that the Welsh had once their pig taboo too. The association of the pig with Hallowe'en is of special interest.

In Scotland the eel is still tabooed, although it is eaten freely in England. The reason may be that an

---

[1] The south-western Scottish pork trade dates only from the latter part of the eighteenth century. There was trouble at Carlisle custom house when the Lowland Scots began to export cured pork, because of the difference between the English and Scottish salt duty. "For some time", complained a Scottish writer on agriculture, in June, 1811, "a duty of 2s. per hunderweight has been charged." Dublin was exporting pork to London in the reign of Henry VIII. A small trade in pork was conducted in eastern Scotland but was sporadic.

ancient goddess, remembered longest in Scotland, had
an eel form.   Julius Cæsar tells that the ancient Britons
with whom he came into contact did not regard it lawful
to eat the hare, the domestic fowl, or the goose.   In
Scotland and England the goose was, until recently,
eaten only once a year at a festival.   The tabooed pig
was eaten once a year in Egypt.   It was sacrificed to
Osiris and the moon.   An annual sacrificial pig feast
may have been observed in ancient Scotland.   It is of
special interest to find in this connection that in the
Statistical Account of Scotland (1793) the writer on the
parishes of Sandwick and Stromness, Orkney, says:
"Every family that has a herd of swine, kills a sow on
the 17th day of December, and thence it is called 'Sow-
day'."   Orkney retains the name of the Orcs (Boars), a
Pictish tribe.

There are still people in the Highlands who detest
"feathered flesh" or "white flesh" (birds), and refuse
to eat hare and rabbit.   Fish taboos have likewise persisted in the north of Scotland, where mackerel, ling,[1]
and skate are disliked in some areas, while in some
even the wholesome haddock is not eaten in the winter
or spring, and is supposed not to be fit for food until
it gets three drinks of May water—that is, after the
first three May tides have ebbed and flowed.

The Danann deities of Ireland were the children of
descendants of the goddess Danu, whose name is also
given as Ana or Anu.   She was the source of abundance and the nourisher of gods and men.   As "Buan-
ann" she was "nurse of heroes".   As Aynia, a
"fairy"[2] queen, she is still remembered in Ulster,

---

[1] King James I of England and VI of Scotland detested ling as he detested pork.
The food prejudices of the common people thus influenced royalty, although earlier kings
and Norman nobles ate pork, eels, &c.

[2] The Gaelic word *sidh* (Irish) or *sith* (Scottish) means "supernatural" and the
"peace" and "silence" of supernatural beings. "Fairy", as Skeat has emphasized,
means "enchantment". It has taken the place of "fay", which is derived from fate.
The "fay" was a supernatural being.

while as Aine, a Munster "fairy", she was formerly
honoured on St. John's Eve, when villagers, circulating a mound, carried straw torches which were afterwards waved over cattle and crops to give protection
and increase.

A prominent Danann god was Dagda, whose name
is translated as "the good god", "the good hand", by
some, and as "the fire god" or "fire of god" by others.
He appears to have been associated with the oak. By
playing his harp, he caused the seasons to follow one
another in their proper order. One of his special
possessions was a cauldron called "The Undry", from
which an inexhaustible food supply could be obtained.
He fed heavily on porridge, and was a cook (supplier of
food) as well as a king. In some respects he resembles
Thor, and, like him, he was a giant slayer. His wife
was the goddess Boann, whose name clings to the
River Boyne, which was supposed to have had its
origin from an overflowing well. Above this well were
nine hazel trees; the red nuts of these fell into the well to
be devoured by salmon and especially by the "salmon
of knowledge". Here again we meet with the tree
and well myth. Brigit was a member of the Dagda's
family. Another was Angus, the god of love.

Diancecht was the Danann god of healing. His
grandson Lugh (pronounced *loo*) has been called the
"Gaelic Apollo". Goibniu was a Gaelic Vulcan.

Neit, whose wife was Nemon,[1] was a Fomorian god
of battle. The sea god was Manannán mac Lir. He
was known to the Welsh as Manawydan ab Llyr, who
was not only a sea god but "lord of headlands" and
a patron of traders. Llyr has come down as the
legendary King Lear, and his name survives in
Leicester, originally Llyr-cestre of Cær-Llyr (walled
city of Llyr). His famous and gigantic son Bran

---

[1] From the root *nem* in *neamh*, heaven, *nemus*, a grove, &c.

became, in the process of time, the "Blessed Bran" who introduced Christianity into Britain.

Another group of Welsh gods, known as "the children of Don", resemble somewhat the Danann deities of Ireland. The closest link is Govannon, the smith, who appears to be identical with the Irish Goibniu. As Irish pirates invaded and settled in Wales between the second and fifth centuries of our era, it may be that the process of "culture mixing" which resulted can be traced in the mythological elements embedded in folk and manuscript stories. The Welsh deities, however, were connected with certain constellations and may have been "intruders" from the Continent. Cassiopea's chair was Llys Don (the court of the goddess Don). Arianrod (silver circle), a goddess and wife of Govannon, had for her castle the Northern Crown (Corona Borealis). She is, in Arthurian romance, the sister of Arthur. Her brother Gwydion had for his castle the "Milky Way", which in Irish Gaelic is "the chain of Lugh". The Irish Danann god Nuada has been identified with the British Nudd whose children formed the group of "the children of Nudd".

There were three groups of Welsh deities, the others being "the children of Lyr" and "the children of Don". Professor Rhys has identified Nudd with Lud, the god whose name survives in London (originally Cær Lud) and in Ludgate, which may, as has been suggested, have originally been "the way of Lud", leading to his holy place now occupied by St. Paul's Cathedral. Lud had a sanctuary at Lidney in Gloucestershire, where he was worshipped in Roman times as is indicated by inscriptions. A bronze plaque shows a youthful god, with solar rays round his head, standing in a four-horsed chariot. Two winged genii and two Tritons accompany him. Apparently he was identified with Apollo. The

Arthurian Lot or Loth was Lud or Ludd. His name lingers in "Lothian".

Gwydion, the son of Don, was a prominent British deity and has been compared to Odin. He was the father of the god Lleu, whose mother was Arianrod. The rainbow was "Lleu's rod-sling". Dwynwen, the so-called British Venus, was Christianized as "the blessed Dwyn" and the patron saint of the church of Llanddwyn in Anglesey. The magic cauldron was possessed by the Welsh goddess Kerridwen.

A prominent god whose worship appears to have been wide-spread was connected with the apple tree, which in the Underworld and Islands of the Blest was the "Tree of Life". Ancient beliefs and ceremonies connected with the apple cult survive in those districts in southern England where the curious custom is observed of "wassailing" the apple trees on Christmas Eve or Twelfth Night.[1] The "wassailers" visit the tree and sing a song in which each apple is asked to bear

> Hat-fulls, lap-fulls,
> Sack-fulls, pocket-fulls.

Cider is poured about the roots of apple trees. This ceremony appears to have been originally an elaborate one. The tom-tit or some other small bird was connected with the apple tree, as was the robin or wren of other cults with the oak tree. At the wassailing ceremony a boy climbed up into a tree and impersonated the bird. It may be that in Pagan times a boy was sacrificed to the god of the tree. That the bird (in some cases it was the robin red-breast) was hunted and sacrificed is indicated by old English folk-songs beginning like the following:

---

[1] Rendel Harris, *Apple Cults*, and *The Ascent of Olympus*.

BRONZE URN AND CAULDRON (*circa* 500 B.C.)
(British Museum)

Vessels such as these are unknown outside the British Isles.

Old Robin is dead and gone to his grave,
   Hum! Ha! gone to his grave;
They planted an apple tree over his head,
   Hum! Ha! over his head.

In England, Wales, Scotland, and Ireland a deity, or a group of deities in the Underworld, was associated with a magic cauldron, or as it is called in Gaelic a "pot of plenty". Heroes or gods obtain possession of this cauldron, which provides an inexhaustible food supply and much treasure, or is used for purposes of divination. It appears to have been Christianized into the "Holy Grail", to obtain possession of which Arthurian knights set out on perilous journeys.

Originally the pot was a symbol of the mother goddess, who renewed youth, provided food for all, and was the source of treasure, luck, victory, and wisdom. This goddess was associated with the mother cow and the life-prolonging pearls that were searched for by early Eastern prospectors. There are references to cows and pearls in Welsh and Gaelic poems and legends regarding the pot. An old Welsh poem in the *Book of Taliesin* says of the cauldron:

By the breath of nine maidens it would be kindled.
The head of Hades' cauldron—what is it like?
A rim it has, with pearls round its border:
It boils not coward's food: it would not be perjured.

This extract is from the poem known as "Preidden Annwfn" ("Harryings of Hades"), translated by the late Professor Sir John Rhys. Arthur and his heroes visit Hades to obtain the cauldron, and reference is made to the "Speckled Ox". Arthur, in another story, obtains the cauldron from Ireland. It is full of money. The Welsh god Bran gives to a king of Ireland a magic cauldron which restores to life those dead men who are

placed in it. A Gaelic narrative relates the story of
Cuchullin's harrying of Hades, which is called "Dun
Scaith". Cuchullin's assailants issue from a pit in the
centre of Dun Scaith in forms of serpents, toads, and
sharp-beaked monsters. He wins the victory and carries
away three magic cows and a cauldron that gives inexhaustible supplies of food, gold, and silver.

The pot figures in various mythologies. It was a
symbol of the mother goddess Hathor of ancient Egypt
and of the mother goddess of Troy, and it figures in
Indian religious literature. In Gaelic lore the knife
which cuts inexhaustible supplies of flesh from a dry
bone is evidently another symbol of the deity.

The talismans possessed by the Dananns were the
cauldron, the sword and spear of Lugh, and the Lia
Fail (or Stone of Destiny)[1], which reminds one of the
three Japanese symbols, the solar mirror, the dragon
sword, and the tama (a pearl or round stone) kept in
a Shinto shrine at Ise. The goddess's "life substance"
was likewise in fruits like the Celestial apples, nuts,
rowan berries, &c., of the Celts, and the grapes, pome-
granates, &c., of other peoples, and in herbs like the
mugwort and mandrake. Her animals were associated
with rivers. The name of the River Boyne signifies
"white cow". Tarf (bull) appears in several river
names, as also does the goddess name Deva (Devona)
in the Devon, Dee, &c. Philologists have shown that
Ness, the Inverness-shire river, is identical with Nestos
in Thrace and Neda in Greece. The goddess Belisama
(the goddess of war) was identified with the Mersey.

Goddess groups, usually triads, were as common in
Gaul as they were in ancient Crete. These deities were
sometimes called the "Mothers", as in Marne, the
famous French river, and in the Welsh *Y Mamau*, one
of the names of the "fairies".

---

[1] Called also *clach na cineamhuinn* (the fatal stone).

Other names of goddess groups include Proximæ (kinswoman), Niskai (water spirits), and Dervonnæ (oak spirits). The Romans took over these and other groups of ancient deities and the beliefs about their origin in the mythical sea they were supposed to cross or rise from. Gaelic references to "the coracle of the fairy woman" or "supernatural woman" are of special interest in this connection, especially when it is found that the "coracle" is a sea-shell which, by the way, figures as a canopy symbol in some of the sculptured groups of Romano-British grouped goddesses who sometimes bear baskets of apples, sheafs of grain, &c. When the shell provides inexhaustible supplies of curative or knowledge-conferring milk, it links with the symbolic pot.

Most of the ancient deities had local names, and consequently a number of Gaulish gods were identified by the Romans with Apollo, including Borvo, whose name lingers in Bourbon, Grannos of Aquæ Granni (Aix la Chapelle), Mogounus, whose name has been shortened to Mainz, &c. The gods Taranucus (thunderer), Uxellïmus (the highest), &c., were identified with Jupiter; Dunatis (fort god), Albiorix (world king), Caturix (battle king), Belatucadros (brilliant in war), Cocidius, &c., were identified with Mars. The name of the god Camŭlos clings to Colchester (Camulodunun). There are Romano-British inscriptions that refer to the ancient gods under various Celtic names. A popular deity was the god of Silvanus, who conferred health and was, no doubt, identified with a tree or herb.

It is uncertain at what period beliefs connected with stars were introduced into the British Isles.[1] As we have seen, the Welsh deities were connected with certain star groups. "Three Celtic goddesses", writes Anwyl,

[1] There is evidence in the Gaelic manuscripts that time was measured by the apparent movements of the stars. Cuchullin, while sitting at a feast, says to his charioteer: "Laeg, my friend, go out, observe the stars of the air, and ascertain when midnight comes".

referring to Gaul, "whose worship attained to highest development were Damona (the goddess of cattle), Sirona (the aged one or the star goddess), and Epŏna (the goddess of horses). These names are Indo-European." An Irish poem by a bard who is supposed to have lived in the ninth century refers to the Christian saint Ciaran of Saigir as a man of stellar origin:

> Liadaine (his mother) was asleep
> On her bed.
> When she turned her face to heaven
> A star fell into her mouth.
> Thence was born the marvellous child
> Ciaran of Saigir who is proclaimed to thee.

In the north and north-west Highlands the aurora borealis is called *Na Fir Chlis* ("the nimble men") and "the merry dancers". They are regarded as fairies (supernatural beings) like the sea "fairies" *Na Fir Ghorm* ("blue men"), who were probably sea gods.

The religious beliefs of the Romans were on no higher a level than those of the ancient Britons and Gaels.

CHAPTER XVII
Historical Summary

The evidence dealt with in the foregoing chapters throws considerable light on the history of early man in Britain. We really know more about pre-Roman times than about that obscure period of Anglo-Saxon invasion and settlement which followed on the withdrawal of the Roman army of occupation, yet historians, as a rule, regard it as " pre-historic " and outside their sphere of interest. As there are no inscriptions and no documents to render articulate the archæological Ages of Stone and Bronze, they find it impossible to draw any definite conclusions.

It can be urged, however, in criticism of this attitude, that the relics of the so-called "pre-historic age" may be found to be even more reliable than some contemporary documents of the " historic " period. Not a few of these are obviously biassed and prejudiced, while some are so vague and fragmentary that the conclusions drawn from them cannot be otherwise than hypothetical in character. A plainer, clearer, and more reliable story is revealed by the bones and the artifacts and the surviving relics of the intellectual life of our remote ancestors than by the writings of some early chroniclers and some early historians. It is possible, for instance, in consequence of the scanty evidence available, to hold widely diverging views regarding the Anglo-Saxon and Celtic problems. Pro-Teutonic and pro-Celtic protagonists involve us invariably in bitter controversy. That contemporary documentary evidence, even when somewhat voluminous, may fail to yield a clear record of facts is evident from the literature that deals, for instance, with the part played by Mary Queen of Scots in the Darnley conspiracy and in the events that led to her execution.

The term "pre-historic" is one that should be discarded. It is possible, as has been shown, to write, although in outline, the history of certain ancient race movements, of the growth and decay of the civilization revealed by the cavern art of Aurignacian and Magdalenian times, of early trade and of early shipping. The history of art goes back for thousands of years before the Classic Age dawned in Greece; the history of trade can be traced to that remote period when Red Sea shells were imported into Italy by Crô-Magnon man; and the history of British shipping can be shown to be as old as those dug-outs that foundered in ancient Scottish river beds before the last land movement had ceased.

The history of man really begins when and where we find the first clear traces of his activities, and as it is possible to write not only regarding the movements of the Crô-Magnon races, but of their beliefs as revealed by burial customs, their use of body paint, the importance attached to shell and other talismans, and their wonderful and high attainments in the arts and crafts, the European historical period can be said to begin in the post-Glacial epoch when tundra conditions prevailed in Central and Western Europe and Italy was connected with the North African coast.

In the case of ancient Egypt, historical data have been gleaned from archæological remains as well as from religious texts and brief records of historical events. The history of Egyptian agriculture has been traced back beyond the dawn of the Dynastic Age and to that inarticulate period before the hieroglyphic system of writing had been invented, by the discovery in the stomachs of the bodies of proto-Egyptians, naturally preserved in hot dry sands, of husks of barley and of millet native to the land of Egypt.[1]

The historical data so industriously accumulated in Egypt and Babylonia have enabled excavators to date certain finds in Crete, and to frame a chronological system for the ancient civilization of that island. Other relics afford proof of cultural contact between Crete and the mainland, as far westward as Spain, where traces of Cretan activities have been discovered. With the aid of comparative evidence, much light is thrown, too, on the history of the ancient Hittites, who have left inscriptions that have not yet been deciphered. The discoveries made by Siret in Spain and Portugal of unmistakable evidence of Egyptian and Babylonian cultural influence, trade, and colonization are, therefore, to be welcomed. The comparative evidence in this connection provides a more reliable basis than has hitherto been available for Western European archæology. It is possible for the historian to date approximately the beginning of the export trade in jet from England—apparently from Whitby in Yorkshire—and of the export trade in amber from the Baltic, and the opening of the sea routes between Spain and Northern Europe. The further discovery of Egyptian beads in south-western England, in association with relics of the English "Bronze Age", is of far-reaching importance. A "prehistoric" period surely ceases to be "prehistoric" when its relics can be dated even approximately. The English jet found in Spain takes us back till about 2500 B.C., and the Egyptian beads found in England till about 1300 B.C.

The dating of these and other relics raises the question whether historians should accept, without qualification, or at all, the system of "Ages" adopted by archæolo-

[1] Elliot Smith, *The Ancient Egyptians*, p. 42.

gists.   Terms like "Palæolithic" (Old Stone) and "Neo-lithic" (New Stone) are, in most areas, without precise chronological significance.   As applied in the historical sense, they tend to obscure the fact that the former applies to a most prolonged period during which more than one civilization arose, flourished, and decayed.   In the so-called "Old Stone Age" flint was worked with a degree of skill never surpassed in the "New Stone Age", as Aurignacian and Solutrean artifacts testify; it was also sometimes badly worked from poorly selected material, as in Magdalenian times, when bone and horn were utilized to such an extent that archæologists would be justified in referring to a "Bone and Horn Age".

Before the Neolithic industry was introduced into Western Europe and the so-called "Neolithic Age" dawned, as it ended, at various periods in various areas, great climatic changes took place, and the distribution of sea and land changed more than once.   Withal, considerable race movements took place in Central and Western Europe.   In time new habits of life were intro-duced into our native land that influenced more pro-foundly the subsequent history of Britain than could have been possibly accomplished by a new method of working flint.   The most important cultural change was effected by the introduction of the agricultural mode of life.

It is important to bear in mind in this connection that the ancient civilizations of Egypt and Babylonia were based on the agricultural mode of life, and that when this mode of life passed into Europe a complex culture was transported with it from the area of origin.   It was the early agriculturists who developed shipbuilding and the art of navigation, who first worked metals, and set a religious value on gold and silver, on pearls, and on certain precious stones, and sent out prospectors to search for precious metals and precious gems in distant lands. The importance of agriculture in the history of civilization cannot be overestimated. In so far as our native land is concerned, a new epoch was inaugurated when the first agriculturist tilled the soil, sowed imported barley seeds, using imported implements, and practising strange ceremonies at sowing, and ultimately at harvest time, that had origin in a far-distant "cradle" of civilization, and still linger in our midst as folk-lore evidence, testifies to the full. In ancient times the ceremonies were regarded as being of as much importance as the implements, and the associated myths were connected with the agriculturists' Calendar, as the Scottish Gaelic Calendar bears testimony.

Instead, therefore, of dividing the early history of man in Britain into periods, named after the materials from which he made implements and weapons, these should be divided so as to throw light on habits of life and habits of thought. The early stages of civilization can be referred to as the "Pre-Agricultural", and those that follow as the "Early Agricultural".

Under "Pre-Agricultural" come the culture stages, or rather the industries known as (1) Aurignacian, (2) Solutrean, and (3) Magdalenian. These do not have the same chronological significance everywhere in Europe, for the Solutrean industry never disturbed or supplemented the Aurignacian in Italy or in Spain south of the Cantabrian Mountains, nor did Aurignacian penetrate into Hungary, where the first stage of Modern Man's activities was the Solutrean. The three stages, however, existed during the post-Glacial period, when man hunted the reindeer and other animals favouring similar climatic conditions. The French archæologists have named this the "Reindeer Age". Three later industries were introduced into Europe during the Pre-Agricultural Age. These are known as (1) Azilian, (2) Tardenoisian, and (3) Maglemosian. The ice-cap was retreating, the reindeer and other tundra animals moved northward, and the red deer arrived in Central and Western Europe. We can, therefore, refer to the latter part of the Pre-Agricultural times as the "Early Red Deer Age".

There is Continental evidence to show that the Neolithic industry was practised prior to the introduction of the agricultural mode of life. The "Early Agricultural Age", therefore, cuts into the archæological "Neolithic Age" in France. Whether or not it does so in Britain is uncertain.

At the dawn of the British "Early Agricultural Age" cultural influences were beginning to "flow" from centres of ancient civilization, if not directly, at any rate indirectly. As has been indicated in the foregoing pages, the Neolithic industry was practised in Britain by a people who had a distinct social organization and engaged in trade. Some Neolithic flints were of Eastern type or origin. The introduction of bronze from the Continent appears to have been effected by sea-faring traders, and there is no evidence that it changed the prevailing habits of thought and life. Our ancestors did not change their skins and their ideas when they began to use and manufacture bronze. A section of them adopted a new industry, but before doing so they had engaged in the search for gold. This is shown by the fact that they settled on the granite in Devon and Cornwall, while yet they were using flints of Neolithic form which had been made elsewhere. Iron working was ultimately introduced. The Bronze and Iron "Ages" of the archæologists can be included in the historian's "Early Agricultural Age", because agriculture continued to be the most important factor in the economic life of Britain. It was the basis of its civilization; it rendered possible the development of mining and of various industries, and the promotion of trade by land and sea. In time the Celtic peoples—that is, peoples who spoke Celtic dialects—arrived in Britain. The Celtic movement was in progress at 500 B.C., and had not ended after Julius Cæsar invaded southern England. It was finally arrested by the Roman occupation, but continued in Ireland. When it really commenced is uncertain; the earliest Celts may have used bronze only.

The various Ages, according to the system suggested, are as follows:—

1. **The Pre-Agricultural Age.**

   Sub-divisions: (A) the *Reindeer Age* with the Aurignacian, Solutrean, and Magdalenian industries; (B) the *Early Red Deer Age* with the Azilian, Tardenoisian, and Maglemosian industries.

2. **The Early Agricultural Age.**

   Sub-divisions: (A) the *Pre-Celtic Age* with the Neolithic, copper and bronze industries; (B) the *Celtic Age* with the bronze, iron, and enamel industries.

3. **The Romano-British Age.**

   Including in Scotland (A) the *Caledonian Age* and (B) the *Early Scoto-Pictish Age*; and in Ireland the *Cuchullin Age*, during which bronze and iron were used.

The view favoured by some historians that our ancestors were, prior to the Roman invasion, mere "savages" can no longer obtain. It is clearly without justification. Nor are we justified in perpetuating the equally hazardous theory that early British culture was of indigenous origin, and passed through a series of evolutionary stages in isolation until the country offered sufficient attractions to induce first the Celts and afterwards the Romans to conquer it. The correct and historical view appears to be that from the earliest times Britain was subjected to racial and cultural "drifts" from the Continent, and that the latter outnumbered the former.

In the Pre-Agricultural Age Crô-Magnon colonists
reached England and Wales while yet in the Aurignacian
stage of civilization.   As much is indicated by the
evidence of the Paviland cave in South Wales.   At a
later period, proto-Solutrean influence, which had
entered Western Europe from North Africa, filtered into
England, and can be traced in those caverns that have
yielded evidence of occupation.   The pure Solutrean
culture subsequently swept from Eastern Europe as far
westward as Northern Spain, but Britain, like Southern
Spain and Italy, remained immune to it.   Magdalenian
culture then arose and became widespread.   It had
relations with the earlier Aurignacian and owed nothing
to Solutrean.   England yields undoubted traces of its
influence, which operated vigorously at a time when
Scotland was yet largely covered with ice.   Certain
elements in Aurignacian and Magdalenian cultures
appear to have persisted in our midst until comparatively
recent times, especially in connection with burial customs
and myths regarding the "sleeping heroes" in burial
caverns.

The so-called "Transition Period" between the Upper
Palæolithic and Neolithic Ages is well represented,
especially in Scotland, where the land rose after early
man's arrival, and even after the introduction of shipping.
As England was sinking when Scotland was rising,
English traces of the period are difficult to find.   This
"Transition Period" was of greater duration than the
archæological "Neolithic Age".

Of special interest is the light thrown by relics of the
"Transition Period" on the race problem.   Apparently
the Crô-Magnons and other peoples of the Magdalenian
Age were settled in Britain when the intruders, who had
broken up Magdalenian civilization on the Continent,
began to arrive.   These were (1) the Azilians of Iberian
(Mediterranean) type; (2) the Tardenoisians, who came

through Italy from North Africa, and were likewise, it would appear, of Mediterranean racial type; and (3) the Maglemosians, who were mainly a fair, tall people of Northern type. The close proximity of Azilian and Maglemosian stations in western Scotland—at the Mac-Arthur cave (Azilian) and the Drumvaragie shelter (Maglemosian) at Oban, for instance—suggests that in the course of time racial intermixture took place. That all the fair peoples of England, Scotland, and Ireland are descended from Celts or Norwegians is a theory which has not taken into account the presence in these islands at an early period, and before the introduction of the Neolithic industry, of the carriers from the Baltic area of Maglemosian culture.

We next pass to the so-called Neolithic stage of culture,[1] and find it affords fuller and more definite evidence regarding the early history of our native land. As has been shown, there are data which indicate that there was no haphazard distribution of the population of England when the Neolithic industry and the agricultural mode of life were introduced. The theory must be discarded that "Neolithic man" was a wanderer, whose movements depended entirely on those of the wild animals he hunted, as well as the further theory that stone implements and weapons were not used after the introduction of metals. There were, as can be gathered from the evidence afforded by archæological remains, settled village communities, and centres of industry in the Age referred to by archæologists as "Neolithic". The Early Agricultural Age had dawned. Sections of the population engaged in agriculture, sections were miners and workers of flint, sections were hunters and fishermen, sections searched for gold, pigments for body paint, material for ornaments of religious

[1] It must be borne in mind that among the producers and users of Neolithic artifacts were the Easterners who collected and exported ores.

value, &c., and sections engaged in trade, not only with
English and Scottish peoples, but with those of the
Continent.   The English Channel, and probably the
North Sea, were crossed by hardy mariners who engaged
in trade.

At an early period in the Early Agricultural Age and
before bronze working was introduced, England and
Wales, Scotland and Ireland, were influenced more
directly than had hitherto been the case by the high
civilizations of Egypt and Mesopotamia, and especially
by their colonies in South-western Europe.   The recent
Spanish finds indicate that a great "wave" of high
Oriental culture was in motion in Spain as far back as
2500 B.C., and perhaps at an even earlier period.   Included among Babylonian and Egyptian relics in Spain
are, as has been stated, jet from Whitby, Yorkshire,
and amber from the Baltic.   Apparently the colonists
had trading relations with Britain.   Whether the "Tin
Land", which was occupied by a people owing allegiance
to Sargon of Akkad, was ancient Britain is quite uncertain.   It was more probably some part of Western
Europe.   That Western European influence was reaching
Britain before the last land movement had ceased is
made evident by the fact that the ancient boat with a
cork plug, which was found in Clyde silt at Glasgow,
lay 25 feet above the present sea-level.   The cork plug
undoubtedly came from Spain or Italy, and the boat is
of Mediterranean type.[1]   It is evident that long before
the introduction of bronze working the coasts of Britain
were being explored by enterprizing prospectors, and that
the virgin riches of our native land were being exploited.
In this connection it is of importance to find that the
earliest metal artifacts introduced into our native islands
were brought by traders, and that those that reached
England were mainly of Gaulish type, while those that

[1] The boat dates the silting process rather than the silting process the boat.

reached Ireland were Spanish. The Neolithic industry does not appear to have been widespread in Ireland, where copper artifacts were in use at a very early period.

A large battle-axe of pure copper, described by Sir David Brewster in 1822 (*Edinburgh Philosophical Journal*, Vol. VI, p. 357), was found at a depth of 20 feet in Ratho Bog, near Edinburgh. Above it were 9 feet of moss, 7 feet of sand, and 4 feet of hard black till-clay. "It must have been deposited along with the blue clay", wrote Brewster, "prior to the formation of the superincumbent stratum of sand, and must have existed before the diluvial operations by which that stratum was formed. This opinion of its antiquity is strongly confirmed by the peculiarity of its shape, and the nature of its composition." The Spanish discoveries have revived interest in this important find.

As has been indicated, jet, pearls, gold, and tin appear to have been searched for and found before bronze working became a British industry. That the early prospectors had experience in locating and working metals before they reached this country there can be little doubt. There was a psychological motive for their adventurous voyages to unknown lands. The distribution of the megalithic monuments and graves indicates that metals were found and worked in south-western England, in Wales, in Derbyshire, and Cumberland, that jet was worked at Whitby, and that metals were located in Ireland and Scotland. Gold must have been widely distributed during the period of the great thaw. It is unlikely that traces of alluvial gold, which had been located and well worked in ancient times, should remain until the present time. In Scotland no traces of gold can now be found in a number of districts where, according to the records, it was worked as late as the fifteenth and sixteenth centuries. Some of the surviving Scottish megalithic monuments may mark the sites of ancient goldfields that were abandoned in early times when the supplies of precious metal became exhausted. The great circles of Callernish in Lewis and Stennis in Orkney are records of activity in semi-barren areas. Large communities could not have been attracted to these outlying islands to live on the produce of land or sea. Traces of metals, &c., indicate that, in both areas in ancient times, the builders of megalithic monuments settled in remote areas in Britain for the same reason as they settled on parts of the Continent. A gold rod has been discovered in association with the " Druid Temple " at Leys, near Inverness. The Inverness group of circles may well have been those of gold-seekers. In Aberdeenshire a group of megalithic monuments appears to have been erected by searchers for pearls. Gold was found in this county in the time of the Stuart kings.

The close association of megalithic monuments with ancient mine workings makes it impossible to resist the conclusion that the worship of trees and wells was closely connected with the religion of which the megalithic monuments are records. Siret shows that the symbolic markings on typical stone monuments are identical with those of the tree cult. Folk-lore and philological data tend to support this view. From the root *nem* are derived the Celtic names of the pearl, heaven, the grove, and the shrine within the grove (see Chap. XIII). The Celts appear to have embraced the Druidic system of the earlier Iberians in Western Europe, whose culture had been derived from that of the Oriental colonists.

The Oriental mother goddess was connected with the sacred tree, with gold and gems, with pearls, with rivers, lakes, and the sea, with the sky and with the heavenly bodies, long centuries before the Palm-tree cult was introduced into Spain by Oriental colonists. The symbolism of pearls links with that of jet, the symbolism of jet with that of Baltic amber, and the symbolism of Baltic amber with that of Adriatic amber and of Mediterranean coral. All these sacred things were supposed to contain, like jasper and turquoise in Egypt, the "life substance" of the mother goddess who had her origin in water and her dwelling in a tree, and was connected with the sky and "the waters above the firmament". Coral was supposed to be her sea tree, and jet, amber, silver, and gold were supposed to grow from her fertilizing tears. Beliefs about "grown gold" were quite rife in mediæval Britain.[1]

It should not surprise us, therefore, to find traces of Oriental religious conceptions in ancient Britain and Ireland. These have apparently passed from country to country, from people to people, from language to language, and down the Ages without suffering great change. Even when mixed with ideas imported from other areas, they have preserved their original fundamental significance. The Hebridean "maiden-queen" goddess, who dwells in a tree and provides milk from a sea-shell, has a history rooted in a distant area of origin, where the goddess who personified the life-giving shell was connected with the cow and the sky (the Milky Way), as was the goddess Hathor, the Egyptian Aphrodite. The tendency to locate imported religious beliefs no doubt provides the reason why the original palm tree of the goddess was replaced in Britain by the hazel, the elm, the rowan, the apple tree, the oak, &c.

On the Continent there were displacements of peoples after the introduction of bronze, and especially of bronze weapons. There was wealth and there was trade to attract and reward the conqueror. The Eastern traders of Spain were displaced. Some appear to have

---

[1] The ancient belief is enshrined in Milton's lines referring to "ribs of gold" that "grow in Hell" and are dug out of its hill (*Paradise Lost*, Book I, lines 688-90).

migrated into Gaul and North Italy; others may have found refuge in Ireland and Britain. The sea-routes were not, however, closed. Ægean culture filtered into Western Europe from Crete, and through the Hallstatt culture centre from the Danubian area. The culture of the tribes who spoke Celtic dialects was veined with Ægean and Asiatic influences. In time Continental Druidism imbibed ideas regarding the Transmigration of Souls and the custom of cremation from an area in the East which had influenced the Aryan invaders of India.

The origin of the Celts is obscure. Greek writers refer to them as a tall, fair people. They were evidently a branch of the fair Northern race, but whether they came from Northern Europe or Northern Asia is uncertain. In Western Europe they intruded themselves as conquerors and formed military aristocracies. Like other vigorous, intruding minorities elsewhere and at different periods, they were in certain localities absorbed by the conquered. In Western Europe they were fused with Iberian communities, and confederacies of Celtiberians came into existence.

Before the great Celtic movements into Western Europe began—that is, before 500 B.C.—Britain was invaded by a broad-headed people, but it is uncertain whether they came as conquerors or as peaceful traders. In time these intruders were absorbed. The evidence afforded by burial customs and surviving traces of ancient religious beliefs and practices tends to show that the culture of the earlier peoples survived over large tracts of our native land. An intellectual conquest of conquerors or intruders was effected by the indigenous population which was rooted to the soil by agriculture and to centres of industry and trade by undisturbed habits of life.

Although the pre-Celtic languages were ultimately

displaced by the Celtic—it is uncertain when this process was completed—the influence of ancient Oriental culture remained. In Scotland the pig-taboo, with its history rooted in ancient Egypt, has had tardy survival until our own times. It has no connection with Celtic culture, for the Continental Celts were a pig-rearing and pork-eating people, like the Ægæan invaders of Greece. The pig-taboo is still as prevalent in Northern Arcadia as in the Scottish Highlands, where the descendants not only of the ancient Iberians but of intruders from pork-loving Ireland and Scandinavia have acquired the ancient prejudice and are now perpetuating it.

Some centuries before the Roman occupation, a system of gold coinage was established in England. Trade with the Continent appears to have greatly increased in volume and complexity. England, Wales, Scotland, and Ireland were divided into small kingdoms. The evidence afforded by the Irish Gaelic manuscripts, which refer to events before and after the Roman conquest of Britain, shows that society was well organized and that the organization was of non-Roman character. Tacitus is responsible for the statement that the Irish manners and customs were similar to those prevailing in Britain, and he makes reference to Irish sea-trade and the fact that Irish sea-ports were well known to merchants. England suffered more from invasions before and after the arrival of Julius Cæsar than did Scotland or Ireland. It was consequently incapable of united action against the Romans, as Tacitus states clearly. The indigenous tribes refused to be allies of the intruders.[1]

In Ireland, which Pliny referred to as one of the British Isles, the pre-Celtic Firbolgs were subdued by Celtic invaders. The later "waves" of Celts appeared

[1] *Agricola*, Chap. XII.

to have subdued the earlier conquerors, with the result that "Firbolg" ceased to have a racial significance and was applied to all subject peoples. There were in Ireland, as in England, upper and lower classes, and military tribes that dominated other tribes. Withal, there were confederacies, and petty kings, who owed allegiance to "high kings". The "Red Branch" of Ulster, of which Cuchullin was an outstanding representative, had their warriors trained in Scotland. It may be that they were invaders who had passed through Scotland into Northern Ireland; at any rate, it is unlikely that they would have sent their warriors to a "colony" to acquire skill in the use of weapons. There were Cruithne (Britons) in all the Irish provinces. Most Irish saints were of this stock.

The pre-Roman Britons had ships of superior quality, as is made evident by the fact that a British squadron was included in the great Veneti fleet which Cæsar attacked and defeated with the aid of Pictones and other hereditary rivals of the Veneti and their allies. In early Roman times Britain thus took an active part in European politics in consequence of its important commercial interests.

When the Romans reached Scotland the Caledonians, a people with a Celtic tribal name, were politically predominant. Like the English and Irish pre-Roman peoples, they used chariots and ornamented these with finely worked bronze. Enamel was manufactured or imported. Some of the Roman stories about the savage condition of Scotland may be dismissed as fictions. Who can nowadays credit the statement of Herodian[1] that the warriors of Scotland in Roman times passed their days in the water, or Dion Cassius's[2] story that they were wont to hide in mud for several days with nothing but their heads showing, and that despite their

[1] *Herodian*, III, 14.   [2] Dion Cassius (*Xiphilinus*) LXXVI, 12.

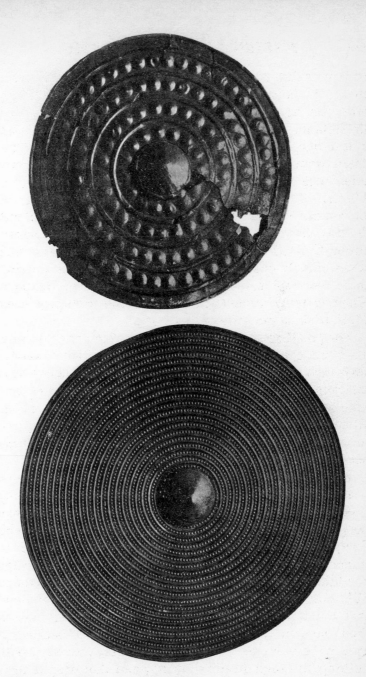

BRONZE BUCKLERS OR SHIELDS
(British Museum)

Upper: from the Thames.   Lower: from Wales.

fine physique they fed chiefly on herbs, fruit, nuts, and the bark of trees, and, withal, that they had discovered a mysterious earth-nut and had only to eat a piece no larger than a bean to defy hunger and thirst. The further statement that the Scottish "savages" were without state or family organization hardly accords with historical facts. Even Agricola had cause to feel alarm when confronted by the well-organized and well-equipped Caledonian army at the battle of Mons Grampius, and he found it necessary to retreat afterwards, although he claimed to have won a complete victory. His retreat appears to have been as necessary as that of Napoleon from Moscow. The later invasion of the Emperor Severus was a disastrous one for him, entailing the loss of 50,000 men.

A people who used chariots and horses, and artifacts displaying the artistic skill of those found in ancient Britain, had reached a comparatively high state of civilization. Warriors did not manufacture their own chariots, the harness of their horses, their own weapons, armour, and ornaments; these were provided for them by artisans. Such things as they required and could not obtain in their own country had to be imported by traders. The artisans had to be paid in kind, if not in coin, and the traders had to give something in return for what they received. Craftsmen and traders had to be protected by laws, and the laws had to be enforced.

The evidence accumulated by archæologists is sufficient to prove that Britain had inherited from seats of ancient civilization a high degree of culture and technical skill in metal-working, &c., many centuries before Rome was built. The finest enamel work on bronze in the world was produced in England and Ireland, and probably, although definite proof has not yet been forthcoming, in Scotland, the enamels of which may have been imported and may not. Artisans could not have manufactured enamel without furnaces capable of generating a high degree of heat. The process was a laborious and costly one. It required technical knowledge and skill on the part of the workers. Red, white, yellow, and blue enamels were manufactured. Even the Romans were astonished at the skill displayed in enamel work by the Britons. The people who produced these enamels and the local peoples who purchased them, including the Caledonians, were far removed from a state of savagery.

Many writers, who have accepted without question the statements of certain Roman writers regarding the early Britons and ignored the evidence that archæological relics provide regarding the arts and crafts and social conditions of pre-Roman times, have in the past written in depreciatory vein regarding the ancestors of the vast majority of the present population of these islands, who suffered so severely at the altar of Roman ambition. Everything Roman has been glorified; Roman victories over British "barbarians" have been included among the "blessings" of civilization. Yet "there is", as Elton says, "something at once mean and tragical about the story of the Roman conquest. . . . On the one side stand the petty tribes, prosperous nations in minature, already enriched by commerce and rising to a homely culture; on the other the terrible Romans strong in their tyranny and an avarice which could never be appeased." [1]

It was in no altruistic spirit that the Romans invaded Gaul and broke up the Celtic organization, or that they invaded Briton and reduced a free people to a state of bondage. The life blood of young Britain was drained by Rome, and, for the loss sustained, Roman institutions, Roman villas and baths, and the Latin language and

[1] *Origins of English History,* pp. 302-3.

literature were far from being compensations. Rome was a predatory state. When its military organization collapsed, its subject states fell with it. Gaul and Britain had been weakened by Roman rule; the ancient spirit of independence had been undermined; native initiative had been ruthlessly stamped out under a system more thorough and severe than modern Prussianism. At the same time, there is, of course, much to admire in Roman civilization.

During the obscure post-Roman period England was occupied by Angles and Saxons and Jutes, who have been credited with the wholesale destruction of masses of the Britons. The dark-haired survivors were supposed to have fled westward, leaving the fair intruders in undisputed occupation of the greater part of England. But the indigenous peoples of the English mining areas were originally a dark-haired and sallow people, and the invading Celts were mainly a fair people. Boadicea was fair-haired like Queen Meave of Ireland. The evidence collected of late years by ethnologists shows that the masses of the English population are descended from the early peoples of the Pre-Agricultural and Early Agricultural Ages. The theory of the wholesale extermination by the Anglo-Saxons of the early Britons has been founded manifestly on very scant and doubtful evidence.

What the Teutonic invasions accomplished in reality was the destruction not of a people but of a civilization. The native arts and crafts declined, and learning was stamped out, when the social organization of post-Roman Britain was shattered. On the Continent a similar state of matters prevailed. Roman civilization suffered decline when the Roman soldier vanished.

Happily, the elements of "Celtic" civilization had been preserved in those areas that had escaped the blight of Roman ambition. The peoples of Celtic speech had preserved, as ancient Gaelic manuscripts testify, a love of the arts as ardent as that of Rome, and a fine code of chivalry to which the Romans were strangers. The introduction of Christianity had advanced this ancient Celtic civilization on new and higher lines. When the Columban missionaries began their labours outside Scotland and Ireland, they carried Christianity and "a new humanism" over England and the Continent, "and became the teachers of whole nations, the counsellors of kings and emperors". Ireland and Scotland had originally received their Christianity from Romanized England and Gaul. The Celtic Church developed on national lines. Vernacular literature was promoted by the Celtic clerics.

In England, as a result of Teutonic intrusions and conquests, Christianity and Romano-British culture had been suppressed. The Anglo-Saxons were pagans. In time the Celtic missionaries from Scotland and Ireland spread Christianity and Christian culture throughout England.

It is necessary for us to rid our minds of extreme pro-Teutonic prejudices. Nor is it less necessary to avoid the equally dangerous pitfall of the Celtic hypothesis. Christianity and the associated humanistic culture entered these islands during the Roman period. In Ireland and Scotland the new religion was perpetuated by communities that had preserved pre-Roman habits of life and thought which were not necessarily of Celtic origin or embraced by a people who can be accurately referred to as the "Celtic race". The Celts did not exterminate the earlier settlers. Probably the Celts were military aristocrats over wide areas.

Before the fair Celts had intruded themselves in Britain and Ireland, the seeds of pre-Celtic culture, derived by trade and colonization from centres of ancient civilization through their colonies, had been sown and had borne fruit. The history of British civilization begins with neither Celt nor Roman, but with those early prospectors and traders who entered and settled in the British Isles when mighty Pharaohs were still reigning in Egypt, and these and the enterprising monarchs in Mesopotamia were promoting trade and extending their spheres of influence. The North Syrian or Anatolian carriers of Eastern civilization who founded colonies in Spain before 2500 B.C. were followed by Cretans and Phœnicians. The sea-trade promoted by these pioneers made possible the opening up of overland trade routes. It was after Pytheas had (about 300 B.C.) visited Britain by coasting round Spain and Northern France from Marseilles that the volume of British trade across France increased greatly and the sea-routes became of less importance. When Carthage fell, the Romans had the trade of Western Europe at their mercy, and their conquests of Gaul and Britain were undoubtedly effected for the purpose of enriching themselves at the expense of subject peoples. We owe much to Roman culture, but we owe much also to the culture of the British pre-Roman period.

INDEX

Achæans, Celts and, 111, 112.

Acheulian culture, 13, 14.

Adonis, killed by boar, 197.

Ægean culture, Celts absorbed, 112.

— — in Central Europe, 96.

Æstyans, the, amber traders, 161.

— worship of mother goddess and boar god, 161, 162.

Africa, Crô-Magnon peoples entered Europe from, 35.

— ostrich eggs, ivory, &c., from, found in Spain, 96.

— transmigration of souls in, 143

Age, the Agricultural and pre-Agricultural, 213.

— the Early Red Deer, 214, 215.

— the Prehistoric, 217.

— the Historic, 217.

— the Reindeer, 213.

Ages, Archæological, new system of, 215.

— — problem of Scottish copper axe, 219.

— the Mythical, colours and metals of, 121. See also *Geological* and *Archæological Ages*.

Agriculture, beginning of, in Britain, 217.

— importance of introduction of, 212.

— history of, 210.

— Neolithic sickles, 4.

— barley, wheat, and rye cultivated, 5.

Aine, the Munster fairy, 202.

Airts (Cardinal Points), the, doctrine of, 145. See also *Cardinal Points*.

Akkad, Sargon of, his knowledge of Western Europe, 96, 218.

Alabaster, Eastern perfume flasks of, in Neolithic Spain, 96.

Albertite, jet and, 164.

Albiorix, the Gaulish god, 207.

All Hallows, Black Sow of, 200.

Amber, associated with jet and Egyptian blue beads in England, 104, 105 (*ill.*), 106.

— Celtic and German names of, 162.

— as magical product of water, 162, 163.

— eyes strengthened by, 165.

— imported into Britain at 1400 B.C., 106; and in first century A.D., 114.

— jet and pearls and, 22.

— as " life substance ", 80.

— Megalithic people searched for, 93.

— origin of, in Scottish lore, 162.

— Persian, &c., names of, 163, 164.

— Tacitus on the Baltic Æstyans, 161.

— connection of, with boar god and mother goddess, 161.

— as " tears " of goddess, 161.

— trade in, 219.

— the " vigorous Gael " and, 163.

— connection of, with Woad, 163.

— white enamel as substitute for, 165.

America, green stone symbolism in, 34.

Angles, 126.

— Celts and, 227.

Anglo-Saxon intruders, our scanty knowledge of, 209.

231

Crô-Magnon Races, Mother-goddess of, 42.
— — "Tama" belief, 44.
— — not in Hungary, 50.
— — "Red Man" of Wales, 19.
— — Red Sea shells imported by, 210.
— — history of, 210.
— — relations of, with Neanderthal man, 14.
— — in Wales, 19.
— — sea-shell necklace (*ill.*), 39.
— — trade of, in shells, 40.
— — tall types, 24.
— — high cheek bones of, 25.
— — tallest types in Riviera, 35, 36.
Crô-Magnon skulls (*ill.*), 24.
Crô-Magnons, Azilian intruders and, 62.
— heart as seat of life, among, 32.
— in Britain, 67, 125, 216.
— English Channel land-bridge crossed by, 67.
— hand-prints and mutilation of fingers, 47.
— modern Scots and, 137.
— Selgovæ and, 139.
Crow, and goddess of grove and sky, 160.
Crows, Celtic deities as, 195.
Cruithne, in Ireland, 224.
— the Irish, not Picts, 132.
— the Q-Celtic name of Britons, 132.
Cuchullin, and Scotland, 224.
— dog god and, 64.
— goddess Morrigan and, 195.
— his knowledge of astronomy, 175, and also note 1.
— pearls in hair of, 163.

Dagda, the god, 202.
— connection with oak and fire, 202.
— cauldron of, 202.
— Thor and, 202.
— a giant-slayer, 202.
Damnonians. See *Dumnonii.*
— an early Celtic "wave", 107.
— Fomorians as gods of, 198.
— settlements of, in metal-yielding areas, 89.
Damona, Celtic goddess of cattle, 208.

Danann deities, 201.
— — not in Scotland, 199.
— — talismans of, 205.
— — Japanese talismans, 205.
— — war against Fomorians, 198.
— — Welsh "Children of Don" and, 203.
Dandelion, as milk-yielding plant of goddess Bride, 187.
Danes, in Britain, 126.
Dante, moon called "eternal pearl" by, 159.
Danu, the goddess, 198.
Danube valley trade route, 114.
Danubian culture in Central Europe, 96.
— — Celts as carriers of, 111, 112.
Decantæ, The, 129.
Deer, as goddess, 154.
Demetæ, The, in Wales, 129.
Demeter, The black, 196.
Demons, dogs as enemies of, 65.
Derbyshire, Magdalenian art in, 53.
Deva, Devona, Dee, Rivers, 206.
Devil as "Big Black Pig" in Scotland, 200.
— as Black Sow in Wales, 200.
— as pig, goat, and horse, 191.
Devon, Damnonians in, 89.
— Magdalenian art in, 54.
Diamond, The night-shining, 160.
Diana of the Ephesians, fig tree and, 193.
Diancecht, Irish god of healing, 202.
Diarmid, Gaelic Adonis, 197.
Diodorus Siculus, on gold mining, 90.
— — reference to British temple to Apollo, 177.
Disease, deity who sends also withdraws, 179.
— ancient man suffered from, 2.
— "Yellow Plague", 2.
Dog, The Big, god Indra as, 196.
— The Sacred, 154, 155 (*ill.*).
— taboo to Cuchullin, 154, and also note 3. See *Dogs.*
Dogger Bank, ancient plateau, 68.
— — animal bones, &c., from, 57, 61.
— — Island, 69.
Dog gods, 64.